HEAVEN, HELL, & HISTORY

HEAVEN,
HELL,
&
HISTORY

A Survey of Man's Faith
in History from Antiquity to the Present

JOHN T. MARCUS

THE MACMILLAN COMPANY, *New York*

COLLIER-MACMILLAN LTD., *London*

To Emilie, Peter and Ruth

ACKNOWLEDGMENTS

MANY friends have kindly read and criticized this manuscript. They have provided me with invaluable help in areas that often lay beyond my own field of study. I should like to express my particular gratitude to the following colleagues: Professor Frank Wekerle for his suggestions on the passages on philosophy, notably Hegel and Nietzsche, and Professor John Gilmour for his review of other philosophical materials, including Heidegger and Whitehead; Professors Joseph LaLumia, Leon Pearl and Harry Siller for their constructive criticisms on sections dealing with science and the philosophy of science; Professor George D. Jackson, Jr. for his reading of the section on Marx; Professor Harold Yuker for his advice on the materials on psychology, and Professor Herbert D. Rosenbaum for his helpful comments on Hobbes and Locke.

I am indebted to my departmental colleagues, Professors John C. Moore, Robert A. Davison and Robert Sobel for their general comments and suggestions on style and expression. I am particularly appreciative of Professor John W. Follows' detailed comments on clarity and form, and the assistance and encouragement of the Chairman of my department, Professor Gerrit P. Judd IV, who read the bulk of the manuscript. May I add my appreciation for the encouraging conditions at Hofstra University which made it a pleasure to undertake a long-range project of several volumes. Finally, I would like to thank Mrs. Rhoda Shulman and my wife for their patient typing of such words as "historicity" and "detranscendentalization."

Hofstra University
January, 1967

ACKNOWLEDGMENTS

CONTENTS

INTRODUCTION

1. The Historical Crisis of Our Time

Is history the latest and last of the human gods that have failed? Is the despair of finding any meaning in man's experience the most starkly revealing discovery of the mind, and the sense of futility the end result of our civilization? These pessimistic questions, which are explicitly raised or half-consciously implied in many key elements of modern thought, reflect the anxiety and sense of purposelessness underlying much of contemporary life. Disillusion in its most general form manifests itself through a pervasive nihilism, destructive of all human values and hopes. In its more limited and specific form, it expresses itself as a profound alienation from the traditions, values and, in particular, the historical aspirations of Western culture. Fear of the abyss arises above all from disenchantment with our glorified historical expectations. History appears as the tragic story of human failure, devoid of the redemptive role of classic tragedy, from Orestes or Job to Faust.

Since the appearance of Spengler's *Decline of the West*, a concern with the pathology of our civilization has become a morbidly fascinating theme for historical philosophers and the literate public. Cultural introspection has been refined, and sometimes overrefined. Under the stress of the historical crises and the chaos of recent years, social comment has gone from pessimism about Western civilization to pessimism about man.

New political movements, wars and revolutions have confirmed many of the social prophets' hypotheses of irrationalism and violence. These forces seem to have taken on in our time a new universality and relentlessness. The assumption that violence and irrationalism are the ultimate reality of man is the basic premise of some modern ideologies and is implicit in others. Such ideological currents have led to growing apprehension that the problems confronting our civilization cannot be resolved through hope, work and time, but are not capable of solution at all—that the human condition, in sum, is uncontrollable. Confronted today with the possibility of omnicide on one hand and the growing rejection of all suprahuman values on the other, we have watched the age-old philosophical theme of the possible futility of existence take on new psychological immanence in Western life and thought. Doubt has become the common solvent of many contemporary attitudes, both among intellectual elites and among the mass. Totalitarian movements have sought escape from the frustration of our aborted hopes of social redemption through identification with the charismatic will of the leader and the forced certitude of imposed beliefs. Meanwhile, the deep-seated uncertainty of an influential part of the intelligentsia has turned into a pervasive sense of moral chaos, or a nihilistic philosophy of absurdity. The survival of Western civilization is held in jeopardy. It is significant that cultural historians have taken a renewed interest in the study of late Rome, and that some social philosophers find disturbing comparisons between the temper of our own time and that of the decaying Roman Empire.

At the heart of this crisis of values lies a crucial problem of ideology and psychology: the repudiation of all sense of order and meaning in human experience. The course of civilization is seen as an incoherent sequence of events, or as a relentless movement of superhuman forces against which the individual and humanity itself are helpless. In its intellectualized expression, this anxiety has manifested itself in repeated proclamations of the ultimate purposelessness of man's existential condition *in history*, i.e., that there exists no redemption from man's meaningless role as an historical being. The denial of a meaningful continuum in history has fostered a sense of void. Individual life appears futile in the larger context of man's lack of destiny. This loss of the sense of an historical objective seems to deprive human experience of its moral *raison d'être*. Indeed, when history as a whole seems futile, the notion of coherent purpose in the individual is shattered, and each event seems an isolated, purposeless phenomenon in the abyss of time. In this view there is no escape from death, no lingering effect from the light of one's own brief candle. This fear cuts to the very heart of the ideological drive in man, namely his yearning to transcend his present state and to "break free." In short, the present crisis of values has its root in an intimation of the untranscendability of the human condition in an historical world devoid of rhyme or reason.

The sense of incoherence and untranscendability is mirrored in a host of intellectual movements. It is clearly evidenced in the shock techniques and aggressive irrationality characteristic of much of modern art. Twentieth-century aesthetic forms have been rife with expressions of the chaotic unconscious within us, and of the mindless chaos around us. Each successive art movement has manifested to some degree man's fear of alienation in modern industrial society and of the imprisonment of each individual psyche in a permanently unfulfilled state.

Science, for all its intellectual and technological successes, has also contributed substantially to the climate of anxiety. Conclusions drawn in a vulgarized form from the revolution in the physical sciences—conclusions often misapplied or misinterpreted —have proved to be influential intellectual forces. Based on imprecisely understood scientific concepts of time and space, certain social philosophies proclaim that, in a universe where all positions are relative, subjective and indeterminate, man can find little hope of escape from his own mortal frame of reference into an absolute and eternal Being.

Of all the sciences, however, it is psychology which has most reenforced the fear of the inherent untranscendability of the human condition. The rationalism of early psychoanalytic clinical theory was overshadowed by the emphasis on man's unconscious drives as the decisive elements in his life and culture. This notion was readily distorted in popularized form into a new determinism that reduces human actions to the play of irrational forces within the psyche. In this view, civilized man is still chained to his baser self and its aggressive impulses. According to Freud, he is irretrievably trapped in the contradiction between his basic urges and his guilt feelings.

This pessimism is also reflected in contemporary philosophic movements. From Plato through the mid-nineteenth century, the predominant mode of philosophical enquiry was the quest for some absolute truth and for an ultimate good. Through philosophical knowledge, man hoped to find justification for his life. Socrates' remark that the purpose of philosophy is to teach men how to die suggests the implicit psychological motivation towards metaphysics, epistemology and ontology, not to mention ethics, social philosophy and theology. The goal of philosophy was to reach towards immortality by somehow apprehending the eternal, for the notion of seeking an absolute has an inherently redemptive aspect, insofar as it appears to offer access to a transcendent truth beyond the individual's subjective experience and a purpose beyond his mortal life. But most twentieth-century philosophers reject the idea of a transcending absolute. Indeed, this repudiation provides one of the few common elements between such generally unrelated philosophical movements as the positivist and existentialist schools.

That this disorientation among intellectuals has also affected larger groups of society is clear from the history of two world wars and the repeated social and political crises of contemporary industrial civilization. The rise of various totalitarian movements provides especially devastating testimony of man's apprehension about his "imprisonment" in history and his fear of being trapped in an aimless existence. Industrial mass society, economic dislocation and total war have created mass values susceptible to totalitarian ideologies as a counterattack on the despair born of historical futility and purposelessness. The irony is that this reaction adopts the very weapons of irrationalism and violence which it purports to counteract.

The nihilism suggested in much of contemporary literature appears related to the major events of modern history. Despite its frequently pretentious forebodings and artificial mood of self-pity, the literary vogue of despair touches a real chord in modern experience. It is particularly noteworthy that Western man's sense of anxiety arose as a direct consequence of the collapse of our sense of historical purpose: it emerged from the inherent self-contradiction in seeking human redemption within history. The full dilemma is revealed in the individual's vain attempt to escape mortality within the frame of historical time and in terms of specific historical expectations. The problem of meaning in historical consciousness becomes crucial in a civilization which has come to place upon the individual's conception of historical destiny the full burden of his vicarious transcendence of death. It is largely the fear of history and the loss of hope in historical redemption that has brought the crisis of our time.

2. *The Problem of Self-Transcendence and Historical Consciousness*

Why should the sense of history play such a key role in our scale of values? What has made it serve in Western society as the fulcrum of our ideals? Why did history provide, for a while, a sense of order in human experience and purpose in individual life? To answer these questions, we must consider the nature of man's yearning for transcendence. We must see how the desire for eternity is related to man's impulse to seek unity and coherence in his world, and how sometimes it manifests itself in the awareness of time. Then we can discuss the role of redemptive aspirations of history in the life-forms of Western culture.

Like all biological organisms, man seeks direct gratification of his basic drives. As he develops towards civilization, he formulates a consciousness of time. He develops a collective memory and a sense of individual self-projection into the future. He no longer lives solely in the present moment and in the immediate satisfaction of wants. With the development of a sense of temporality, the wish to gratify present impulses is transformed psychologically into a wish to ensure their future satisfaction. Death, which will put an end to the fulfillment of desire, becomes relevant to his present life—a prospect he strives desperately to veil from his consciousness even if, as Freud argues, another force within his psyche drives him towards it. Fear of an absolute end to his being alters the life principle itself from a present-centered survival impulse into an overpowering yearning for immortality, or for "presence" through the eternity of time.

To gratify this urge for perpetuity, the individual seeks to transcend himself and his finite, temporal span. The notion of an afterlife appears. There emerges the idea of a distinct "spirit" that will survive the mortal body. Since the encounter with death and the desire to transcend it are common to all civilizations, this "spirit" finds universal expression, from the Egyptian *ka* to the Christian soul. The universality of funeral rites, apparent even in prehistoric cultures, attests man's concern with some form of posthumous identity. Many of man's great endeavors and cultural triumphs rise from the psychological impulse to immortality through preservation of the individual's spirit or in eternalizing his memory, whether in the form of the pyramids or of the Taj Mahal. Were there no sense of transcending death, there would be no occasion for burial ceremonies, monuments and elegies. Even in secular perspectives, entombment in a shrine is intended to perpetuate the memory of the dead hero. It symbolizes a human transcendence within an historical frame. A similar function is performed for some individuals by ideals and goals. Such hopes of transcendence often arouse a true altruism and self-sacrifice. They may awaken a person's love of country, of humanity, or of God. For some people, these sentiments are unselfish in that they love their nation solely for the sake of its destiny, humanity purely for the sake of man, and God for His perfection. For most others, however, the sentiments represent more self-centered values, being essentially an idealized egocentricity in disguised form—a hope of salvation through self-denial and sacrifice. But in any case, all such values stem, psychologically, from a person's desire to achieve somehow the immortalization of his own identity and the identification with eternal Being.

Self-transcendence, then, means primarily man's going beyond himself and his moment in time—his reaching for identification with something beyond his own finite and mortal ego. It entails the development of an idealized alter ego that signifies his eternal identity, either directly as a spiritual being or indirectly in some human legacy. Transcendence, we will see, depends upon the power of empathy and fellow-feeling; it involves an imaginative displacement of the psyche, for example, in the capacity to envisage a perfect or heavenly state. It appears in countless forms of religious beliefs, and myths of immortality. It appears also in immortalizing objectives, such as the raising of sons who will duly worship their ancestors, or the passing on of a moral legacy to men who will admire their legendary and historical heroes. We may conclude that the urge to self-transcendence is basic to civilization, for it is one of the most fundamental impulses of the psyche, namely to secure its own being from extinction.

Man's desire for vicarious immortality manifests itself in his conception of the ideal. Identification of oneself with an ideal object, such as the spirit of an ancestor, or with an ideal value, such as the good society, constitutes an indirect method of eternalization. For the quest of ideality expresses the universal desire for a self-transcending objective. Thus, while prevalent contemporary thought holds that moral values can exist only in relation to particular cultures and contexts, and that their forms are necessarily transitory, it does not deny that the quality of idealness—or some conception of good and right—is a basic element in human consciousness and a notable force in history. Indeed, no society is without both its ethical consciousness and its ritual forms representing some kind of enduring value transcending individual life.

The desire to find some coherence in life, or to evoke a semblance of order out of chaos, constitutes a general aspiration of mankind. It is reflected in the myths, archetypes and sacred rituals of all primitive cultures. This universality arises from the function that the ideal of unity performs in enabling the individual to formulate a sense of his own place and purpose, and to conceive of some meaning to his experience extending beyond his mortal existence. By providing the person with an intimation of his role, the particular conception of order, in effect, defines his social and cultural identity. Thus the distinctive unifying ideals in a civilization indirectly frame its transcendent goals and establish the concrete forms of the individual's aspiration to eternity.

In each culture, specific values and rituals give shape to man's underlying urge for unity and order, and to his desire for harmony with the transcendent forces of life. *In our own secularized civilization, this urge has found its basic expression in historical consciousness.* Indeed, one of the ways of seeking unity and meaning in things is through *the coherent organization of experience in historical time.* The unifying principle then becomes the temporal structure; the organizing theme of thought and action becomes man's conception of an evolutionary development that can be directed towards achieving a moral order in history. For example, much of the impetus behind our traditional social and political ideals has been the expectation of attaining morally rewarding historical goals, such as manifest destiny, social justice or universal peace.

These historical objectives seemed to confer upon the disconnected or erratic elements of life some consistency and redemptive meaning. They served an eternalizing function because men tended to presume that their historical goals, for example the British Empire, the Thousand-Year Reich or the Classless Society, would extend indefinitely into the future. Each of these historical ideals thus appeared to confer a symbolic immortality upon those who associated themselves with its historical triumph. In short, the basic yearning for eternity comes to manifest itself in redeeming objectives, whether these take mythical, religious or historical form. Particular historical ideals merely serve as the means through which the individual seeks a self-transcending identification with the encompassing unity that gives purpose to human existence and a form of vicarious release from death.

In historical consciousness, the individual's desire to identify himself with an immortal object expresses itself in his contributing to a transcended state—a state occurring within the historical process. That is, the redemptive value must have here a temporal quality. In sacred archetypes, the transcendent objective is eventual removal of the self *from* the process of time. In the secular-historical model (epitomized by Faust), the transcendent objective is the unending record of one's presence *in* time. Historical redemption offers not an other-worldly existence of the spirit but a moral goal embodied in the anticipated society of the future. It envisions an ideal world of human creation, if not as an attainable reality, at least as a desirable goal. In contrast to those forms of self-transcendence that seek an atemporal communion with nature or the spirit world, or which proclaim the undifferentiated-ness of being, historical redemption calls for a personal impact upon the contemporary course of events. It requires a distinctive legacy to posterity, such as memorable acts and creations that carry the name of their author into the unending future, or the unsung contributions of countless anonymous individuals to the destiny of a nation or of mankind. But in any case, it is marked by the uniqueness of each person's role in the linear unfolding of events and in the cumulative process of culture. By projecting his idealized alter ego upon the vision of a redeeming future state, the individual seeks to overcome the sense of alienation induced by the prospect of his own mortality. He achieves through historical consciousness a feeling of personal liberation and of eternal worth.

When the sense of history, which we shall hereafter call historicity, serves in this self-transcending capacity, its concern is not the past for its own sake. Its focus is rather the relation between the past and the future, whether as an inevitable process of destiny or as an opportunity for man's fulfillment and ideal aspirations. Here the past presents not a model for emulation in some cyclical regeneration of time, but the source out of which the future state arises. The process of history is seen as drawn towards certain teleological goals, in reference to which the "meaning" of present events is to be evaluated. In some historical perspectives, the teleology appears predetermined and inevitable, arising out of a divine plan or a law of historical necessity. In others, it appears simply as the unpredestined consequence of conflicting human wants and desires. Thus under given material and social conditions, such as industrialization, nationalism or the demand for social justice, these wants channel men's actions in a particular direction. According to this view, there is no single movement of history immutably imposed upon man by Providence or by the inherent order of things; but there is still a teleological quality to the historical process, in the sense that men are possessed of intentions and that, within the limiting frame of cultural and economic circumstances, they pursue goal-directed activities. The various ideal objectives to which individuals and groups direct their efforts provide the distinctive "futuricity" of our historical consciousness, which enables it to serve in a redemptive capacity.

Redemptive historicity implies the presence of inherent tendencies and immanent forces within the historical process, even if they do not predetermine the course of events. For example, an acorn has the inherent potential to become an oak, but fulfillment of this potential depends upon external conditions, or contingencies, which cause the acorn to germinate into a new tree, or to rot on the ground. Similarly, based upon past developments, the historical process may be seen as exhibiting certain tendencies which limit the future range of choices. These tendencies become manifest in occasional momentous events, such as the French and Russian Revolutions, which reveal to the believer the "immanent forces in the historical process." They provide the faithful with a sense of security in their conception of historical destiny. But these tendencies depend upon individual acts in order to be realized or completed. In the cumulative legacy of the historical past, there are always implicit certain unfinished tasks of the moment. Our responses to them, which depend upon circumstances and culturally formed values and individual desires, may lead towards certain historical objectives, such as democracy and freedom. In the transcendent conception of history, the process of developing these inherent capacities into actual realities (such as the *risorgimento*) gives a sense of redemptive purpose to individual existence. Thus historical consciousness comes to serve as a unifying principle in human experience. It answers man's basic need for a meaningful ordering of things. In the end, it seems to transcend even its secular origins, as in the case of the patriot who finds a religious quality in his national ideal.

It is evident that, given such a perspective of history, the collapse of the sense of historical destiny would provoke an acute moral disorientation. It would engender a fear of the philosophical void and a crisis of identity. If there is no historical meaning or continuity in the succession of experiences, then little seems left, psychologically, on which to anchor a person's sense of place and role. The individual is still conditioned by our culture to search for the nature of his identity within a coherent historical world. But he is deprived of traditional historical goals—hence the severe aggravation of the sense of alienation in our society. Indeed, we may propose that the crisis of values of our time is basically a consequence of our loss of a redemptive historical hope.

3. Purpose and Organization

The theme of this study is historical transcendence. Our concern is the use of historical consciousness as a redemptive faith. We shall seek to uncover the particular attributes that distinguish an historical perspective on transcendence from the other forms of immortalizing aspirations. Our key consideration will be the nature of redemptive historicity. How does it serve to convert the profane into the sacred? In what way does the rise of historical consciousness affect the character of a civilization and the form of its values? Our chief aim will be to show why, in the secularized values of modern Western civilization, the characteristic form of immortalization came to be the approach to transcendence through historical consciousness—why personal redemption was so often identified with historical objectives, notably with social and political ideals. This will enable us to examine the various consequences of this distinctive relationship. In conclusion, let us define transcendent historicity in terms of the meaning that has emerged from our discussion. It is:

> any historical ideal beyond the present reality, which serves
> to give purpose to life, and offers the hope of redemption
> from our mortal existence, because it represents a symbolic
> form of perpetuating our identity and presence.

The first volume of this work is devoted to the rise and decline of historical consciousness in Western thought, and will deal with the impact of historicity on the character of values and ideals in our civilization. Our study will focus on the development of historical thinking as revealed in historical literature, and especially as it appears in other cultural expressions of life. In tracing the origins of the historical outlook from its Greek and Hebrew roots through the history of Rome and of the Middle Ages, we will see different uses of historical consciousness for redemptive purposes, noting at the same time the non-historical forms of self-transcendence in both Hellenic and medieval Christian values.

The main part of this study will be devoted to the period from the seventeenth to the nineteenth century. Until the French Revolution, historicity remained the prerogative of educated elites. It was primarily associated with the rational current of the Enlightenment. After the French Revolution, it became a mass phenomenon in urban Western society, parallel to but distinct from the idea of progress. The ideal of historical redemption came to a climax in the nineteenth century, with the movements of liberalism, nationalism and socialism. It found its philosophical statement in the ideas of Hegel and Marx, its scientific expression in evolutionary theory and its artistic form in romanticism. It expressed itself in political and social expectations, at first in the familiar idea of progress, but subsequently also in the conservative ideal of authoritarian nationalism.

Our historical survey will conclude with an account of the disintegration of historical faith in recent years. The failure of historicity will be described against the background of events of the period, and shown in the currents in the arts, sciences and philosophy, and especially in the crises of war, depression and totalitarianism. The collapse of historical consciousness affected the whole structure of Western values and life. It aroused the fear that man could not transcend himself or his mortality. If man's being-in-time was meaningless, there could be no redeeming legacy to the future, and hence no symbolic "presence" after death. Anxiety became the price of man's historical version of secular salvation. The loss of the historical hope that man could break out of the human condition and end the isolation of the individual left a profound moral and psychological void. Historical faith had imposed upon worldly objectives and secular aspirations a redemptory and immortalizing function they could not fulfill.

We must leave to another volume a discussion of some of the non-historical forms of transcendence found in other civilizations, and the subsequent effect of Western historical consciousness upon them. There we will see how, under the impact of imperialism, Western influence directed non-Western societies towards specifically historical goals, such as nationalism.

Then we will be able to consider transcendent historicity in terms of its structure. There, too, we will shift from the chronological approach of the present volume to the categorical analysis of the forms and functions of historical consciousness. A central point of concern will be the role of what we may call *mystiques*, a type of historical awareness in which an event appears transformed into the incarnation of a transcendent ideal, and the transcendent objective of history appears immanent in the historical process, as for example, the Jacobin ideal embodied in the French Revolution. Above all, we shall see the distinctive relation of historical transcendence to the impulse to creative action and individualism, characteristic of Faustian historical culture.

In the end we will address ourselves to the key question of this study, namely, whether it is possible to reestablish a sense of historical purpose and self-transcending aspiration without presupposing the discredited assumptions of nineteenth-century historicity. Can we find moral value in history without placing upon it the unwarranted burden of achieving a transcendent state through secular objectives and ideals?

Let us now begin our view of Western historical thought with a brief discussion of the growth of historical consciousness out of ancient and medieval civilizations.

PART I

PLATE I

I

THE TWO CURRENTS

Historicity and Transcendence

1. Roots of the Western Tradition

The Hebrews were the first people to seek transcendence through historical experience. In the Old Testament, the very identity of the Jews, summed up in the special bond of their religious tradition, is forged out of their national history. It is not a coincidence that the Jews preserved with such detail and accuracy first an oral and then a written account of their historical experience.

It is true that the Chinese of the Shang and Chou dynasties had already laid the foundations for the splendid historical literature of Confucian civilization. Here there developed a record, not only of chronicles, but of rituals, customs and life that rivals the historical production of any Western civilization. But the style and intention of Chinese and Hebrew historiography remained clearly distinct. Their respective approaches, which may be crudely distinguished as cyclical and linear, suggested the more general differences in their historical perspectives and worldviews, notably on the nature and function of history itself. Thus each civilization was to leave a unique form of historical writing, attesting its particular conception of historical purpose.

The distinctiveness of the Jewish sense of history is found in the central notion of the *covenant*—the idea that God had promised the Jews a unique destiny through time. This covenant is the basis of the relationships of Moses and Abraham with God, and is reaffirmed by the prophets. Thus a linear view of history is suggested by the idea that the events of Jewish historical experience constitute a non-cyclical process. The Old Testament is seen as a manifestation of Divine Providence in which the ultimate goal is already implicit in the covenant from the beginning of time. That is why, in the Old Testament, the Jews fused their religion with their national history, which they viewed as the working out of their covenant with the Lord.

The distinctly historical cast of ancient Judaism is demonstrated in the history of Yahweh Himself. Successive historical experiences led to an ethical maturation which was reflected in the Jews' changing image of His character. The Lord first appears as a warrior-deity in the days of Joshua; by the time the Jews had experienced their brief national independence, the Assyrian conquest and the Babylonion exile, however, He had become the God of justice and love. The significance of this drastic change is that it was not a matter of theology or mystic intuition, but rather of the historical experience of faith. The transformation of Yahweh is completely bound up with the historical record of the Hebrew nation. The ultimate expression of this historical relationship is found in the post-Exilic transcendence of the national deity. It is manifest in the ethical monotheism that culminates in the idea of one universal God. The moral implications of this transfiguration are best illustrated by the contrasting characterizations of the Lord of Abraham, Who orders His servant to immolate his own son and thus suspends His moral law, and the God Who asks in Micah: "What doth the Lord require of thee, but to do justly and to have mercy, and to walk humbly with thy God?"

The historical evolution of Judaism is of concern to us not only for its own sake, but because it led to the formulation and development of the concept of historicity. In their own way, all major religions have undergone a process of spiritual and moral development. The uniqueness of the Hebrews' faith is the way in which it postulated man's creative participation in the moral order. Abraham entreated God to save Sodom and Gomorrha for the sake of fifty good men, then of forty and eventually of ten—by implication, even of one. The Patriarch here fulfilled the historical function of man as spokesman of an ethical ideal of divine justice and the voice of the Jews' moral consciousness. For the Hebrews, this moral ideal did not lie outside time and history in some eternal mystical order, but in the providential destiny of the Jewish people in the historical world. In the matured Judaic view, there is an end to history. It is the eschatological expectation of the coming of the Messiah that makes the Biblical conception of history linear and redemptive. Jewish historicity is transcendent because it is predicated on reaching a goal that lies beyond the historical realm, yet is inherent in it. The last moment of secular time, already implicit in the first, gives a unique meaning to each instant:

> And there shall be a time of trouble, such as never was since there was a nation *even* to that time: and at that time thy people shall be delivered, every one that shall be found written in the book. (Daniel, XII:1)

In short, the Hebrews gradually fashioned out of their historical and moral experiences their conception of the universal God. They identified the redemptive meaning of life with the moral purpose of their history, apprehended as an eschatological drama. Historical prophecy, not in the sense of prediction but of the attestation to God's will and moral law, was the expression of Yahweh's covenant with His people. History thus assumed a unique importance for them. From our perspective, they left a distinctive legacy of historical consciousness to Christian thought and to modern Western civilization.

In contrast to Judaism, Hellenic civilization is usually seen as ahistorical. There is much evidence to support this view. Where the Hebrews looked for an historical ordering of experience, the Greeks looked for a logical coherence in the ordering of reality. Where the Hebrew moral sense was focused upon the covenant, Greek moral consciousness was embodied in the *polis* and in a transcending moral law that ultimately bound both the gods and men. One of the notable impulses of Greek rational philosophy was to escape change and the impermanence of things by finding an absolute and unchanging ideal behind the appearances of motion and instability. Greek scientific and philosophical thought sought unity and coherence in nature through a geometric ordering of space and a rational explanation of the physical world. The philosophers hoped thereby to understand the ideal symmetry and equilibrium of the universe. It is clear that the quest for such a fixed order embodied their yearning for an eternal perfection and for a vicarious immortality.

A humanist value accompanied the Greek philosophical predisposition for seeking absolute order in nature. Hellenic rationalism expressed itself as much in the quest for an absolute moral law as for an absolute physical law. Moral consciousness, manifest in the political ideal of the Hellenic city-state, was represented on one hand in Spartan patriotism, and on the other in the great dramatic tragedies of Periclean Athens. The existence of an absolute good was affirmed by Socrates. These currents converged in Platonic idealism, which contains the Socratic concern with justice and the Spartan concept of civic virtue. We see also the joining of an abstract geometric order of nature with an ethical philosophy of the perfect state.

In the work of the great Athenian dramatists, notably Aeschylus, and in Plato's philosophy of man, there appears one of the most significant aspects of Greek civilization, the idea of self-transcendence. It takes many forms, from the Eleusinian mysteries to the ideal of the *polis*. It manifests itself in the rationalist quest for a coherent universe and the principle of unity in all being. It emerges also in the mysticism and irrationality never far beneath the surface of Greek culture. The Dionysiac element of the mysteries, which provided a psychological counterpart to the Apollonian traits of balance and proportion, constituted an attempt to transcend the present time and the mortal frame of life. A dialectical movement of rational and irrational currents marked the Hellenic attempt to reach a transcendent value such as we find in Aeschylus' *Oresteia* or in the *Antigone* of Sophocles.

The singular quality of the Hellenic vision is characterized by the intimation that there exists an absolute moral order which transcends both man and the gods. The psychological tension in

Greek civilization arose from the inherent conflict between human destiny and the moral objective of man. The unique humanism and individualism of Greek life expressed itself in the tragic vision of the hero who affirms his dignity by opposing the gods and the decrees of fate, and upholds the moral law. The significance of the fact that the deities of Mount Olympus are fallible beings, often motivated by jealousy and lust, is that it permits man to formulate his own redemptive vision of the good, as Plato did in the *Republic*. One of the crucial legacies of Greek civilization is its conception of justice standing beyond the human condition and beyond fate, yet intelligible to the human mind.

We can see that the idea of transcendence was intrinsic to much of Greek thought. But it seemed to have no relation to historical consciousness. Its geometric quality and its implication of a timeless order appeared to preclude a serious concern with history. Aristotle's interests, for example, lay closer to the considerations of historians than did those of most Greek philosophers. He undertook a comparative analysis of constitutions. He was deeply involved in the explanation of process, in the sense of the natural fulfillment of the potentialities of a living organism. Yet it is revealing that Aristotle had little use for history. He approached constitutions in terms of political categories, not historical development. He applied his notions of process, or *entelechy*, to nature but not to the history of man. What makes his indifference all the more striking is that he lived through some of the most momentous changes of the ancient world and scarcely took note of them in his political philosophy.

Are we to conclude that Greek civilization was irrelevant to the development of historical consciousness? Before we do so, we might note that the term "history" is itself of Greek derivation. Furthermore, much of our historical sense and critical methodology stem from two Hellenic writers, Herodotus and Thucydides. The Greeks were probably the first people in Western civilization to approach the study of the past as a systematic account of the development of present human society. They were the first to seek in history a rational explanation of the major crises of their day. We must therefore consider historicity in relation to the other

aspects of Greek culture. Apart from the ahistorical current we
have been considering, there was a Greek tradition of historical
awareness. Contrasting with the Platonic view, there was the Homeric tradition which had the most profound impact on Greek life.

With Homer, we come back to the centrality of historical
consciousness, though presented in the poetic and mythical forms
typical of an heroic age. We need not elaborate on the influence of
the *Iliad* and the *Odyssey* in shaping Hellenic culture. We might
note that in the aristocratic warrior ethic of the Homeric age,
the quest for vicarious immortalization of the hero's identity took
a typically historicist form. It manifested itself in the yearning for
fame which would guarantee to the individual a kind of continuing presence in the "living memory" of succeeding generations.
Later, immortality came to mean a sharing in the perpetual life of
the *polis*. Confronted with the somber prospects of the under-
world, the Greek tended to look to such expectations of civic
glory as his great redeeming hope.

Essential to Greek historical consciousness is the affirmation
of the dignity of man. Though life is tragic and each individual is
bound by fate, he can attain freedom. Man becomes morally free
not by overcoming his destiny but by responding to it with human
dignity. The archetypal myth of man's freedom and dignity is the
Prometheus legend which has a distinctly historicist quality,
though its chief protagonist is a god. The theme of Prometheus is
the transcendence of the human condition through revolution
against oppressive authority. Shelley noted this meaning when in
the context of the French Revolution he entitled his drama on the
deliverance of mankind, *Prometheus Unbound*.

The ideal of moral freedom expressed itself in political forms.
In the civilization of the *polis*, the political world was the moral
world, and the good man participated in the life of his city-state.
The affirmation of the self-transcending dignity of the individual and the moral worth of the citizen achieved its most sophisticated expression in Athenian democracy. In the Periclean vision,
the individual develops himself as a free moral being. All the
elements of Athenian versatility are but the means through which
this end is to be realized. It was a foreign-born Athenian historian

who saw in the sweep of history a process culminating in the Hellenic ideal of free citizenship. For Herodotus, history had a transcendent, religious meaning exemplified in Athenian values. In the Persian wars, he sees the Greeks, pitted against the powerful Persian empire, successfully defending their supreme moral ideals of civic independence and of human liberty. History thus seemed to give purpose and a transcendent value to the individual's actions.

The Athenian world Herodotus had glorified was in full decline by the time Thucydides analyzed the Peloponnesian War. Where Herodotus had looked upon history through a religious framework in terms of some transcendent meaning, Thucydides saw it as a clinical study in the pathology of power. He was concerned with the analysis of political decay. Frequently anticipating the insights of Machiavelli, Thucydides developed many of the historian's techniques of critical historical thinking and of rational treatment of evidence. But he had his own suprahistorical frame of reference, namely the constancy of human nature and of selfish ambition. This view imposed upon him a cyclical conception of history in contrast to the implicit lineality in Herodotus' historical thought.

What are we to conclude? We have seen that Hellenic culture, though nonhistorical by comparison with Judaic traditions, developed its own form of historical awareness. A society which identifies the political life as the moral life, and active citizenship as the primary ideal, can hardly remain indifferent to its historical past or to the "meaning of history." Hellenic historical thought, notably in Herodotus and Thucydides, left an important legacy to Western historicity. In conclusion, we may say of the Hebrews and the Greeks that each of these civilizations gave distinctive elements to the Western historical consciousness and to the sense of transcendence. Both developed the idea of absolute moral value and tied it in different ways to a transcendent vision of the ideal. The Greeks left the conception of meaningfulness in history susceptible to rational analysis. The Hebrews left the conception of historical eschatology.

2. The Development of the Western Tradition

In the culture of patrician Rome, history played a crucial part, as befitted a civilization that glorified stoic patriotism and service to the state. During the days of the Republic, the patrician ideal vaunted the citizen's duty to the city: *Dulce et decorum est pro patria mori.* The Roman achieved vicarious immortality by identifying himself with the undying majesty of Rome. Hence honor and reputation were vital to him. The prose of Cicero and Livy contained something of this transcendent quality, and it is found especially in the patriotic epic of Vergil. This relationship is expressed in the emblems of the legions, the triumphs of generals, the words of the magic formula: *Senatus Populusque Romanus.* But there is a quality missing here for a true sense of transcendence. There is no messianic vision, no impulse to a state of being higher than the contemporary Roman world, no sense of lifting oneself out of one's present form of consciousness. In the context of Roman pragmatism, the idea of liberating man from the human condition seems a strangely romantic illusion.

This does not deny the Stoic idealism of the Roman elite, nor the historians' criticism of their society in terms of refined patrician values. Many Latin historians were at their best in elegant descriptions of political degeneracy. Livy deplored the erosion of Republican virtues which he sought to recapture in the history of past Roman triumphs. He presented the typical civic-heroic view of a patrician class, which uses history for the education of rulers and statesmen. Sallust, supporting the plebeian cause, had focused attention on the moral laxity of the patricians. Tacitus subsequently attacked the rise of despotism under the Empire and the decline of civic virtue in all classes, including his own. Yet the objectives and values of these historians did not constitute a transcendent principle. Their work was not marked by either the universal scope of Herodotus' panorama of ancient civilizations or by the religious unity found in the prophetic literature of the Old Testament. For a new sense of transcendent and redemptory meaning in man's historical experience, we must turn to the rise of Christian civilization.

Christianity built upon the eschatological sense of the Jews. It also encompassed the rational legacy of Hellenic Greek culture. A fundamental dualism thus pervaded Christian life. Reduced to its essential terms, it consists of the dialectical tension between a passive, other-worldly contemplation, and an active messianic commitment. The passive position generally seeks withdrawal from the material and historical world, and receptiveness to the divine presence; the active position involves participation in secular concerns and the calling to God's work, in the sense of carrying out a divine plan for the world. These two religious approaches are not mutually exclusive. In Western Christendom, in fact, the affirmation of one approach has almost always included some element of the other. Both positions lend themselves to the mystic intuition of a direct knowledge of God. Both lend themselves to ascetic self-denial and sacrifice. But they do represent opposing tendencies. They constitute real differences of emphasis in the Christian balance of the contemplative and the active life. Many of the changes which, under the impact of economic and political forces, have transformed Christianity over the past millennia have done so by shifting the equilibrium from one pole towards the other.

Christian attitudes towards history have reflected this duality. In general, tendencies that emphasize radical withdrawal from the world leave little room for concern with secular history. Even religious history may appear as a distraction from man's contemplation of the true City of God. Conversely, the tendencies that emphasize the world as a divine creation and stress God's redemptive purpose in human affairs are more concerned with the social implications of Christian teachings. They find religious significance in the individual's historical task. In contrast to the passivity of the contemplative outlook, the messianic drive often emphasizes revolutionary goals of social justice and equality. The ideal of a community of brothers was frequently limited to the elect, that is to say, to a particular sect, but at other times it was extended to all of Christianity. Then it might lead to politically revolutionary implications. Thus the messianic outlook, though ahistoric in itself, often led to historical consciousness. Millenarianism is future oriented. It has little concern with the historical past, or with the time before the New Dispensation. But messianism narrows the gap between contemplative religion and social objcctives. Here history becomes important as the scene of Divine Providence manifest in human events.

Early Christianity was largely ahistorical. The Second Coming was deemed imminent. In terms of the world, there was no real past or future. There was only the extended present from the Resurrection to the Day of Judgment. But gradually, Christians had to face the realization that the world would continue for an indefinite period. The consequence of this recognition was a revival of concern with time and with the process of man's historical development. The new perspective presupposed a divine meaning manifest in previous human events, especially in the history of the Old Testament, of the Church and of Rome. How was God's will shown in the rise of Christianity and in the decline of the Roman Empire? In response to this question, which had become insistent by the fifth century, Augustine wrote *The City of God*.

Augustine's best-known theological treatise is not an historical work. The history of the worldly city held no intrinsic interest for him. His criterion of historical truth and evidence was conformity to the revealed word of God. He had little or no concern with historical events as such, or with other criteria of historical objectivity, because the study of secular history was of no use to man's salvation. Yet history is the stage where the reality of the other, eternal city has been made manifest to man. In this earthly life, the two cities interact with each other, and man cannot free himself from his involvement as a social animal. History thus acquires meaning in the framework of Christian providence. In the history of the Jews, of pagan civilization and of the Church, Augustine saw the hand of God.

Many divergent influences were to flow from Augustine's great impact on medieval Christianity. Manicheaen undercurrents appeared in the strong impulse to reject the material and sensual world. A new formulation of history and Christianity also emerged gradually from Augustine's thought. A new postulation of historical consciousness arose in the emphasis on eschatology, for eschatological history related itself to the sacred and profane backgrounds of Christian teachings and experiences. Thus indirectly, a transcendent form of historicity eventually emerged from Christian doctrine, and from the dialectical antithesis of its mystic and worldly tendencies.

The society of the High Middle Ages gradually worked out a distinctive but variable balance between the two themes of withdrawal and of participation. Implicit in the values of medieval culture was the self-transcending ideal of Christian salvation. The purpose of life was the love of God and the salvation of one's soul. The theme of medieval other-worldliness is undoubtedly exaggerated in our popular historical perspective. Secular objectives played a greater part in the life of all classes, including the clergy, than is suggested by our romanticized picture of a mystic age. Yet there is little doubt that the aspiration to personal redemption pervaded much of medieval civilization. It was inherent in the institutional structure, rituals and doctrines of the Church. It lay behind the traditions, superstitions and simple faith of popular folk culture. In this sense, the concept of self-transcendence through eternal salvation was an existential reality of medieval Christian experience.

It is significant that the primary forms of value in medieval Christianity involved little or no sense of historical consciousness. The teachings of the Church in the High Middle Ages emphasized the non-historical aspect of the Christian dialectic. Church doctrine considered society a divinely fixed structure. In the corporate social theory of the scholastics, particularly Thomas Aquinas, the ideal organic hierarchy of social institutions reflected the unchanging order of divine creation. In this conceptual framework, there was little room for a doctrine of historical evolution. The view of society as an organic whole presupposed a coordinated relation of its members, but a not a sense of social growth or a continuing process of change. Thus, despite the great dynamism of the High Middle Ages and the dramatic changes in many aspects of medieval life and culture, historical thought barely began to appear. While logic and art, architecture and theology, attained remark-

able greatness, historical writing remained essentially at the level of
chronicles.

Early medieval civilization was based on an agrarian economy. A manorial society geared to the seasons and the powerful
force of tradition is not a likely source for a lineal view of time or
a sense of historical movement. It does not lend itself to the
conception of historical destiny. Rural communities dependent
upon the recurring phases of nature tend to develop a cyclical
view of life. With the rise of an urban culture in the High Middle
Ages and the renewed vitality of intellectual currents, a new consciousness of time arose. The clock gradually became a regulator
of urban living. A standardized system of dating with reference to
the Christian calendar focused attention on the linear chronology
of events. It was accompanied by a rising concern with man's
active role in history. Spengler looked back upon this period as the
source of a "Faustian" spirit of dynamic creativity characteristic
of Western culture and of its distinctively historical outlook. The
twelfth-century humanist John of Salisbury believed that his generation had surpassed the wisdom of the ancients—the essence of
the idea of historical progress. Expressing the distinctively historicist notion of a cumulative development of man, he suggested
that if men could see further than their predecessors, it was because they sat on the shoulders of giants. But it was especially the
twelfth-century Bishop Otto of Freising who, in his remarkable
work *The Two Cities*, presented a panoramic view of history given
unity by his sense of Christian destiny and the inexorable approach of the New Jerusalem.

In radical Christian thought, new millenarian movements appeared that anticipated progress towards a heavenly kingdom on
earth. The mystic recluse, Joachim of Floris, envisioned progressive stages of Christianity towards an ideal state of redemption for
all mankind in which the organized Church would cease to be
necessary for salvation. His implicitly optimistic faith appealed to
the imagination of certain revolutionary sects which developed
largely within the communes of the thirteenth and fourteenth
centuries.

The new urbanism of the High and Late Middle Ages was

not a sufficient condition to generate historicity; otherwise every urban civilization would have produced historical mindedness. The historical outlook was still an infrequent view against the prevailing ahistoricity of medieval civilization. But it had its consequences, and it suggested the shape of things to come.

With the coming of the Renaissance, the historicist features of Western thought were clearly accentuated. The humanists' addiction to the literature of antiquity and to the rediscovery of ancient manuscripts reinstated historical literature as a notable cultural expression. The histories of Machiavelli and Guicciardini indicate a new level of historical interest and awareness. Historical thought became a significant element in the attempt to find new meaning in experience, particularly political experience. New techniques of historical and textual criticism and rational analysis of evidence appeared, for example, in the work of Lorenzo Valla.

Characteristic Renaissance objectives and ideals had a distinctly historical quality, of which historical writing was only one expression. Though the idea of progress clearly was not the predominant intellectual current of the age, a certain sense of hope in man's future developed, if only as a countermovement to the prevailing skepticism about human nature. The key to the historicist implications of the period is the subtle but profound transition from the emphasis on the individual as a soul to the emphasis on his unique ego.

In the values of the Renaissance elite, individualism meant the fulfillment of the potentialities of the self, and the achievement of a new self-consciousness. What man created, particularly in terms of his life and personality, constituted a new ideal of self-transcendence and led to a new conception of immortality. The man who created a work of art and the patron whose name it glorified could achieve immortality by bequeathing a unique legacy to the ages. In the pursuit of individual distinctiveness, activism and individuality became the key qualities of a Faustian striving to create something enduring. According to the popular saying, the artist "lived on in his work," and "existed" in the memory of men. The uniqueness of a man's historical contribution became the measure of his hope for a perpetual identity in men's minds.

Through his sense of creativity, man imagined himself a participant with God in the process of creation. Christian neo-Platonists like Ficino made a central theme of man's participation in the divine order. Pushed to its demonic extreme, this conception leads to man becoming his own god. He formulates his own values, his own world and his own vision of self-aggrandizement. As prince-despot, he creates the state in his own image. As adventurer, he determines his own standards. As individualist, he fashions his own personality. For in this view of self-transcendence, man ultimately identifies himself with what he makes, which is why he must above all "make himself." In short, it is the individual's "divine" accomplishment in life that frees him from finiteness and mortality. It permits him to transcend in his imagination the inevitability of death by extending his vicarious self into the open-ended historical future.

With the Reformation and the Counter-Reformation, new political situations developed in Europe, and old religious forces appeared in new forms. The emergence of absolutism and the sovereign state focused increasing attention on the historical character of political institutions. An example is the work of Bodin. The emphasis in certain Protestant teachings on a return to Augustinian theology fostered a renewed concern with Church history. Calvinist interest in the Old Testament and the history of the Jews further stimulated historical awareness. The emphasis on the "calling," which presupposed the individual's active role in life and a concern with the future results of man's labor, indirectly enhanced the interest in history from a religious point of view. Historicity was also stimulated by some of the radical millenarian sects that emerged as Protestant offshoots. In their utopian eschatology, they sometimes anticipated the achievement of a perfect kingdom on earth, and thus suggested a messianic view of progress. Some of the sects proposed radical social and economic ideals, such as those of the Diggers and Levelers of mid-seventeenth-century England. Others, such as the Fifth Monarchy Men, and followers of Jakob Boehme and John of Leyden, proposed fantastic revolutionary schemas. Ahistorical as many of these revolutionary teachings were, they nevertheless promoted the concern with social change and influenced the prevailing consciousness of time. Some sects specifically related the past history of Christianity to their redemptive expectations of the future. It was not only Protestants like Theodore de Beza who concerned themselves with the historical presence of the Church; Bishop Bossuet presented a remarkable panorama of world history from a Catholic point of view, given unity and purpose by a sense of Christian destiny.

The triumph of scientific thinking in the seventeenth and eighteenth centuries affected historical consciousness in several ways. On the whole, the spectacular achievement of Newton in the elaboration of a mathematical order of nature and the new vogue of physics relegated historical and evolutionary thought to the background. The conception of fixed universal order tended to preempt the consideration of organic process. Yet indirectly, the age of Newton had a significant impact on Western historical awareness. Apart from the prevailing trends of scientific thought, there arose expressions of social philosophy that were definitely historical in orientation. They remained undercurrents, sometimes of little influence in their day but of considerable impact on later intellectual developments. Giovanni Battista Vico formulated a significant concept of the process of civilization and of the stages of cultural growth. Using myth and poetry as expressive of the deepest layers of human experience, Vico proposed in his *New Science* an historical order through three major stages of development; the Age of Gods, the Age of Heroes and the Age of Men. Vico's science of society involved both cyclical and linear elements of historical order. His conceptual framework of mythical and poetic analysis influenced later historical and literary thought, from Michelet to Joyce.

The predominant eighteenth-century current of scientific thinking, namely the conception of a mathematically structured universe, also had an impact on historical consciousness, though in an indirect manner. It established the idea of a rational order in nature, which could be applied to the coherent ordering of man's historical experience. History was regarded as subject to the rational patterns of natural law. The sense of a coherent meaning in the historical process gave an apparent purpose to human affairs, which was subsequently translated into the idea of progress.

From mathematical philosophy came a new concern with infinity. It expressed itself in the notion of a perpetual extension of secular time that placed the vision of man's historical future in a new secular frame. The sense of an infinite future gave new meaning to the ideal of eternal human happiness and perfectibility. It provided the hope of redemption in the vision of a rational state emerging from the irrational society of the past. Impressed by the method of Cartesian reasoning, Fontenelle proclaimed that the achievements of the Moderns exceeded those of the Ancients and that, with the continuing advance of knowledge, such a relationship would prove to be true in every subsequent age. Consequently, he argued, men should not lose themselves in a misplaced worship of the past, but should look to their historical youth as the cumulative basis for future progress. In this approach to self-transcendence, the individual identified himself with the unending future good of mankind.

We find in the new perspective the eventual merger of the two major Western currents of self-transcendence and immortalization. On the one hand, we see the Greek ideal of man's moral transcendence of the human condition in a rationally ordered universe. On the other hand, we find the Judaic sense of a moral coherence and meaning in human experience through the eschatological objective of history. In the secularized utopia eventually suggested by some Enlightenment thinkers—even against the prevalent skepticism of their day—these currents are brought together, filtered through both Christianity and the political and scientific developments of the modern age. The absolute ideal of implicitly neo-Platonic inspiration and the sense of future deliverance derived from the Christian view of history were combined in the new historicity of modern Western consciousness. Man's redemption here is his participation in the historical ideal. Self-transcendence then becomes a consequence of historical values and of man's historical faith.

We have come here to the heart of our subject, and the key issue in the use of historical consciousness for a transcendent purpose, namely the idea of an immortalizing projection of the self through historical time. We must now examine the manifestations and consequences of this notion in the cultural and intellectual currents of modern Western civilization.

PART II

II

THE ENLIGHTENMENT

The Road to Historical Consciousness

1. "Nature" and "History"

At first glance, the Enlightenment appears a retreat from historicity. Indeed, its characteristic mode of thought seems to reverse the developing historical consciousness we have traced from medieval Christianity, and to postulate a worldview fundamentally ahistorical. Its rational utopianism was Platonic and Newtonian in that it presupposed a fixed geometry in the fundamental pattern of nature. This view was expressed in a model for an ideal society divorced from specific historical experiences and unique historical contexts. Thus the essence of historical humanism—the emphasis on individual distinctiveness—here was lost in a Cartesian abstractionism fundamentally concerned with the ability of society to mirror the unchanging mathematical symmetry of the natural world.

Critics of rationalism, notably Burke and Carlyle, have attacked the anti-historical character of the Enlightenment and its revolutionary disciples. Utopianism, they argue, is incompatible with historicism. The former involves an exclusive concern with the future and indifference to the historical past. One cannot deny that these critics have put their finger on a real conflict of outlook, especially if one views history from the romantic perspective as the distinctive evolution of each people. Many utopian visionaries have undoubtedly been contemptuous of man's historical record. They see the past as devoid of the true enlightenment—whether revelatory or philosophical—without which it can shed no light on the future, and is of no use to the present. Both chiliastic sects and some of the later revolutionary disciples of the *philosophes* shared this quality of predominant ahistoricity. It was reflected in their impatience and messianic zeal. Of course, certain types of utopianism have been more inclined to emphasize this theme than have others. But to some extent, the predilection appears in all varieties of utopian idealism. Their natural tendency is to postulate a particular vision of the good as the proper condition for the whole of mankind, or at least for the redemption of all the elect, without regard to culture or nationality. Even Marxism, which claims that all knowledge is rooted in the evolutionary context of men's needs and acts, participates in the same outlook. That is why many of its critics term it fundamentally ahistorical, despite its view of history as the master science. How much more may not the Cartesian utopianism of the Enlightenment, with its vision of man's natural state attuned to a timeless universal order, be judged anti-historical?

But in fact this charge is based on the confusion of "history" with "tradition." No less than Burke, the Jacobins had a sense of history, only theirs was basically different from the more conventional historical perspective. It rested on a fundamentally contrasting, unspoken assumption of the nature of the relation between past and future. The revolutionists also looked back in time, especially to the age of Rome, as their use of classical symbolism amply testifies. The backdrops of antiquity, the flowing white robes and garlands of their naïvely neo-pagan festivals, were expressions of an allegedly Greco-Roman humanism. The evocation of republican civic pride and glory, and the ideal of the free city-state were grafted onto their national patriotism. To be sure, this view constituted a largely mythical picture of classical times. But it was no more distorted than the avowedly "historical" panoramas of the romantic Victor Hugo. If the revolutionists' historical vision failed to bring Greek and Roman values back to life, it fell short no more than that of Walter Scott and other historicist romantics who were unable to "re-create" medieval Europe. The point is that eighteenth-century rationalists evoked their own historical models, which functioned in part as moral ideals. Like Carlyle, who felt their rationalizing and analyzing propensities reduced the inherent mystery of things to counting-house relationships, the disciples of the Enlightenment believed that the future was conditioned by the past. Perhaps that is why some *philosophes* found a typical outlet for their ideas in historical studies, many of them landmarks of historiography. There are the examples of Diderot and Voltaire, and of course of Hume and Gibbon. Of these gentlemen, the most illustrious names of their time, several not only wrote histories, but made them the key to their work.

What was it that converted some of the *philosophes'* rational philosophy of nature into something we may term an awareness of history? For one thing, the emergent notion of progress rested on a sense of historical movement brought about not by some providential, extra-historical force, but by man learning from his historical experience how to overcome the past and transform the present. The secular utopianism of the Enlightenment had no explanation for human advance other than man's record of learning and progressive rational achievement, culminating in eighteenth-century scientific knowledge. Thus Condorcet saw the successive ages of civilization expressed in man's increasing understanding and his power of reason. From this historical momentum, Condorcet projected man's future progress towards a state of fully realized rational capabilities. Thus the faith in progress is different from religious millenarian movements. The latter remain truly ahistorical because their "new time" is brought about by direct divine intervention and consequently owes nothing to man's previous history or accumulation of knowledge.

An instance of the historical bent of the Enlightenment is the use of the term "natural history" to refer to the study of nature. Voltaire, in his article on history for Diderot's *Encyclopedia*, comments that the term is a misnomer, and that a more appropriate designation of the topic would be "physics." But the fact that it was in use is revealing in itself, just as our use of the term social science is revealing of our culture. Certainly, much eighteenth-century thought about organic nature tended towards a fixed categorization in line with the Cartesian legacy. Linnaeus' botanical classification reveals this quality. But the wider and more flexible zoological classification of Buffon brings us back to the intimation of a natural history. The conception of historical process is confirmed in the revealing titles of some of his works, such as *The Epochs of Nature* and *The History of the Earth*. Here we encounter a definitely evolutionary view, anticipating Goethe, Lamarck and Erasmus Darwin. Buffon even suggests some sort of transcendent-historical vision that would find in "the archives of the world" the milestones of "the everlasting highway of Time."[1]

One reason for the development of this evolutionary-historical sense in the Enlightenment ironically was the success and universality of its mathematical and scientific thought. For the triumph of reason convinced much of the intelligentsia that it stood on a higher peak of rational knowledge than did preceding ages. Even skeptics who had little faith in humanity as a whole because they saw human nature as constant and held crime and misery to be the irremediable conditions of life, could generally agree that in the realms of science and natural philosophy, the intellectual elite of their age had scaled the highest mountains. This view of their own mental progression naturally inclined them to see a rise in the achievements of the human mind. The occasional optimists among them went a step further. They combined their conception of an eternally fixed, clocklike universe with the ideal goal of a rational political and social organization moving towards harmony with the universal order of nature. In short, Enlightenment philosophy put together an unchanging and a-historical pattern in the physical world with an historical-evolutionary development of the human mind—even when it denied the general advance of culture and regarded with skepticism or resignation the constancy of man's misery and oppression. This ambivalence characterized many of the intellectuals of the age, notably Voltaire, Hume and Gibbon, who rejected any utopian view of the future. Yet to the extent that these men saw a measure of political balance and satisfaction attained in the present age or sought to explain the rise of intellect to its present level, they were inclined to think in historical terms.

We must trace the distinctive historicity of the eighteenth century from the preceding ahistorical legacy of natural rights and social compact upon which were grounded the ideals of the state and of political freedom. For these ideals were to become the new secular vehicles of man's historicized and transcendent purpose. Political ideals were to become the common denominator through which natural law would affect men's consciousness of past and future, the link of social evolution to the rational cosmos. In other words, it was primarily political concerns and the developing political awareness that functioned as the instrument through which historical values came to embody a self-transcending and quasi-religious meaning in Western consciousness.

It was Hobbes who, in mid-seventeenth century, proposed the modern myth of the sovereign state. In the appropriately violent setting of the Cromwellian revolution, Hobbes gave birth to that new "mortal god," the *Leviathan*. But Hobbes and historicity, Hobbes and freedom! One might as well write of Locke and the divine right of kings! Why then begin with a contradiction? The answer is that the deification of the state and the secular religion of national patriotism which have stamped our own times so decisively, owe their origin to seventeenth-century political ideals and were partly inspired by the historical experiences of national monarchies, notably of France and England. Some of these currents are reflected in Hobbes' rationalized secular demigod, ironically in a non-transcendent materialism and thoroughly utilitarian political philosophy. In an age when moral issues were identified with man's natural state, the state of nature with the moral character of political society, and political society with human destiny—in such an age when moral ideas and political ideals became virtually synonymous, and political passions often governed the lives of educated men—it was Hobbes who formulated the state as the most crucial creation of man, outside of which there could be neither society nor civilization.

The *Leviathan* clearly reflects the mechanistic currents of the age of Newton although it was published thirty-six years before

the *Principia*. It constructs a philosophy of the sovereign state that
is inherently non-transcendent and notably ahistorical; indeed,
indifference to history and repudiation of transcendence were perhaps its chief characteristics. The new absolute could have served
Hobbes, as it was to serve others, in the role of a transcending
ethical ideal. But it didn't, perhaps because the only universal
that fitted his particular materialist philosophy of man was physical self-preservation, which does not readily lend itself to transcendentalization.*

Writing in the context of civil war and under the impact of
the execution of Charles I, Hobbes depicted man in a state of
nature that is nothing but the war of "every man against every
man." Here the fundamental conditions of life consist of a corrosive insecurity and the terror of death. While Hobbes talks of the
natural law, he does not use the term in the conventional sense,
i.e., derived from stoicism and Christian scholasticism, an inherent
yet transcending ethical principle in the order of nature underlying
human moral consciousness and the legitimate laws of society.
Hobbes' natural law did not involve any innate sense of fairness
and justice, let alone a romantic or sentimental urge to sympathy
and fellow-feeling. In line with the requirement of his materialist-
utilitarian philosophy, natural law was simply the self-preservation
of the organism erected into policies of self-interest. In his classic
phrase, life in the state of nature is "solitary, poor, nasty, brutish,
and short."[2]

Purely out of the survival instinct, man, in Hobbes' view,
craves security and peace. He enters into a compact with his
fellowmen by which he establishes the state, and transfers to it
virtually all of his personal rights. Outside this state there can be
no creative undertaking, because in nature all man's activities are
impeded by the fear and prevention of a violent end. The prepara-
tion for the struggle that is always imminent remains man's unending concern. Does it help him in such a condition, to "enjoy"
natural rights? Of what use is a freedom defined by man's power

---

* True, for Spinoza it did, but self-preservation was certainly not the only
human motive that fitted his transcendental rational ethics.

momentarily to impose his will, before inevitably surrendering to a stronger rival? Hobbes concludes that when individuals establish the sovereign power, they must transfer to it *all* their previous rights, save that of self-preservation itself. Only in this way can the state have the unchallenged authority necessary to maintain order and keep civil society away from the ever-threatening abyss. From this argument follows the distinctive trait of Hobbes' social philosophy, namely that the *Leviathan*, which man himself has created, holds not only unlimited power but also unlimited right. Indeed, it is the sovereign's will that establishes right, for outside the civil compact there exists no moral obligation. Here, rather than in the mere fact of absolute monarchy or the unlimited power of the sovereign, we find what makes of Hobbes' state a model of despotic government and the new tyrannical god.

Hobbes' collective state, it should be noted, is purely the creation of men and derives its authority solely from their individual needs. The initial act in which each individual accepts his subjection to the state is a voluntary abdication of his own future will in favor of the will of the sovereign because it lies in his rational self-interest to do so. That such a sorry bargain would be voluntarily undertaken, and such a surrender offered testifies to the intolerable character of life in the condition of nature. Hobbes' sovereign despot therefore emerges as nothing but an inside-out expression of unbridled individualism, and of the individual's desire to overcome his natural condition. Like the liberals who were to berate his conception of the state, Hobbes remains fundamentally an individualist who sees the function of government in terms of the self-interests of its subjects. The dilemma of his rational and supposedly scientific political philosophy is that he had reduced individualism to the only elements he found inherent in human nature: aggressiveness, fear and the instinct of survival. It is not Hobbes' affirmation of the centralization of all legal authority in the absolute legislator that distinguishes his thought from that of his liberal critics—his view of political life was not so far removed from theirs—but rather his claim of the sovereign's power to define the moral right as a function of enforcing civil order. Hobbes' political philosophy presents a remarkable juxtaposition of overbearing statism and radical self-centeredness that, despite recent efforts to "rehabilitate" him, constitute an interesting psychological insight into absolutism as a response to individual insecurity, amid what is conceived to be man's natural state of war.

But if Hobbes' *Leviathan* could serve as a rationalization of absolutism, it could serve as well to justify successful revolution. His concern was the maintenance of order against the predatory tendencies of men; if a revolution occurred, it constituted proof that the government had failed. The social compact compelled obedience to authority only so long as this obligation remained in the subject's rational self-interest, i.e., so long as his peace and security were preserved. Here is an implicit justification of revolution that is at least as radical as the more famous defense of consent by Locke. In Hobbes' view, the will of the sovereign defines the moral order. Consequently, a successful revolt followed by a new compact is by definition "morally" justified— though not in the transcendent sense of an ethical law of nature such as forms the underlying moral presupposition of democratic society. One may wonder why Cromwell, who seems a far closer approximation to Hobbes' sovereign than was any Stuart king, did not become his model ruler! The Protector certainly imposed the order which Hobbes saw as the only justification for the state. In the nature of Hobbes' philosophy, his opposition can hardly have come from any sentimental attachment to the fortunes or historic claims of Charles. But the fact remains that for Hobbes any challenge or resistance to the authority of the sovereign, such as was exemplified by Parliament and the Puritan faction, constituted an open invitation to the dreaded war of each against all. The problem with Hobbes' utilitarianism is not that he precluded empathy because of his cynical rejection of motives other than self-preservation; it is rather that he interpreted this elemental drive solely at the lowest common denominator of physical survival. He overlooked the key question of whether even self-interest may not prompt, as it seemed to Spinoza to do, a vicarious identification and fellow-feeling. In Hobbes' rigorously materialist philosophy, even the *Leviathan* has no inherent ethical value, and fails to achieve any transcendent quality or function.

Hobbes grounded his materialist-utilitarian political system on a mathematical-mechanical structure quite befitting his time, and devoid of historical consciousness, or of any sense of "becoming." He structured his original state of nature as a universal condition of pre-civil man, devised universal psychological "laws" of human behavior, and created his abstracted structure of sovereign monarchy as a universal model. The physical balance of opposing forces translated itself into a neat geometrical order. Hobbes' state of nature was not an anthropological reality, as he admitted, but a logical exercise of necessary suppositions, once granted the basic axiom of human aggressiveness. In other words, both his state of nature and his civil society are essentially myth archetypes, not attempts to re-create man's actual prehistorical condition or existing political communities. Both are hypothetical relationships, deduced from Hobbes' axioms about the essential nature of human beings. His state of nature is not really a condition in time so much as the natural predilection within man at all times. It co-exists with the civil state built upon it, but always lurks threateningly beneath civilized life. Thus the formation of the body politic is not really a distinct act at a specific moment. It is an "initial" compact in the sense of a primordial consent which permits the characterization of two distinct, parallel and timeless forms. In any case, history is not a relevant factor here; politics have become a subdivision of physical mechanics.

But the *Leviathan* did embody an unspoken view of history. Its historical frame rested upon the qualities Hobbes considered the natural tendency of men beneath their terrified craving for peace, the somber qualities of his cheerless jungle. Hobbes' philosophy of history, like that of Thucydides and Machiavelli, was correspondingly fatalistic on the central issue of any historical faith, namely the possibility of the moral improvement of man. The sovereign assumed the responsibility of educating and caring for his subjects. But progress could have no significant meaning where the only justification of government is the prevention of chaos. Thus, the pessimistic perspective of history—quite different from the tragic view—crystallized into the impossibility of man's transcendence of his animal nature. If he has successfully overcome the overt form of natural war in the peaceful state of the

Leviathan, he remains trapped in the state's grip. He can over-come a despotic civil society based on rational egoism only by regression to the more terrifying state of nature. In the absence of any true process of historical becoming, man is confined, in the fixed world of material forces, to two possibilities. Either he must bear the effective absence of individual freedom and suffer the arbitrary, compassionless might of the legislator or he must face the only alternative: constant terror and sudden death.

2. The Changing View of Man: From Aggressive to Benign

The Hobbesian formula revealed a powerful originality, and exer-cised considerable influence. Hobbes' arguments became those with which other political thinkers had to deal, his relationships those they had to account for or refute. Above all, Hobbes' con-ceptions of the sovereign state and the absolute monarch were to become the standard models of political life, eventually transcen-dentalized into the romantic nation-state of the nineteenth century. It is revealing that Rousseau, who was to disagree so vio-lently with Hobbes' view of the state of nature, and diametrically to oppose his own principle of popular democracy to Hobbes' despotism, was nonetheless to share Hobbes' key doctrine of the unlimited power and authority of the sovereign legislator. Indeed, by investing Hobbes' social compact with a moral rather than merely rational value, Rousseau's formulation of the general will was further to strengthen the claim of the state. He would convert Hobbes' *Leviathan,* based on ultilitarian interest, into the moral cohesion of the community. Thus he provided the ethical quality Hobbes' materialism had rigorously excluded. He furnished the modern state with the transcendent function that Hobbes' mortal god lacked.

In his own day, however, Hobbes remained a solitary politi-cal figure, no doubt because of the starkness of his despotic ideal. As Hobbes' concern with power was reminiscent of Machiavelli's, so was his unpopularity, notably with those whose cause he would serve. In the century leading up to the Enlightenment, the prevail-ing political tone in England became increasingly one of hope that history might lead to a more civilized, i.e., more rational, life.

There were solid reasons for this upturn after the tumultuous years of the seventeenth century. Politics became a less dangerous sport, with the relative consensus of 1689. For the Whigs, life was marked by increasing mercantile prosperity, while the landed gentry retained power and greatly added to its wealth. Prestige and a sense of political responsibility, or of *noblesse oblige,* characterized the new elites within the parliamentary "club." Not only was there something for everybody in the ranks of the Whig oligarchy, but their class fortunes went hand-in-hand with the rising power of the nation. Britain's destiny seemed demonstrated at the Treaty of Utrecht of 1713—which marked a hiatus in the threatening French advance—and in the rapid expansion of English colonies. The tangible progress of science in the country that had already produced Bacon and Newton was a consoling thought. Restoration comedies added zest to London coffee-house conversations. The inhabitant of Newgate may not have been better off than before, but he wrote no political tracts and few people expected his lot to improve. His fate did not seem to weigh too heavily on the consciences of his betters or to put a real crimp in their general self-satisfaction.

Foreshadowing this new, post-'89 note was the empirical touch of Locke's *Second Treatise of Civil Government.* Its comparative lack of originality was evidence of the representativeness of his political ideas. It thus provided a popular and easy-going counterweight to the pessimistic rationalism of the *Leviathan* and proved to be more readily exportable. In it, we find several of the key propositions that were to culminate later on in the distinctive view of the Enlightenment. Though Locke himself showed little concern for history, hardly using it in his own major works, his political theory nevertheless was to leave a significant imprint on the subsequent historical consciousness and expectations of the *philosophes.*

Locke took his stand against absolutism by deriving his political society from the same stock notions of social compact, state of nature and natural law as Hobbes had done, but giving to these terms quite different meanings—meanings more in keeping with the conventional style of an ethical principle of natural justice. Starting with a different psychology, he conceived of the state of nature as a condition of contentment, a near-utopia, or golden age, in which man had lived in equality and freedom. Where Hobbes had seen the fundamental human urge as self-preservation, Locke saw it as happiness; the two ideas are not antithetical, but they do represent a difference of focus and a change in style. To Locke, "life, liberty and property" constituted the natural rights of man. Accordingly, he conceived of the natural law as a condition of freedom under a sort of negative golden rule in which each individual had the right to do as he chose so long as he did not injure the "life, health, liberty or possessions" of another.[3] This was certainly a more engaging formula than Hobbes' natural state of war. It permitted Locke not to make his commonwealth a tyrant. In his double social contracts, one setting up civil society out of the state of nature and the other organizing a government,* Locke, unlike Hobbes, stipulated a limited sovereign power confined to the minimum authority consistent with public order. Hobbes, we should note, had seen the actual *functions* of government in much the same way as did Locke, notably in allowing the citizen to conduct his private affairs with a minimum of interference.** Where they differed was in the unlimited *power* Hobbes had assigned to his absolute ruler, and in the claim that the state established, rather than manifested, the moral law. What permitted Locke's different approach was his different appraisal of the natural motives of men. He took Hobbes' social compact and cast it in a new mold, bearing the stamp of a different psychology and concluding with a different form of civil order. The difference between Hobbes' and Locke's state of nature is the transition from pessimism to optimism.

In Hobbes and Locke, we have seen two forms of the social compact, the key political concept of its day, based on two notions of the so-called natural law. Each was predicated on a mythical archetypal model of the human condition in the original state of nature. Upon similar assumptions were built the subsequent polit-

---

* Whether the second step was a true contract need not concern us here.

** That is why it is incorrect to ascribe to Hobbes' political thought a totalitarian, as distinct from an absolutist, quality.

ical conventions of the Enlightenment. As in both the *Leviathan* and the *Second Treatise on Civil Government,* the character of the archetype is in direct accord with the individual's implicitly pessimistic or optimistic approach to political society and historical change. There were to be as many conceptions of history as there were conceptions of man in the natural state. It is here that we find the focal point of impact of the new sciences. For rationalism pervaded psychology, political thought and the forms of historicity in that each was seen in terms of a universal order. Therefore those who, like Locke, wished to argue against Hobbes' virtually unreserved commitment of the self to the state, with its absolutist implication and pessimistic view of human motivation, had to formulate a different social compact. They had to devise another model of nature, and a contrasting universal paradigm of the human psyche. The implicit optimism of Locke hinged upon his view of man's natural condition as a state of mutual assistance, goodwill and peace. Here, rather than in the mechanisms of power, lay the crucial difference between him and Hobbes, and the significance of their respective legacies to subsequent historical aspirations grounded in rival political ideals.

The compact theory which Locke proposed is generally seen as connecting historically with the legacy of medieval government. Both rested upon the recognition of mutual obligations between ruler and ruled. Both involved a division of sovereign power, away from the notion of absolute, centralized authority. In fact, however, Locke's balanced weights in the separation of powers is more akin to the balance of Aristotle's *Politics.* Where the feudal contract of the Middle Ages had consisted of a set of traditional and morally sanctioned reciprocal personal duties, the seventeenth-century compact was an equation of units. Where the feudal contract had expressed an organic unity of living parts, the compact theory of the age of Newton represented a mechanical equilibrium of political forces. All this bore the stamp of the third law of motion more than of Bracton's conception of medieval kingship.

The scientific vogue, however, produced its own contradictions. In the anomalies of compact theory, two quite different notions of law became hopelessly confused. Upon the old convention of "natural law" as a superior, guiding ethical principle was superimposed the incompatible meaning of "laws" in science. That the so-called "law of nature" was in fact something quite different from the natural laws of physics, because the one dealt with supposed causal necessities and an inviolable relationship, the other with a prescription for behavioral norms or an assumed injunction, constituted a distinction that seems to escape most contemporary notice. But it is precisely this confusion which attests the desire in much of late seventeenth-century thought to reduce all principles, including moral ones, to a universal rational system modeled on a geometric order, as in Spinoza's ethics and Hobbes' politics. Such was to be the embracing mission of compact theory in the new age of science!

If the influence of medieval tradition thus appears vestigial in seventeenth-century political ideals, Locke's notion of compact does nonetheless connect with the old legacy in one key sense: the notion that government must ultimately rest upon consent and moral right. From medieval experience he partly revived the claim that political life ought to be based on a decentralization of sovereign authority and on participation in government. In a word, Locke's legacy to the changing forms of historicity was that he, a moderate, gave the doctrine of consent a quasi-democratic form which eventually would promote a radically optimistic view of man's historical expectations.

How did this inversion come about? Why did Locke's unhistorical and atranscendent political objective furnish the substance for a later transcendentalized conception of democracy and of historical destiny? Locke grounded his discussion of practical political matters in a theoretical deduction from the state of nature. From the universal attributes of mankind, he deduced the qualities of civil society—in fact, he was rather to invest both with those human qualities he had already determined, and to provide them with a suitable dress. But the form remained essentially analytic rather than synthetic. Thus even Locke, the pragmatist, succumbed to the Cartesian approach. But Locke was, after all, an empirically minded thinker, and he soon reverted to this outlook, found in the pragmatic considerations of his psychological notions. It is common knowledge that in his *Essay Concerning Human Understanding*, Locke conceived of the human mind as a *tabula rasa*, a "white paper, void of all character," to use his own words, or a "yet empty cabinet," devoid of all innate ideas and principles which experience alone would provide.[4] How this view could be reconciled with his argument about the state of nature is not entirely clear. In any case, the blankness of the mind at birth left room for the development of a consciousness of man's natural rights to equality and freedom in a way which Hobbes' psychology of natural aggressiveness had not. So the neutrality of the *tabula rasa* could be fitted into a hopeful view of man's political capacity. At the same time, the utilitarian empiricism of his psychology of experience left Locke little room for transcendent aspirations. Even freedom here is a serviceable commodity rather than a romantic vision.

Hobbes and Locke shared at bottom a utilitarian approach to politics, even if Locke's was the more pragmatic and optimistic in its outcome. Locke's commonwealth, like Hobbes' *Leviathan*, was the outgrowth of a social compact that provided a strictly manmade base for society and government. Thus both were products of self-interest. When all is said and done, "happiness" may be a more attractive objective than self-preservation but it is hardly a less utilitarian one, and perhaps what it gains in appeal it only loses to superficiality. In short, ethical rationalism here is a new style; it is not yet a new faith.

The significant point for us is that Locke's pragmatic work had the effect of a polemical tract because of the subsequent conditions in which its ideas reverberated. The conventional claim that his famed Treatises are merely *pièces d'occasions*, or *ad hominem* discussions foreshadowing the settlement of 1689 from a Whig point of view may be exaggerated. But the fact remains that Locke's ideas anticipated the status about to be achieved in the Glorious Revolution. Here we discover the revealing ahistoricity of his method. Writing in relation to a specific historical situation, he turned his theme into a universal argument. He avoided any claim on the basis of precedent or of English history, or any mention of the specific issues between the Stuarts and Parliament.

It simply wasn't done that way; a self-respecting political position had to be based on Scripture, or on nature, or on the example of the ancients. Apparently Locke did not want to trivialize his discussion by historicizing it. Even in his empiricism, the historical method was not compatible with the requisite universal predicates of natural law and human psychology. Yet despite this fact, the consequence of Locke's discussion and its relation to English constitutional practice was to turn the attention of some of the *philosophes*, notably Montesquieu and Voltaire, to the investigation of their own governmental institutions in the comparative light of English history and political precedents.

The irony is that Locke thereby achieved a radical influence as a defender of revolution oddly out of keeping with his own moderate inclinations. It is a commonplace nowadays to point out that Locke was something of a conservative liberal, as perhaps were most Whigs once they had achieved a satisfying *modus vivendi*. His separation of the powers of government, and his limiting of one by another in a form of checks and balances, served to limit the popular branch as well as to restrain the monarchy. In its executive function, the crown remains an important principle of government. Indeed, Locke introduced what appears to be a significant concession to Hobbes in stipulating the sovereign's prerogative to take whatever means necessary for the defense of the community from outside attack. Locke does not suggest that he intends to defend a pure mass democracy. Perhaps it was only an accident that in his day the basic challenge to English constitutional practice seemed to come from the Stuart kings, and that in attempting to redress the balance he compensated by stressing the role of the populace. Thus it was other people's reading of Locke that selected, or at least emphasized, the liberal aspects of his political thought, and that used them to justify democratic aspirations. But the fact remains that his theoretical *a priori* vindication of the Glorious Revolution became in many people's minds a general defense of democratic consent. It was Locke's words that made the people the judge of whether or not the ruler was living up to the trust they had placed in him. A power they had conferred was a power they could withdraw. It was Locke's chapter on the right of revolution which introduced into the mechanical balance of his stable system a built-in mechanism of change and a self-perpetuating principle of movement. Because of Locke's upbeat view of man's yearning for freedom and equality, this carefully qualified invitation to political change could but lend itself, despite the ahistoricity of his argument, to a popularized interpretation of progress. Where revolution had figured in Greek thought, at least for Thucydides and Polybius, as the frustratingly repetitive cycle of civic life, and in Hobbes' political philosophy as frightful degeneration into chaos, it meant something quite different to Locke, namely the progressive political solution of human problems.

Locke provided the vehicle of popular consent which later, in the absolutist environment of France, served as an instrument of revolutionary innovation. In an ironic inversion of the conventional categories, one may say that where Hobbes' absolutist state arose from a pessimistic radicalism, Locke's liberal commonwealth arose from an optimistic conservatism. Between them they had furnished man with the natural "right" to create his own utilitarian political state in response to his needs and interests. Each had provided in his own way a rationalization of revolution, though Hobbes saw it as a disintegration into war and fear while Locke saw it as a legitimate renewal of the social contract in order to preserve man's natural freedom. If Locke's ahistorical view became implicitly progressive, it was clearly neither transcendent nor utopian. It did, however, bring the idea of nature to bear on man's aspirations for a future political society; it did give historical "presence" to the concern with natural rights, and to the widespread notion of the natural order of the cosmos; it did make of natural law the cornerstone of an ideology of political change and of the acceptance of an implicitly progressive historical movement. Perhaps we should, then, reverse the emphasis of our previous conclusion, and note that, if Locke's social contract represented neither a transcendent ideal nor an historical conception, its principles eventually served to promote a utopian expectation of man's political future.

3. The Enlightenment and Historicity

The intellectual elite of mid-eighteenth-century France found itself in an enviable position. It lived in a remarkably intellectualized society which feted and revered its savants, particularly its literary wits. The world of the salons provided a highly polished stage for the sophisticated culture in which a royal mistress and legendary beauty protected philosophers and had her portrait painted holding a book. A notably cosmopolitan European society furnished leading minds with an international audience, the pleasures of travel, and the self-satisfaction of expecting the adulation of Potsdam to be renewed in St. Petersburg. A select few of these minds enjoyed the respect of kings and empresses who patronized their works, or listened to their theories and pretended to be one of them. The numerous lesser figures basked in the reflected light of a stream of correspondence with the great. Above all, the intelligentsia could enjoy the confident knowledge that it was beginning to understand a cosmos built according to plausible scientific laws an intelligent layman could grasp. It could flatter itself to be among the pioneers opening the windows of reason.

Here were grounds for conformity and smugness. Why, then, did the *philosophes* conspicuously display the second quality and not the first? Why did revolutionary thought, first religious, then social and finally political, become the passkey to their intellectual world? The reasons are innumerable. Many are given in their own writings; others, more subtle perhaps, are not. The artificiality of the society that lionized them both attracted and repelled them, even as they were part of it and could no more have separated themselves from its customs than Tacitus could have dreamt of joining the Germanic bands. Most of them loved the polished manners of the aristocracy they charged with artificiality and an inverted order of values. Most had had close calls with the censors if not with prison, but this fact seems more a sign of their nonconformity than a cause of it.

The slowly grinding machinery of state was proving itself inefficient and arbitrary. The contradictions of absolute monarchy, dependent upon the personal qualities of the king and the uncertain factor of heredity, became evident. Irritations which had been obscured by the dazzle of the Sun King's court broke out towards the end of his reign, and became increasingly dramatic under the rule of his successors. Louis XV reversed his predecessor's policy of appointing the bourgeois to official posts of state. A class grown used to social climbing through bureaucratic employment, cut off from its prospects of social mobility and its entré into noble ranks, turned against a regime of which it had previously been the most loyal, because most interested, supporter. To the *philosophes'* audience of intellectual noblemen and of educated bourgeois bordering on the nobility, were added the larger numbers of the bourgeoisie proper. Their discontent was reflected in the alienation of intellectuals who came from middle-class ranks: Diderot, Voltaire, Rousseau. Criticism of the class structure became one of the staples of Enlightenment literature, even among those who sought ardently to be accepted into aristocratic society.

The well-known weaknesses of the *ancien régime* concern us here only insofar as they contributed to the historical consciousness and transcendent ideals of the *philosophes*. The anomaly of the richest nation in Europe heading towards governmental bankruptcy, the grandiose waste of the court and the fruitless debts of war undermined the basic loyalties of classes that had traditionally supported the monarchy and the state. The arbitrariness of government and the petty artificiality of court society increasingly offended the sense of order of intellectuals devoted to the notion of a rational world. The creeping economic paralysis of the countryside and the patchwork tax system which often made reinvestment in productivity a severe burden had a devastating effect. The frustrations of a peasant class, generally the most prosperous on the Continent, made the bulk of the population restive or sullen under exactions and humiliations it was now sufficiently self-conscious to resent. These conditions left much of the intelligentsia with two primary forms of reponse. One was indifference to the condition of things and escape into the social pleasures of aristocratic society. The other was a commitment to reform, or to the creation of a new social and economic order. The physiocrats, for example, sought an economic rationalism which would restore the prosperity of French agriculture. They tried to apply the new techniques of science to the productive organization of society. An attempt to reform the agricultural and tax systems of France constituted the first rational step towards progress vainly undertaken by Turgot. It is significant that this approach to enlightened social reform meshed with Turgot's philosophy of history. For in fact, the great agrarian and economic reformer wrote one of the more remarkable eighteenth-century histories on the progress of the human mind, and thus linked the preceding ideas of Fontenelle to the later views of Condorcet and Comte.

The psychological conditions of mid-eighteenth-century French society drove many intellectuals to find decreasing satisfaction in the service of established cultural values. The defense of political institutions and the established religious order held progressively less effective appeal. The zeal of a Bossuet in defending the Gallican Church seemed out of place amid the prevailing intellectual fashions of the Enlightenment. The consequent feeling of cultural alienation induced the noted crisis of conscience of the age. Under these circumstances, the commitment to change soon became a commitment to revolution, first in the Church, secondly in society, and lastly in politics.

Of all the elements of philosophical conflict, opposition to the religious institution in France and criticism of religious doctrine had by far the most pervasive effect and most far-reaching consequences. Since the middle of the seventeenth century and the end of the wars of religion, traditional Catholic loyalties and beliefs had had only spasmodic effect among the new intellectuals. Much of the dogma and the ideas built upon the dogma seemed out of joint with the trend of scientific rationalism. Thus the Church provided the most visible target for rationalist critics and the new pride in the self-sufficient power of man's reason. But the Church of the *ancien régime* was not simply an institution. It was a thoroughly integrated part of French society and a deep-rooted element in French culture. Consequently the *philosophes'* assault upon it soon broadened into wider areas of conflict. Eventually new social ideals and political utopianism became the natural goals of those thinkers who had started as critics of religious "superstitions." From their new perspective, they regarded history as the process of development of man's rational capabilities.

Do these tensions suffice to explain the fact that the most well-placed and favored of intellectual elites turned against the established values and institutions of the society in which they had been educated, and amid which they had reached the intellectual leadership of the Western world? The crucial influences of life always remain, in part, psychological intangibles. It is often the particular characteristics and experiences of individuals that make rebels of them, as in the case of Jean-Jacques Rousseau, for example. Intellectual dissent is rarely a phenomenon of conscious decison or of rational argument. It is generally a consequence of accidental circumstances, unconscious predispositions and perhaps veiled self-interest. There have been revolutionary idealists in virtually all generations of our modern history. But these considerations do not account for the fact that at a certain time and place, a disinctive constellation of restive minds emerges—a situation that must lie beyond individual propensities and particular personalities.

Among the ultimate sources of the Enlightenment spirit was the concern for the redemptive assurance of having true knowledge in scientific terms. The pervasive yearning for certitude in rational world order, proposed in Cartesian and Newtonian thinking, placed the *philosophes* at odds with the institutionalized irrationalities in which they lived. As deists, the eighteenth-century rationalists shared at least one basic conviction with Christianity, ancient Judaism and Platonic thought: the belief that there exists some absolute standard of truth. Placed in a temporal setting, this impulse to true knowledge called for an historical explanation of man's transcendent insight into the rational order of things, and a projection of his unlimited capacity to reason.

But perhaps there remained above all one central cause of revolutionary dissidence leading to utopian aspirations: frustration with a society that had reached the internal limits of its conventional capacities. Where no other transcendent objectives seemed left within the structure of a culture, the natural result was the feeling of futility and boredom. The sense of being shut up in one's world led to the alienation of sensitive minds. The new scientific rationalism and the new political ideology provided an escape from jaded sentiments. At the same time, it was inherent to the secularized values of scientific knowledge and of political idealism that they could only offer a worldly fulfillment. Consequently the men of the Enlightenment found meaning in the conviction of their destiny to promote the progress of mankind.

Just as many of the transcendent values which emerged from revolutionary English political thought ironically originated among conservatives with little sympathy for transcendent or redemptive ideals, or for messianic politics, a comparable phenomenon arose in the transmission of redeeming political expectations to the new currents of French intellectual life. Transcendent aspirations were occasionally born of conservative ideas, initially expressed by moderate thinkers temperamentally unsuited to be cast as prophets of a new secular utopia. The common denominator of their revolutionary influence was the penchant for social criticism and the desire for a more rational ordering of society. But reason has many forms. The abstract universalism of most of the *philosophes* was occasionally offset by a more comparative and empirical perspective with distinctly historicist implications.

The Baron Louis de Montesquieu was born into the ranks of a nobility that had been driven from power and political responsibility by the centralization of absolute monarchy. It is not surprising that he should feel ill-disposed towards political conditions in France and view the regime as a form of despotism swayed by the arbitrary whims of court. Disdainful of the artificiality of public life during the reign of Louis XV and the erratic absolutism of France in mid-eighteenth century, Montesquieu spent much of his time in retirement. The two articles of his social and political faith were the superiority of virtue over pleasure, and the passion for liberty. We might note here the contrast with Hobbes' conception of the state. The author of the *Leviathan* denied right except as a determination of the sovereign, and eliminated freedom from his monarchical commonwealth. Montesquieu held right and freedom to be the two ultimate values. Appropriately, he adhered to a political system opposed to that of Hobbes. Like Locke, he opposed the idea of an unlimited sovereign and proposed the separation of powers, and the return to a traditional participation in government in order to preserve liberty.

England! Here was a country where the aristocratic elites had preserved their political functions, authority and responsibility to serve, and where royal pretensions had been curbed. England was a state where the constitutional practice of the eighteenth century had produced a political order based on participation of privileged groups. That is to say, public life was dominated by individuals favored by birth and wealth, or who had somehow been accepted into the educated ranks of the dominant classes. By this standard, Montesquieu and most of the other *philosophes* would qualify for admission into the ruling aristocracies and oligarchies. The parliamentary state was not a democracy. But few men in the circle of the Enlightenment doubted that government ought to be in the hands of those who were qualified to govern by their breeding, wit and education. The ideal of a more rational society put a premium on the vanity of intellectuals, convinced that they understood the mechanism of the universe and the order of nature. The *philosophes* generally believed that the goal of a more enlightened society would not be achieved by turning government over to the "rabble" who were mostly ruled by irrational passions and appetites. The limited popular participation in the English Parliament represented the balance that intrigued many of France's would-be reformers. Above all, England after the Glorious Revolution symbolized a political society based on consent. If anything, it was the consensus of political classes that characterized a regime which had selected its own monarch on its own terms. Thus freedom seemed the great quality of English political life, even more when viewed from across the Channel. One leading *philosophe* had tasted its effective meaning when he found English asylum from a French prison. It is not surprising that eighteenth-century English parliamentary government, which from the inside suggests a petty game of factional, corrupt politics played by small in-groups defending their respective privileges, fascinated French thinkers as a living contrast to their own monarchy, and a model of a free society.

For Montesquieu, the English example was revealing. Both

his concern for the powers and responsibilities of an active aristocratic elite and his passion for liberty seemed particularly served
by the constitution of 1689. Montesquieu's political philosophy
placed Locke's social compact in the new setting of Bourbon absolutism. It is obvious that Locke's formulation of balance and consent, whose moderate tones blended in with its original Whig
background, stood out in sharp relief against the background of
Louis XV's absolute and inefficient rule. How Montesquieu fastened upon the English separation of powers, and perhaps misread
them, is a well-known story. More important for our purpose is
how Locke's almost prosaic conception of a free commonwealth
was converted into a shining ideal of liberty. Through Montesquieu, who inadvertently became a hero of eighteenth-century
revolutionary ideology, a dispassionate analysis of law and government was transmitted to the thought patterns of other *philosophes*, who changed it into a vision of a transcendent historical goal.

Montesquieu first came into public notice with the publication of his popular *Persian Letters*. Under the guise of notes written home by two Persian travellers describing the strange culture
of Western Europe, Montesquieu satirizes the beliefs, prejudices
and foibles of eighteenth-century life. These writings suggest some
of his political ideals. In the eleventh letter, which constitutes
Montesquieu's indirect answer to Hobbes, he presents the myth of
the Troglodytes, a people living according to the crudest precepts
of survival and self-interest. They consume themselves in their
egoism. Because of their wickedness, they are abandoned by others to their mortal fate. That is the path, Montesquieu suggests, of
those who would organize a political community totally devoid of
ethical ideals and of moral principles.

In letter eighty-three, Montesquieu argues that equity and
justice are the supreme virtues of man, remaining valid independ-
ently of any divine sanction. Moral right, embodied in the higher
moral law, has its own rational compulsion. It serves as a dispassionate, yet transcending, objective and meaning to life. For
Montesquieu, the transcendent moral principle finds its primary
expression in social ideals and values. He saw the forms of moral

values, not as abstract universals, but as particulars varying with climate, social conditions and historical experience.

Of all Montesquieu's writings, *The Spirit of the Laws* is his most notable work, and the one which indirectly had the most significant consequences for our approach to history. Law, for Montesquieu, expresses the essential order of things and constitutes the principle of coherence in human affairs. It is thus intrinsic to being, and in this sense exhibits the quality of necessity. In the first paragraph of the book, Montesquieu explains that laws are "the necessary relations resulting from the nature of things." The laws of society are merely the particular expression of these inherent relationships applied to the varying conditions under which men live. Montesquieu's primary concern lay in grasping the character and the reasons of their distinctiveness. His explanation presented a departure from the intellectual presuppositions of the Enlightenment. He did not develop his argument from theoretical deductions or from a mythical and universal state of nature, nor seek to justify a uniform pattern of political rights or principles of government. His primary consideration went to the singularities of climate, social conditions and culture. From a strictly rationalist point of view, Montesquieu's approach was disturbing, for it precluded the idea of universal order and symmetry in human affairs. No wonder that many of the *philosophes* came to regard him as strange, and that in the end only Diderot among them followed his bier.

It is Montesquieu's method that is of particular concern to us. His arguments are based on a mass of sound and unsound data from a great variety of nations and cultures. Montesquieu's approach is essentially comparative, and his type of analysis has been regarded as an early exercise in sociology, notably by Durkheim. His evidence is largely historical. From Book Twenty-eight on, he traces the origins of French civil jurisprudence through a detailed account of the laws and feudal customs of the Franks up to the Capetians. Yet *The Spirit of the Laws* is not historical in spirit. The comparative evidence is snatched from one culture or another, and the dimension of time and evolution is conspicuously missing.

Elsewhere, however, Montesquieu showed awareness of a process of becoming, and exhibited the historical sense which his concern for the particular, and his consciousness of the importance of precedent and tradition, had suggested. In his brief book, *Considerations on the Causes of the Grandeur of the Romans and of Their Decay*, he, like many another historian, turned to Roman civilization in order to find the general secret of cultural growth and decline. He drew lessons applicable to his own time from the military valor and moral fiber of the Romans. From the example of Rome's military deterioration he concluded rather strangely that Denmark's defeat by Swedish armies was due to the congenital weakness of the Danish government. On a more general level, he concluded from Roman history the following "historical" maxim:

> Owing sometimes to the cowardice of emperors, more often to the weakness of the empire, efforts were made to appease with money the peoples threatening invasion. But peace cannot be bought because the seller only comes into a better position to force its repurchase.[5]

Here history may be said to serve Montesquieu as "The Spirit of Morals." But it remains an auxiliary discipline.

In sum, we find in the Enlightenment the complex and occasionally confused counterpoint of ahistorical rationalism and distinct historicity. This tension is revealed, for example, in Bayle's *Philosophical and Historical Dictionary*. On the one hand, Bayle sought to follow the method of Descartes, and on the other to establish a sort of positive truth-value of historical facts, or more accurately, to apply Cartesian rationality to wider realms of "truth," including the historical one. The point here is not Bayle's clouded distinction between synthetic and analytic propositions, but rather that for all his championing of historical criticism and the truth of historical fact when it is uncovered according to proper scientific method, he remained inhibited from formulating any relationship between our knowledge of history and the nature of human experience. Consequently, he was never able to develop, as was Voltaire, a sense of history.

III

THE ENLIGHTENMENT

History and Utopia

1. Skepticism and Progress: Voltaire and Gibbon

François-Marie Arouet was the most influential figure in setting the tone of the Enlightenment. He brought together the Cartesian tendency of his native France and the Newtonian tendency of his one-time adopted England. He borrowed heavily from the empiricism of Locke, and on this intellectual combination he superimposed his own distinctly historical view. The ideas of the Enlightenment were synthesized in Voltaire's writings, which joined the conception of a fixed natural order ruled by a god-mathematician with that of the historical evolution of human society. In Voltaire's work, therefore, we find the dilemma of eighteenth-century historicity, in the conflict between the skeptical view of human nature and the hope of a more rational social order. In his approach to history, Voltaire expressed the contradictions between the prevalent skepticism and the increasing outcroppings of the notion of progress.

Voltaire manifests his philosophy of history (he invented the term) principally in two works, *The Age of Louis XIV* and the vast *Essay on the Customs and Spirit of Nations*. In the *Essay*, a panoramic view of the evolution of European society from medieval "barbarism" to modern civilization, Voltaire develops his conception of the progress of the human mind. It is a progress that has not been constant, and indeed has seen periods of decline and even of collapse, but that, on the whole, has marked the history of man from his primitive condition to his present state.

In approaching his great historical undertaking, Voltaire wanted to avoid the old historical style of chronicling royal achievements; his was essentially a cultural, not a political history. Not for him "the precise year in which the brutal sovereign of a barbarous people was succeded by a prince unworthy of historical notice!" Not for him the "chronological series of all the dynasties" which, if one could master it, "would be a jumble of words!"[1] But if Voltaire rejected history as a chronicle of kings and asserted that the true greatness of an historical age lay in the diffusion of creativity among artisans, artists and philosophers, his own principal heroes nevertheless remained kings and conquerors. Louis XIV was *le grand Monarch*, despite his grave faults. Voltaire, after all, had delighted in his role as featured attraction of the courts of Frederick and Catherine, and the Prussian king had even "forgiven" him after their celebrated quarrel, returning to the ranks of Voltaire's royal fans. Why should M. Arouet not look to crowned heads as the patron-spirits of their age? We must remember the political ambivalence in which he sympathized with republican institutions while looking to the expected reforms of enlightened despots acting as philosopher-kings. In any case the enlightened ruler functions as the catalyst of his period. He becomes the agent through which its powers, accumulated from preceding phases, are sparked to a new vitality that permits the most recent age to rise above earlier achievements. Yet the king is only the prompter; the real advance is made by men of genius in art and thought. It is properly found in the customs and ideas of the society. True history itself remains a unity, a whole, consisting of the progressive advance of the human spirit.

Voltaire identified four great ages of man, namely those of Pericles, Augustus, Mohammed II, and Louis XIV. They represent successive peaks of human achievement, each higher than its predecessor. He implied that this process could be continued in the future. He saw his own time as a temporary decline from the great age of the Sun-King. Yet this period outshone all previous great ages in its release of man's creative energies. Above all, it excelled in the development for the first time of a general philosophy based on reason. Such was the prevailing conceit he shared with the cosmopolitan intelligentsia of his day.

Did this complacency about the scientific and general intellectual achievements of modern man, which reminds us of Fontenelle's argument of the superior knowledge of the Moderns over the Ancients, mean that Voltaire saw in history the prospect of human perfectibility? Did he formulate an optimistic view of human destiny, to be fulfilled in the moral improvement of mankind?

Optimism! What was more insufferable to Voltaire than the fatuous faith of Pangloss in the inveterate goodness of things? *Candide* brings Voltaire's skepticism about human nature into sharp focus. Satire is generally a device of those who criticize present conditions in order to improve them. But Voltaire mocks as much the utopian hopes of the reformer as the satisfied pretension that this is "the best of all possible worlds"; Eldorado presents a caricature of the ideal state, just as Candide's other adventures present a caricature of our own. Voltaire's conclusive word on the perfect society of human reason seems to be that man would gladly seek escape from its rational harmony to the travails and passions of this world.

Thus Voltaire's criticisms do not eventuate in an ideal social order, but lead rather to a resigned acceptance of an imperfect world and a wiser understanding of the irrationality of men. His conception of progress in history is consequently limited by his belief in the unchanging character of human nature. All ages, he informs us, are filled with misfortunes and vices. It was Voltaire who characterized history as a record of human crimes and a trick played upon the dead. In such a perspective, there is little room for man's moral redemption through historical ideals.

This skeptical view was not unusual in the historical thought of the Enlightenment. The *philosophes*, with their elitist bias and intellectual detachment, saw history dominated by man's irrational passions and prejudices. Voltaire's pessimism and disillusion with the idea of universal progress were no more skeptical in tone than the most famous historical production of the age, Gibbon's *De-cline and Fall of the Roman Empire*. In this monumental work, Gibbon presented the panorama of a passing civilization. The key-note to his study was the process of decay, deterioration and doom. From the grotesque behavior of emperors to the corruption of military honor, Gibbon offered a discouraging picture of cultural decline. Rome in its glory represented to him the summit of man's cultural achievement. If even this unique empire had fallen, was it not likely that his own culture was also destined to pass away? Gibbon thus doubted the prospect of mankind's escaping the inherent forces of decline which overcame Roman civilization.

Gibbon's study showed his contempt for the fanaticism of believers. It is zeal and passion, in his view, that undermine culture. Even religious virtue and self-sacrifice become political evils when they sap the basis of civic order and pride. But the dispassionate reason of pagan Rome had also induced skepticism. For Gibbon as for his countryman, Hume, reason constituted less a new value than a form of analysis that could destroy false beliefs without offering any ultimate purpose or meaning. Rationalism was a method, not a new ideal of hope.

The attitude of an age towards history is not necessarily embodied in the work of its professional historians. Indeed, the popular approaches to history are likely to be quite different, not only in such obvious matters as methods, biases, credulity and degrees of accuracy or subtlety, but also in intent and purpose. Most of all, they tend to differ in the kinds of satisfaction and forms of self-awareness men derive from contemplating the traces of their collective past. History often serves the non-historian more intimately and purposefully, as well as more misleadingly, than it serves the critical professional. Where the technician seeks accuracy and detail, the amateur seeks emotional sympathies and moral significance. In this regard, the non-historian is more apt to find a transcendent meaning in his sense of the past. The notable point for us is that he frequently exercises a greater influence upon the historical consciousness of subsequent generations, and even of later historians, than do the skilled craftsmen of his day. The attitude of hope in much of nineteenth-century historiography derived not from the skepticism of Gibbon but from the optimism of some of the other *philosophes* who approached history with less professionalism.

We have found marked ambiguities within the Enlightenment view of history. It is clear that we cannot accept the popular misconception of the eighteenth century as an age characterized by a consensus of belief in historical progress. The Aurelian detachment of Gibbon and Hume is as typical of the Enlightenment as is the ideal of progress. The view that man should not try to build an illusory city but rather cultivate his own garden is as characteristic of Voltaire as his conception of the progressive evolution of human knowedge and civilization. The remarkable phenomenon is that there eventually emerged from the eighteenth century a conception of human perfectibility which gave shape to the idea of historical self-transcendence. For the Enlightenment exhibits a resilience found even in the more anxious moods of the period. As in the case of M. Arouet, skepticism often gave rise to fatalism, which did not, however, constitute the last word of the age or the man—otherwise Voltaire could not have been posthumously cast as patron saint of the Revolution in a prophetic role he would surely have scorned. The ray of hope in man's reason, often clouded, nonetheless remained an essential part of his humor, and reflected itself upon the style of his time. The eighteenth century was an age of pamphlets and political tracts; it is a psychological self-contradiction for someone to be a pamphleteer of futility.

On balance, we may conclude that the rationalist view of history exemplified by Voltaire did not hold out the hope of an ethical regeneration of man, or an end to his present condition. It involved, rather, the idea of a development of man's creative energies, particularly in the arts and sciences. Above all, it was the achievement of reason and rational philosophy that were seen to mark the greatness of the human mind and the advance of history. Great men master skills and knowledge, but mankind cannot master itself or its passions, for that would mean a qualitative change in human nature. Thus even progress remains essentially untranscendent, and man remains trapped in his egoism. Yet we can learn from history how to avoid repeating our mistakes, for ex-

ample to prevent a new Saint Bartholomew's massacre. Referring
to the most recent of the four great ages of mankind, that of Louis
XIV, Voltaire writes, "It is perhaps that one which, of the four,
most nearly approaches perfection." It has been enriched by the
other three, yet in some ways it surpassed all of them; if a few of
the arts have not gone beyond the heights reached in the days of the
Medici, Augustus or Alexander, the key fact nonetheless remains
that "human reason in general has improved." The result is that
for Voltaire "a sane philosophy dates only from this most recent
time," and that since the age of Louis XIV, a revolution in government, manners, art and thought has taken place "that will
forever mark the true glory of our country." The key to history is
precisely this: that its cumulatively great ages stand as an eternal
example to posterity.[2]

2. Reason, Sentiment and Hope

If Voltaire's view of historical progress was ambivalent, that of
Rousseau was downright contradictory. He had once been one of
the *philosophes*, in the company of Holbach and the entourage
of Diderot, to whose *Encyclopedia* he contributed. Then about
1753, he broke violently with them over their cold deism and
rationalism; he formulated a distinct position of his own, in
opposition to the Enlightenment. It was the appeal to the heart,
or rather the emotionality, which Rousseau voiced, that was to
dominate much of the aesthetic tendencies, political thought and
conception of human nature of the next century.

　　In his case perhaps more than in most, personal experiences
and moods have a direct bearing upon his work. His unhappy
youth in Geneva, his later adventures, a strange dependence on
mother figures, his violent quarrels with a long succession of
friends and would-be well-wishers—all, he felt, seemed to con-
spire against him. He felt himself increasingly victimized by
friends and enemies alike, and thus, despite his fame, he seemed to
revel in feelings of frustration, and perhaps to invent torments for
himself. He found a series of tolerant patrons. The publication of
his two *Discourses* brought him a notoriety which grew immea-

surably with the publication of *The Social Contract*. He was even commissioned as an expert to draw up constitutional models for two abortive regimes. Yet his conviction of his own failures, notably in matters of love, deepened. He underwent a half-hearted conversion to Catholicism, and then redeclared himself a Protestant. But by then his beliefs had become highly colored by his own imagination, and bore only a hazy kinship to traditional Christian doctrine, although his religiosity was not in doubt.

His intensity of feeling so overwhelmed his political and philosophical ideals, that the most preeminent quality of his writing is, perhaps, its tone and vibrancy, although he was not by any means devoid of cogent arguments and strikingly original ideas. Above all, he had caught one key note: the recurrent desire in man for some intimation of a transcendent overtone to his existence. In capturing this crucial theme, Rousseau proclaimed the new age of romanticism.

In fact, however, the distinction between classical reason and romantic sentiment has been overdrawn. Diderot, author of the *Encyclopedia* and high priest of the *philosophes*, was at times a lachrymose sentimentalist who placed the man of passion above the man of reason, because passion is essential to creativity. Even Holbach, who advocated a purely mechanist-materialist philosophy in line with La Mettrie's human robot, the *Machine-Man*, and who purveyed after Condillac a calculus of pain and pleasure that anticipated the drab utilitarianism of Bentham, felt the poet was the truly perceptive man. The man of feeling was not alien to the world of the *philosophes*, therefore, nor was the man of reason alien to the ideal state of Rousseau, who spent most of his life in philosophical argument. But if Diderot's sentimentality was a precursor to Rousseau's emotionality, there was nonetheless a crucially different emphasis between them. The ideal of the preeminently rational man gave way to that of the affective man of fellow-feeling and sympathy for humanity.

At this point we strike the first of many contradictions that characterize Rousseau's implicit consciousness of history, reflecting the ambiguities in his conception of human nature. One moment he affirms that man in the natural state is inherently neither good nor bad. In the *Discourse on Inequality* he remarks that man in the primitive state feels no moral obligation to others, so that he cannot be said to be either good or evil, to have vices or virtues in the accepted meaning of these words. Nature thus has no implicit "moral" qualities; it is neither beneficent nor malevolent, it simply *is*. This ethical neutrality leads Rousseau to reject the idea of natural law as the real source of civil law. He regarded legislation as the product of human intention, and consequently could attribute to man a potential mastery over his own moral destiny.

But at other times Rousseau implies that human nature is fundamentally benevolent in the sense that man in his natural state is predisposed to fellow-feeling and craves justice. These sentiments in effect unbalance the moral neutrality of nature towards a benevolence that reflects the goodness of its Creator. To Rousseau, the predisposition to sentiment and moral consciousness constitutes an *a priori* quality in the human mind. For contrary to Locke, Rousseau proclaims an *a priori* attribute without which man would be unable to respond to the external stimuli, an attribute that consists of his innate capacity to feel: "To exist is to feel," he writes in *Emile*, "our feeling is undoubtedly earlier than our intelligence, and we had feelings before we had ideas."[3] The basic human sentiment which moves natural man, before he has been spoiled by society, is an impulse to sympathy and justice: "There is therefore at the bottom of our hearts an innate principle of justice and virtue, by which, in spite of our maxims, we judge our own actions and those of others to be good or evil; and it is this principle that I call conscience."[4]

Both of these views repudiate the Hobbesian delineation of man as inherently aggressive and pitiless. Each of Rousseau's formulations lends itself to an optimistic historical view. In one case, meliorism becomes the product of the natural cooperative instinct of men, given free rein in the democratic city-state; in the other case, it becomes the product of a sound education that teaches us to resist corruption and to develop our life in harmony with the simplicity of nature. The ideal education described in the *Emile* would preserve the natural goodness in man and open the door to his conscience and capacity for fellow-feeling. In neither case is goodness "automatic." It must always be cultivated and nurtured by man at great difficulty. But we can fashion our moral ideal in line with the mystic, divine force that provides for the believer the security of a benevolent order of things. In *Emile* he has the Savoyard Vicar say: "I believe, therefore, that the world is governed by a wise and powerful will; I see it or rather I feel it, and it is a great thing to know this."[5]

Rousseau was a man of marked religious feelings. Much of his romanticism was tinged by his religious attitude. Presumably his sentiments were of generally Christian derivation. But his faith, as articulated by the Savoyard Vicar, departed so far from both orthodox Protestantism and Catholicism, notably on his repudiation of original sin, that it can best be described as an undogmatic and sentimental religiosity. In its vague appeal to benevolence, his religion remained distinctively personal, a part of his character. It spread a sort of Pelagian trust in the natural goodness of man over portions of his work—a goodness that could but have hopeful overtones. What a strange outgrowth of Swiss Calvinism! Still, Rousseau took his religious feelings seriously and felt his religious convictions, as he did everything, with passion. He detested especially the aloof, impersonal deism of the *philosophes*. Indeed, this attitude was one of the main reasons for his break with Diderot and the Voltairean circle. He had no sympathy with their rationalist concept of a deity who served as an architect and prime mover of the universe but had no direct involvement or personal concern in the moral affairs of man, and was impervious to such human sentiments as love. If Rousseau detested the deism of many Enlightenment thinkers, he despised even more the outright atheism of other rationalists like Holbach and Helvetius.

The importance for our purpose of Rousseau's religious temperament is the transcendent historicism which later utopian democrats and socialists derived from his moral ideals. For as he stated it through the mouth of the Vicar, his religious sentiment induced a fundamental emotional optimism that lay beneath the pessimism with which he frequently viewed the general corruption of civilized mankind. At times he voiced a hopeful view of man's moral and historical destiny. "I have hope," he wrote to Voltaire in reply to the latter's attack on optimism, "and hope makes all things beautiful."[6]

Did Rousseau then regard history as a record of human progress? There are few political philosophers who have asserted the opposite notion with as much forcefulness or conviction. Rousseau was far too preoccupied with the virtually universal corruption of the "civilized" individuals of his time and with the falsity of the society around him to see in man's development from his primordial condition anything but degeneration and moral decline. Far from perceiving humanity on the road to a better state, he sees it mired in corruption from which only the most strenuous efforts offer any hope of rescue. Whatever were Rousseau's romantic views on mankind in the state of nature, he had few illusions about the goodness of man in present society. When he turns from the ideal state of *The Social Contract* to concrete proposals for governing Poland and Corsica, his lack of illusions becomes notably apparent.

Rousseau accounts for the contrast between the potential goodness of men properly educated and the actual degradation of humanity by saying that our civilization is anti-nature, and has thus alienated man from his natural sensibilities and his natural condition of freedom and equality. In his early essay on *The Discourse on the Sciences and the Arts*, he argues that the perfecting of the instruments of human knowledge and control, far from benefiting man, have only tended to cultivate a veiled callousness and aggressiveness. Technology has been directed towards the fruitless pursuit of luxury and leisure. Science and learning, far from improving mankind, have only led to its moral degradation. Rousseau's historical tone is one of pessimism.

In the second and more famous *Discourse on the Origins of Inequality,* he returns to the attack. Civil society, he charges, is the source of human woe. Ever since man came to settle down, develop agriculture and metallurgy and therewith the need for specialization and exchange, he gave up his state of nature for a role in society predicated on an inequality of status and means. It is specifically the notion of property that has set history off on the wrong track. "The first man," he writes in the second part of the *Discourse on Inequality*, "who upon enclosing a plot of land got it into his head to say, *this is mine*, and found persons sufficiently credulous to believe him, he was the true founder of civil society." And he cries out:

> How many crimes, wars, murders, woes and horrors might not humanity have been spared by that man who, ripping out the marker or filling in the ditch, had called to his fellow men: 'Beware of listening to this impostor; you are lost if you forget that the fruits belong to all and the earth to no one!'[7]

Henceforth possession was changed to property, authority to arbitrary power, and natural equality to distinction of classes. Thus against the popular view of progress, Rousseau finds a deep undercurrent of man's alienation from nature and from himself. The hypocrisy and injustice of society mean one thing for man: that he has become enslaved. This is the opening cry of *The Social Contract*: "Man is born free, and everywhere he is in chains. Many a man believes himself a master who is, no less than they, a slave." Society seeks to stamp out what is natural in man and thereby creates evil.

Rousseau sees man himself—not God and not nature—as the source of human misery. "Oh Man!" says the Savoyard Vicar, "seek no further for the author of evil; thou art he."[8] Rousseau finds that there is no ill but that which man does or suffers, and both come from man himself. He sees evil as a product of disorder, while in the order of the universe he discovers "a never-failing system." Therefore it must be that ills exist only in the minds of those who provoke them, and this provocation, he concludes, "is not the gift of nature, but the work of man himself."[9]

The heart of Rousseau's thought is the salvation of man through his return to nature and innocence. The escape from a sophisticated and cosmopolitan social order into an idyll of pastures, simple peasants or innocent primitives is hardly an innovation of the eighteenth century. It is a romantic illusion that has marked the most classic of ages, and it constitutes a recurrent, if not a constant, theme in history. The presence of a comparable Taoist motif in China suggests it may well be a universal notion. In any case, the Noble Savage was proposed by Tacitus, and the intermittent vogue of primitivism goes back at least to his time. It was much in fashion with Rousseau's predecessors, and it is common knowledge that propositions about the state of nature were a staple of political discourse in the seventeenth and eighteenth centuries. Excepting Hobbes' view, the natural state and the law of nature were generally portrayed, after the line of Locke, as an ideal form of primitive equality and freedom. Defoe evoked an exotic dream among his European readers of the adventure of life in primitive surroundings. Diderot had his fantasy-picture of Tahiti. With Rousseau, return to primeval innocence comprises the solution of social ills—enslavement, injustice, class distinctions, hardness of heart, and the destruction of the individual's natural personality. It is romantic. But it is not simply escape, and it is not the rejection of history.

To understand the historical quality of Rousseau's thought, we must realize that the state of pre-civil man never constituted the ultimate object of his search. The return to nature was a necessity, but it was not an end in itself. The theme of human history in the two *Discourses*, as well as in the pedagogy of the *Emile*, is that by finding our way back to nature, past that point where civilization went awry, we will enable ourselves to rebuild civilized society in harmony with the natural order rather than in opposition to it. The characteristics of our vitiated historical evolution are not always clear. Sometimes the key vice of our civilization is located in the institution of private property. At other times, perhaps reflecting his own bourgeois background and the fact that he was the son of a watchmaker, Rousseau deems property essential to any stable order at all. But it should be a property so organized as no longer to impose a moral disability on the poor. In his later works his penchant for socialism, still occasionally alternating with his defense of a purified form of property, becomes more clearly identified both with practical reforms, such as his project for a Corsican constitution, and with utopian vision.

But in any case, the theme of the return to nature here is *not* that of the Noble Savage. While Rousseau characterizes Robinson Crusoe as the most useful reading for his imaginary young pupil, Emile—if, that is to say, one need resort to books at all—the example he obviously has in mind is Robinson, not Friday. And if Rousseau constantly places Emile in woodland surroundings, agricultural pursuits, and "nature settings," it is not to make him a primitive. "When I want to train a natural man," he writes emphatically, "I do not want to make him a savage and to send him back to the woods." Rather, it is Rousseau's object to prepare him to live in society without being carried away "by the passions and prejudices of men." And the philosopher, popularly accused of rejecting rational thought, concludes: "Let him see with his eyes and feel with his heart, let him own no sway but that of reason."[10]

Rousseau advocates that man return to his natural psychological state, not in order to find there, by some irrational cancellation of historical time, a primitive utopia to which he should return, but to discover its natural order so as to be able to erect an ideal state in harmony with it. Thus, history is not only the link between the archetypal state of nature, in which man cannot live because he is a social animal, and our present debased society, but also the link between that society and the potentially ideal republic. The major question, therefore, is: Is the model of the good society historically attainable, or at least approachable? Rousseau's answer, not surprisingly, is ambiguous. He vacillates between hope and a sense of futility or despair at humanity's almost universal corruption. Whenever he deals with the concrete problems of his time and the actual condition of man in contemporary life, he seems resigned to the insuperable difficulties of reform. What conclusion but pessimism can emerge from his view that all the peoples of Europe except the Corsicans lie beyond hope of attaining political or moral redemption through their choices and actions? Yet he could not entirely renounce the vision of the democratic state, and seemed to find consolation in affirmations of hope.

If Rousseau's answer to the question of progress remains

ambivalent, his followers have generally found little difficulty in interpreting him as an historical optimist and even as a utopian moralist. Perhaps this reputation is due to the fact that his best-known works convey not only his disillusionment in the present but also his romantic faith in humanity and in the equality of man, and his implicit trust in the future. In *The Social Contract*, he develops his treatise in a style which indicates that his model for political harmony, freedom and moral unity constitutes an histori-cally meaningful and attainable ideal. It hardly suggests an exer-cise in describing an intentionally chimerical utopia beyond the hopes or destiny of man. His ideal republic transcends history, but remains a morally worthy goal of political development and a relevant historical objective of human endeavor.

It was easy to interpret Rousseau's social philosophy in terms of a view of the past marked by man's moral degeneration from his natural condition, and a view of the future marked by man's democratic aspiration towards the ideal state and to the civic virtue of the citizen's republic. The very starkness of the first phase inspires our hope in the second. Thus in Rousseau's legacy if not in his own thought, it remained for history to resolve the paradox of a past which has produced moral corruption, and a future that contains the potential promise of the ideal society described in *The Social Contract*.

The critical factor in Rousseau's model community is that he secularized the transcendent objective by embodying it in the moral worth of the state. The moral life is manifest in the political ideal. The transcendence of man's presently frustrating condition of self-alienation is to be resolved in the mystic bonds and com-mon purpose that bind the community together. That is why the idealized republic of virtue could not help becoming for Rousseau the embodiment of transcendent value. Despite his aversion to secularism, his moral good is significantly reduced to secular dimensions, namely the good of the nation. For the state is to Rousseau a man-made entity, yet it has a moral quality and func-tion. Law, which is essential to the moral order, emanates from the sovereign legislators, the citizens. It does not pre-exist man or society in the order of nature because it is nothing but the expression of the common good of the community which is basically the consequence of geography and population. But man's predisposition to moral consciousness arises from his transcendent sense of justice which, Rousseau informs us elsewhere, is ordained by a benevolent God. This moral impulse manifests itself in society through the empathy of each citizen with the common good, and his active participation in the civil religion of the state.

Rousseau always preserved in his political thought the love of his native Geneva and its republican virtue. The community ethos of the city-state—one might almost say of the Platonic *polis* —remained with him a romantic counterweight to an exaggerated cosmopolitanism. Individuals who are solely citizens of the world could feel no genuine love, which in Rousseau's view must always be particularistic and partly exclusive, for their compatriots. His is the same feeling for *la patrie* as the revolutionary's passion for his country, namely that it constitutes the hope for the universal moral liberation of man. It invests nationalism with the same crucial transcendentalizing function. But in *The Social Contract*, this aspiration runs up against a wall. And in this encounter is laid bare the conflict in Rousseau's political-historical philosophy: Is transcendence a function of individual freedom, or of the inviolable moral entity, the wholeness, of the sovereign state.

That Rousseau was a fierce individualist on the one hand is beyond doubt. His life, and his autobiographical *Confessions* express an almost morbid concern with the distinctiveness of the self and the uniqueness of his own ego. The lesson of *Emile* is the cultivation of the natural individual personality of the child. Could an introspective mind like Rousseau's, playing with its own states of feeling as in *Julie*, turn out to be something other than an esthetic and psychological individuality? His approach to the study of history exemplifies this concern with each personality. Enough of purely formalized historical biographies with illustrious personages in their parade dress, he taunts in *Emile*. History ought to be biography—yes! What waste is that lugubrious alignment of supposed facts which are but historians' opinions, and which inevitably turns students away from the vital heart of history, the lives of men. But biography must be the full life of the individual,

above all the small, immensely revealing insights of his human gestures. In all this, there was certainly the stamp of individualism.

But here was the great dilemma for Rousseau. On one hand
he wanted to preserve this personality and to make the civil
community the highest expression of human freedom. On the
other hand he wanted to reply to that prevalent egocentricity and
cosmopolitanism which robbed man of the moral satisfaction of
serving the common good. So the community must also provide
the opposite objective, namely the moral cohesion of the sovereign
state that signifies the collective historical transcendence of one's
solitary, isolated ego. Rousseau conceived of the nature of politics
modeled on the Genevan scale of a citizens' republic, or in a form
comparable to the Athenian city-state, where participation in public life and civic responsibility constituted the highest expression
of one's personality, the supreme virtue and obligation of the free
man. How could he reconcile these conflicting tendencies without
compromising one or both? But how could he compromise when
both of his historical objectives carried religious connotations?
Could he abandon the principle of human liberation, or could he
jettison the transcendent function of the political community by
threatening to undermine its inalienable cohesiveness? This was
the great moral paradox for all those who would seek to locate
transcendence in man's relation to the historical destiny of the
political community: the conflict between the sense of "persona"
in the individual and the conception of a "personality" of the
state.

Faced with these alternatives, Rousseau sought to save the
principle, since he could not save the phenomena. If only he could
combine the one aim with the other; if he could transmute the
ideal of freedom into that of moral devotion to the state, so that
the two principles would become one! If he could only resolve the
antithesis of his individualistic leaning and his intense nationalism.
Then by the simple expedient of dissolving the former into the
latter, he could apparently retain the untarnished, if hollow, forms
of both.

His answer was the General Will. In *The Social Contract*, the
guiding political principle is the popular democracy of active citi-

zens embodying in their collective will the character of the state. Seen simply as the principle of popular democratic sovereignty, the idea is hardly scandalous; at this level, the impact of Rousseau's theory upon the democratic and egalitarian ideal of modern mass society is all too familiar. But the General Will is not just a statement of majority rule; it is the key device for transcendence within a political-historical frame, or for the secularization of the transcendent ideal. It articulates the presence in the secular society of that mystic bond of unity so essential to Rousseau. The General Will achieves a moral quality and intensity quite out of keeping with a merely expedient organization of political life. What distinguishes it from the ordinary majoritarian formulation is that the expression of the General Will constitutes the "true" volition of all citizens—even of those who stood in opposition to the decision.

Here at last the General Will appears from behind its mask to reveal itself in its ultimately totalitarian form. It is totalitarian because it must claim that the conscious, willful opposition of individuals in the community is unconsciously an affirmation of what they oppose, if only they had the judgment to understand the decision as the act of the sovereign people. Therefore it is morally binding upon the *active* assent of all. There are no real private wills, only apparent ones; all diversity is mere self-interest, never a distinctive view of the common weal. The General Will is totalitarian in the same sense that is every political view which assigns the spirit of the community to the custody of a legislator even of a near-unanimous majority, in such a way as to claim that it must represent the true patriotic intentions of those who disagree with its policies. Its totalitarian tendency is contained in the moral claim that if the minority only realized what they themselves truly wanted for the common welfare, they would have to admit it to be the very *opposite* of what they think, the opposite of what they are *conscious* of wanting:

> The citizen consents to all the laws, even to those which have been passed in spite of him, even to those which will visit punishment upon him should he dare to violate any of them. The constant will of all the members of a State

is the general will and by virtue of it they are citizens and free men. When a law is proposed in the assembly of the People, what they are asked is not whether they approve or reject the proposal in question, but whether it is or is not in conformity with the general will, which is *their* will. It is on this point that the citizen expresses his opinion when he records his vote, . . . When, therefore, a view which is at odds with my own wins the day, it proves only that I was deceived, and that what I took to be the general will was no such thing. Had my own opinion won, I should have done something quite other than I wished to do, and in that case I should not have been free.[11] [Note: Why? In that case "my" view would, by definition, have *been* the General Will!]

The argument that the collectivity knows my true will better than I do, or that my unknown but real decision is against the very one I make, constitutes the invisible line into the totalitarian state. One may object that the concept of the General Will is not categorically different from the normal obligation of a citizen in a democracy to obey the law even if he opposes it. Does the citizen not expect its enforcement even against his own interests, as Rousseau stipulates? Does he not recognize that as a citizen he is bound by the higher principle of his moral allegiance to the community? How is this relation to be distinguished from the alleged "totalitarianism" of the General Will? The answer is crucial to the understanding of totalitarian transcendence and consciousness of history. The citizen who willingly obeys and enforces the law he has personally opposed does not have to suspend his judgment that the law is wrong and that his own decision was right. He need not abandon his own moral view that the sovereign will was misguided or inequitable. Under the General Will, on the other hand, the expression of the general conscience makes the law right and the individual's private judgment wrong. There is no appeal to one's personal conscience in judgment of the sovereign will. In other words, Rousseau's political principle goes a crucial step beyond the consenting loyalty and obedience of the citizen to the law: it substitutes the General Will for the individual's own moral consciousness. The surrender of the definition of right to the sovereign will, ultimately preempting the private judgment of conscience against its decisions, constitutes the key totalitarian step, whether in democratic or despotic form.

It was the historical character of Rousseau's ideal that trapped him in the totalitarian impasse: the need to find transcendence in the moral bond of the political community and in a new historical reality of the state. Listen to the amazing surrender of person in the oath of allegiance he included for the future citizen of Corsica:

> In the name of God Almighty, and of the holy Gospels, by a sacred and irrevocable oath, I join myself—body, goods, will and all my powers—to the Corsican nation; granting her the full ownership of me—myself and all that depends on me. I mean to live and die for her . . .[12]

The expectation of political redemption meant that a break in the social contract threatened the ethical purpose of the citizens, just as it had done in Plato's view of the corrupt *polis*. Though Plato and Rousseau disagreed categorically on the proper method by which the state ought to define its moral will and the ethical bond of its inhabitants, both agreed that the will of the good state constitutes, by definition, the moral consciousness of its citizens. Rousseau brought hereto an historical dimension which revealed its new totalitarian implications in his definition of the religion of the state and its Erastian church. Where Plato left to his philosopher-king the higher realm of truth from which he reluctantly agreed to serve the common good, Rousseau saw in the state itself the expression of moral truth and the embodiment of religious virtue. His proposal for a civil profession of faith establishes the social sentiment of the community, to which he adds ominously the draconian right of banishment against all who do not share this profession. Then he appends the *coup de grace* of potential totalitarian terror: "Any man who, after acknowledging these articles of faith, proceeds to act *as though he did not believe them,* is deserving of the death penalty. For he has committed the greatest of all crimes, that of lying before the law."[13] (Italics added.)

Rousseau, we see, had radically shifted the emphasis in democratic thought from the right of personal withdrawal to the obligation of conformity with the collective will. While both of these principles are part of the democratic tradition, now the primary concern with the individual's right to a private domain has receded before the concern with majority-rule. Thus the irony of Rousseau's undoubted libertarianism. Because of his desire to preserve both the individual and the state intact, the ideal of freedom was in effect transformed into the totalitarian predisposition of *The Social Contract*. Compare his treatment of the minority's views as mere error or self-interest with Mill's classic generosity for diversity of opinion. For Mill, such diversity was the very source of truth, and he based his defense of liberty on a continuing pluralism in the marketplace of ideas. That Rousseau's formulation was well suited to the psychological needs in the subsequent mass currents of modern society is true. But the real point is that his conception of the General Will is the inescapable consequence of his burdening of the secular political state with the function of transcendent unity and purpose. It is the result of seeing the patriotic bond and fraternity of the civic community as the expression of moral transcendence of the ego—the transcendence of that solitude of the self Rousseau felt so keenly—thus providing a political-historical vehicle for a utopian ideal. How ironic that Rousseau, the romantic mystic, who fulminated against the deadening rationalism and materialism of the Diderot circle and upheld the claim of piety, should have contributed more, perhaps, to the effective secularization of values in the age of the nation-state than did Hobbes!

In the end, despite his lapses into sentimentality and the logical difficulties of the General Will, Rousseau emerges as one of the great creative political philosophers. From our perspective, this influence largely derives from his recognition of man's need to find a transcendent moral meaning in life. But Rousseau's vision also failed him tragically. In fact, if it embodied the grave political dilemmas and totalitarian potentialities of a later age, it was because Rousseau had converted Hobbes' non-transcendent political god into a morally transcendent one, located in a secular objective. He had initiated the identification of a transcendent historical ideal with the nation-state and the modern concept of national patriotism. He had unconsciously fastened upon an inherently non-transcendent goal the function of providing man with a sense of self-transcendent purpose. The course of events which converted his libertarianism into a potentially totalitarian system marked the price of his passionate desire to realize some historical "presence" to the transcendent ideal. It constituted a dramatic precedent for our subsequent history.

3. Perfectibility and Historical Transcendence: The Rationalization of Historical Redemption

If both Voltaire and Rousseau found their views of universal progress inhibited, one by a skeptical appraisal of human nature, the other by his sense of corrupted civilization, Condorcet did not. With him, one of the last figures of the Voltairean circle, we find the appropriate fulfillment of the Enlightenment's conception of history, a composite of reason, progress and transcendence through man's historical future. Thus, just before the century ended and just after its great revolution had begun, its philosophy of history came to a fitting climax in Condorcet's exposition of its new secularized teleology.

An enthusiast of the new form of rationalism, a mathematician notably active in the Institute of Science and the French Academy, Condorcet differed from most of the *philosophes* in that he had the opportunity of applying some of his ideals of progress. He participated in converting them into revolutionary policies for the liberation of mankind. Condorcet was a Girondist member of the Legislative Assembly, who briefly served as its president and, somewhat longer, as its guiding philosophical spirit. Here was the *philosophe*, no longer as an armchair political reformer or a paid luminary of a despot's court, ambivalently espousing republican principles while receiving his pay and prestige from some absolute monarch. Contrast the pallid republican commitments of Voltaire with the active Girondism of the sensitive and idealist marquis who took a leading part in formulating the revolutionary principles of the first French Republic. What an irony that this aristo-cratic mathematician and philosopher of human progress, this great optimist about man's history, about the perfectibility of human society and the achievement of universal freedom, prob-ably missed the guillotine's blade only because he died, perhaps by his own hand, in a Jacobin prison. Having fallen afoul of the followers of Robespierre and been caught up in the relentless dynamism of a revolution veering towards totalitarian terror, he had gone into hiding. It was there, while escaping Jacobin authori-ties and then during the brief weeks after he had been caught while the guillotine of the revolutionary tribunal seemed poised above him, that he dashed off the famous *Sketch for a Historical Picture of the Progress of the Human Mind*. The Jacobins them-selves—added irony—were later to order it published. Thus ap-peared in 1794 this striking essay, representative of the historical faith of the Enlightenment and also of the hopeful psychology of the Revolution, never more so than when the revolutionaries were chopping off heads. The contrast between Condorcet's own fate and his faith in human perfectibility mirrors the contradictions in the revolutionary ideal he served.

Two central ideas dominate Condorcet's record of the growth of civilization: the successive stages of progress in the past, and its unlimited prospects for the future. He divides history into nine previous phases, the last one revealingly spanning the time from Descartes to the French Republic. Upon these he extrapolates a tenth phase still to be realized, when the utopian potentialities of human reason will be achieved through the fulfillment of man's freedom.

But Condorcet's historical evolution, for all of its mecha-nistic order and expectations of utopian realization, remained open towards the future; its worldly teleology of revolutionary redemption still conceived the progress of mankind to go on per-petually. Thus "in the experiences of the past, in the observation of the progress that the sciences and civilization have already made," and above all in the "analysis of the progress of the human mind," Condorcet found "the strongest reasons for believ-ing that nature has set no limit to the realization of our hopes."[14] Not only was society going to become better, but it need never cease to do so. The forces that have made for the improvement of the human race "by their very nature exercise a perpetual influence and always increase their sphere of action," so that Condorcet concludes: "the perfectibility of man is indefinite."[15]

Infinity is psychologically vital to Condorcet's scheme, because otherwise the projection of the self through history only leads to a delayed end of the ego. Perpetualness, in fact, becomes the very key to the transcendent historical function. It is only the presumed eternity of the ideal that can make the vicarious overcoming of physical death take on the saving quality of an apparent immortalization. In the meliorist perspective of history, the process of intellectual evolution fits into an eternally ordered world. Historical consciousness is then forced to take on a new psychological significance and especially a new theological burden. It became *de facto* and *de jure* the new instrument of salvation, the redemption of the individual through his contribution to infinite progress and to the eternal presence of mankind. The sufferings and sins of today will be redeemed by our descendents' happiness, in which we participate vicariously by our present efforts towards reason and freedom. Our traditional religious inclination to glorify self-sacrifice and asceticism would be turned to the psychological satisfaction of denying the present for the future, of offering the sacrifice of our immediate personal happiness on the altar of mankind. History, in short, assumes the central kerygmatic function of incarnating the ultimate redemptory ideal. It provides the "cure of souls" through its secularized transcendence.

Condorcet viewed progress as a phenomenon of Western civilization, since only the West was achieving rational understanding of the scientific order of nature and potential mastery over natural phenomena, as well as the ideal of freedom. Even within the old world of the Roman Empire he found a parallel distinction between East and West. The collapse of the latter was rapid and total in the early Middle Ages in contrast with the slow decline of the former. But in the East, degeneration continued whereas in the West, once the light of reason had reappeared in the new awakening of science, it was never again to be extinguished. Yet if the progress of mankind has been Western in its roots, it is to be universal in its fruits. In the perspective of the Enlightenment, the *philosophes'* sense of the universality of its rational "laws of nature" unselfishly dictated the perfectibility, not only of France or Europe, but of mankind as a whole. The symmetrical counterpart to the equality within nations that Condorcet envisioned would be a new equality and harmony among them. If it was still true that European states tyrannized non-Western peoples, it would soon happen that European influences would be converted into "the beneficient instruments of their freedom." With a certain prophetic insight, Condorcet even added that "the progress of these people is more likely to be rapid and certain than our own because they can receive everything from us we have had to find out for ourselves." Thus he foresaw as inevitable a time when tyrants, slaves and priests would survive only in works of fiction, and when "the sun will shine only on free men who know no other master but their reason."[16]

Is there not still some beguilingly perverse charm in the naïveté of Condorcet's faith? Of education he remarks that it would "rectify natural inequalities." He foresees the establishment of a universal language, the constant advance of knowledge and the arts, and of course of man's faculty for reason. Away with the misgivings of Voltaire and the doubts of Hume! May not the more skeptical twentieth-century reader, painfully aware of the intractable nature of things and especially of himself, perhaps view with a certain nostalgic envy the directness of Condorcet's remedies? Anticipating Buckle and Comte, Condorcet's "calculus of combinations and probabilities" would contribute to the elimination of prejudice and war. Our increasing knowledge would, by the conquest of disease, push back ever further the normal time of a person's death. The very human organism becomes perfected, not through a Darwinian struggle but through the harmonious advance of science. Perhaps, after all, there is nothing intrinsic to the nature of man that prevents the indefinite extension of his longevity. Here the hope of immortalization comes down to its most tangible level in the dimly envisaged prospect that nature may have set no limits on our attainable life span.[17] What a fantastic consequence of the passionate yearning to find some vision of transcendence and immortality in a secularized historical outlook! What a strangely delusory prospect of hope to hold out: the potential indestructibility of our living organisms and physical substance!

We come at last to the heart of the Enlightenment's faith in historical transcendence. It consists not merely in the mechanisms of social progress nor in sheer physical survival, but rather in the essential rational-moral quality that will pervade them both. This is what finally gives to Condorcet's view of history its distinctively transcendent character. Indeed, we might note that Condorcet's contemporary, Holbach, in his work, *The System of Nature*, held out little prospect for a larger meaning of life than pleasurable living. Holbach claimed to translate a potentially resigned stoicism into a philosophical hedonism by arguing that man can attain happiness in a fuller being. But because he argued that only by abandoning the quest for an illusory immortality and accepting death does man achieve the one true happiness—that of living in harmony with his own nature—Holbach's form of progress remained non-transcendent. For him, man might find a happier state of mind released from irrational fears and prejudices, but he could never escape the human condition. For Condorcet, on the contrary, the meaning of history must be found in the answer to the question of whether mankind cannot escape that condition by so transmuting the context of life as to achieve liberation from its alienated state. Would not the "taming" of death in the end transfigure man himself into a morally different sort of being? Will not advance in knowledge "incline mankind to humanity, benevolence and justice" so that "the moral goodness of man, the necessary consequence of his constitution, is capable of indefinite perfection like all his faculties"? May we not believe that "nature has linked together in an unbreakable chain truth, happiness, and virtue"?[18]

According to Condorcet, it is history itself that provides him with the answer, by making meliorism self-sustaining. It has created a causal cycle in which each advance leads to the further acceleration of progress. To be sure, such has not always been the case; the unique achievement of the Greeks was subsequently lost, and the great age of Rome was followed by a collapse of civilization. But setbacks like these cannot recur: our very knowledge, and its diffusion to other peoples, will preclude a new collapse of

culture. Indeed, "the progress of the sciences ensures the progress
of the art of education which in turn advances that of the sciences."[19] It is this reciprocal influence, ceaselessly renewed, that
provides the key to the conviction of future perfection by making
meliorism self-perpetuating. That is why progress was for Condorcet unlimited in extent, universal in human society and infinite
in time. That is why the Enlightenment ultimately came to find in
historicity a promise of human redemption.

The issue here, it must be emphasized, is not the concept of
progress. The idea of meliorism has no inherent transcendent
quality. Technological advance or even political and social reforms have no transcendent meaning in themselves. It is only to
the extent that they prospectively bring about a moral regeneration of man that they serve a transcendent historical function.
Thus the point is not improvement per se but the use of historical
progress for the distinct purpose of eternalizing the ego. The individual's consciousness of his historical role in contributing to political, social and intellectual objectives serves as the means for
immortalizing his own vicarious identity in the ideal state. It is this
moral relationship that constitutes transcendent historicity.

What may we conclude on the *philosophes'* legacy to historical consciousness? At the time that Condorcet was describing the
happy prospects of mankind, an English contemporary of his, the
liberal Protestant Joseph Priestley, wrote:

> That the state of the world at present, and particularly the
> state of Europe, is vastly preferable to what it was in any
> former period, is evident from the very first view of things.
> A thousand circumstances shew how inferior the ancients
> were to the moderns in religious knowledge, in science in
> general, in government, in laws, both the laws of nations
> and those of particular states, in arts, in commerce, in the
> conveniences of life, in manners, and in consequence of all
> these, in *happiness*.[20]

Tying this hope to the consciousness of history and to the sense of
breaking out of the present moment in time, Priestley adds that the
advantage of man's superior intellect is that thereby the individual:

contemplates and enjoys the past and the future as well as the present. This comprehension is enlarged with the experience of every day; and by this means the happiness of man, as he advances in intellect, is continually less dependent on temporary circumstances and sensations.[21]

Along comparable lines, Adam Smith suggests the immortalizing function of historical fame and the comfort it brings:

Men have voluntarily thrown away life to acquire after death a renown which they could no longer enjoy. Their imagination, in the meantime, anticipated that fame which was in future times to be bestowed upon them . . . the thoughts of that admiration whose effects they were never to feel, banished from their breasts the strongest of all natural fears, and transported them to perform actions which seemed almost beyond the realm of human nature.[22]

In the final crystallization of the *philosophes'* rational-historical consciousness, the goals of man's activity appear to transcend the moment and to transcend the self, and to redeem the sacrifices of our present life. History then offers a vision and trust in some Eden of the future that provides man with a meaningful objective. We may note Crane Brinton's comment. Pointing out the intentional overstatement of a view which was not adhered to as such by the most noted thinkers of the age, he nonetheless characterizes the new outlook of the Enlightenment as *"the belief that all human beings can attain here on this earth a state of perfection hitherto in the West thought to be possible only for Christians in a state of grace, and then only after death."*[23] Brinton cites the remark of Saint-Just that happiness is a new idea in Europe and, we may add, a new impetus to historical transcendence.

Historicity has become a powerful force, embodying all of the passion to find meaning in what men do and experience in the sum total of their lives through the vision of a liberated humanity. It provides the individual with coherence, and relates him to a larger unity in time. Thus it comes to be imbued with a messianic quality and a salvatory function. In the new historical eschatology, our sins would be redeemed by our confidence in an enlightened utopian tomorrow for all mankind. Our sacrifices in contributing to its realization atone for the shortcomings of others as well as our own. The old historicity of Christianity is all that remains of the Christian aspiration, once the latter's other-worldly objective and kerygma have been rejected. This historicizing of man's yearning for transcendence is dramatically climaxed in Condorcet's faith, where the historical future gives meaning to the present and the past. The individual can transcend the feeling of imprisonment within the self and his mortality through the link with the humanity which has preceded him, and above all with that humanity which is eternally to follow. Perhaps we can picture Condorcet writing the following words a few weeks before the revolution he had seen as the hope of mankind claimed his life, expressing in them the union of transcendence with historical consciousness, and finding in his luminescent historicity a great redemptive hope:

> How consoling for the philosopher who laments the errors, the crimes, the injustices which still pollute the earth and of which he is often the victim is this view of the human race, emancipated from its shackles, released from the empire of fate and from that of the enemies of its progress, advancing with a firm and sure step along the path of truth, virtue and happiness! It is the contemplation of this prospect that rewards him for all his efforts to assist the progress of reason and the defense of liberty. He dares to regard these strivings as part of the eternal chain of human destiny and in his persuasion he is filled with the true delight of virtue and the pleasure of having done some lasting good which fate can never destroy by a sinister stroke of revenge. . . . Such contemplation is for him an asylum, in which the memory of his persecution cannot pursue him; there he lives in thought with man restored to his natural rights and dignity, forgets man tormented and corrupted by greed, fear or envy; there he lives with his peers in an Elysium created by reason and graced by the purest pleasures known to the love of mankind.[24]

IV

REVOLUTION

Historicity and Mass Expectations

1. Peasants, Aristocrats and Bourgeois: The Translation of Redemptive Historicity into Revolutionary Action

Those who hounded Condorcet to his death and then commanded the posthumous publication of his manuscript had at least one thing in common with him: faith in a utopian future. Indeed, they shared his conviction that man achieves transcendence through active participation in the advance of human progress and freedom. Condorcet believed in the moral perfectibility of man despite his own suffering; they believed it despite their imposition of sufferings upon him. Would even Voltaire or Rousseau, one may wonder, have escaped the same fate? How would Rousseau, glorified by some of the revolutionary leaders, notably Robespierre, have fared in the regime of those who proclaimed themselves his disciples, bringing to realization hopes he could only formulate? How would the author of *Julie* and the *Confessions* have accommodated himself to the puritanical rigidity and iron discipline of the republic militant? What might have befallen the author of *Candide*, ceremonially reburied in the Pantheon with the heroes of the Revolution and sanctified as the patron saint of reason? How would Citizen Arouet, self-styled nobleman M. de Voltaire, who had a penchant for associating with aristocrats and kings and referred to the common people as "the rabble," have escaped suspicion in a situation where suspicion usually meant death? If each remained an enshrined deity of the Revolution, it is partly because they both had the foresight to live in the generation before it broke out.

We are not claiming that the Enlightenment per se was the source of the utopian historicity of some of the revolutionaries, nor that it led directly to the zeal of the Jacobins. We are not attributing to the detachment and toleration of the most eminent *philosophes* even an indirect responsibility for the psychology of the revolutionary tribunals. Nor are we arguing that a school of skeptic thinkers who had a generally low opinion of mankind and its prospects left a predominant legacy of utopian faith. It is an obvious fact that disciples often caricature the ideas of the masters they claim to emulate. The French Revolution, we know, repudiated the fondest historical hopes of many of its own supporters, and ultimately belied many enlightened principles. The Terror proved to be a monstrous deformation of Rousseau's republic of civic virtue, the September Massacres a grotesque distortion of Condorcet's faith in humanity, and the intolerance of the *enragés'* worship of reason a travesty on the skepticism and toleration of Voltaire.

What we are saying is that some of the currents of the Enlightenment, notably those suggested in Condorcet and Rousseau, left two major legacies to the Revolution which subsequently were turned into the elements of a new mass historicity. The first legacy is that the rationalist critique of Christianity, the rise of science and the growing skepticism of the Christian view of immortality induced men to seek a secular form of immortalization. For the yearning to eternity, which is a basic psychological drive in man once he is conscious of the infinity of time, could only express itself in secularized goals, specifically in a redeeming vision of the historical future. The second major legacy is that the thinkers of the seventeenth and eighteenth centuries provided one of the key vehicles through which redemptive aspirations were to function in society, namely the realm of the state. These aspirations were manifest in the transcendentalizing of man's political ideals, seen as the moral expression of natural law. Thus the ideas of liberalism and later of democracy were to be translated into a general conception of human progress, and eventually into a messianic hope of the liberation of man.

It was the economic and social forces of the Revolution that transformed the sense of transcendent historicity into a major historical force. The Girondist and Jacobin phases were profoundly to alter the role of historical values born in the genteel environment of the *philosophes*. The Revolution was to change into a passionate and violent force the redemptive historical expectations that had first taken shape in the dispassionate and cosmopolitan detachment of the age of reason. For under the heat and pressure of increasingly radical revolutionary stages, the attitudes towards history fashioned in the urbane atmosphere of the *salons* was to take on a new psychological intensity. This revolution in semi-conscious attitudes would have a more profound historical effect on our civilization than the more obvious and less durable political changes brought about during the "great days" of the revolutionary decade. There were many conflicting forms of revolutionary ideals and historical vision, but virtually all the revolutionary groups shared a transcendent view of history.

From the French Revolution emerged a new style of historical redemption, which provided one of the primary motive forces behind mass movements that made quasi-religious values out of their historical objectives. Since the French Revolution, mass ideals in Western society have increasingly focused upon historical goals as the supposedly transcendent moral principles giving meaning and purpose to individual lives. This messianic use of historical consciousness has been expressed in many different nationalistic and utopian objectives, and bought at the sacrifice of present pleasures and even life itself. In order to discern how historical ideals once limited to the elites were converted by the course of events into a mass force and into one of the decisive factors of our culture, we must review the attitudes towards history that flowed into and out of the French Revolution. We must therefore consider some of the circumstances of pre-revolutionary Europe, or at least of the conditions of the *ancien régime*, as they related to historical consciousness.

A people's attitude towards history is not necessarily re-

vealed by its historians nor its philosophers. The questions which
shape peoples' sense of history depend only in small measure on
generalized doctrines of progress or decline. Sentiments of historical fatalism, pessimism or hope depend little on the formal intellectual currents of the age. In fact, each group and each individual
is moved not so much by prevailing ideologies as by his own
experience and tangible prospects of social advance or psychological satisfaction. Thus the circumstances that will contribute to a
particular community's historical values consist primarily of its
direct opportunities for some sense of fulfillment or of liberation
from its existential condition. These opportunities obviously differ
for various segments of a society and for individual persons within
them. The intellectual historicism of the elites may have little
relevance to the experience and psychological predisposition of
the peasantry. In mid-eighteenth century it was still largely the
educated upper classes that set the pace of historical development,
of political innovation and of ideological challenge. But by mid-
Revolution, this situation had changed. We must therefore investigate the evolving attitudes of the mass strata of the population,
beginning with the peasant class which constituted the overwhelm-
ing majority of eighteenth-century European society.

The limited and primarily indirect evidence we have of the
outlook and the moods of the rural populations in eighteenth-
century Europe suggests that by and large it had little sense of
general historical progress, or any intimation of a revolutionary
view of history. There was, to be sure, a great range in the conditions of life and the outlook of peasant villages that ran the gamut
from prosperous to virtually famine-stricken. But generally speaking, the conditions under which the peasantry lived, especially in
Central and Eastern Europe, provided little stimulus to a revolutionary conception of social equality or to the hope of historical
meliorism. The rhythm of rural life offered limited opportunity for
fostering historical expectations of liberation from the often oppressive burdens of living. In such a context, ideas of political
freedom and egalitarianism, not to mention the vision of a utopian
social order, appear dimly if at all. Other historicist sentiments
and notions, such as nationalism and manifest destiny, seem

equally anachronistic and irrelevant. Thus the use of historical consciousness for moral or redemptive purposes hardly arises.

Modern social sciences suggest that people living under very adverse circumstances tend to accept their lot passively and often to fear change as endangering the slim hold they have on existence. Those who habitually encounter life on sharply disadvantageous terms may come to accept their servile status with resignation. They may tend to view their inferior condition as natural or ordained, and to regard themselves in the terms and the functions fostered by their social betters. A dominated class frequently adopts towards itself the attitudes prevalent in the society as a whole or in the style-setting dominant minority. Many of its members find psychological comfort in their role of obedience. They not only regard their position as unchangeable but positively find refuge in their dependence, seeing it as a bulwark against the great insecurity of their existence. Thus they tend to give little thought, and often less sympathy, to suggestions of radical reforms which seem to threaten their precarious relationship to the established order. The loyalty of French peasants to their king was notable even during the early days of the Revolution and the growing signs of peasant unrest; it is a familiar phenomenon. Rarely is it a person from the most oppressed classes or one accustomed to abject poverty who organizes and leads a revolutionary movement or who formulates messianic historical expectations. He is generally too preoccupied with the demands of sheer survival to have much time and energy for envisaging the romanticized conditions of an ideal society or historical liberation from his present life. Where the problems of the present loom inordinately large, the vision of the future tends to become nebulous, or to remain essentially at the personal or family level.

For an active yearning for social betterment to become a political reality, it is generally helpful to combine some minimum opportunity of hopeful prospects and revolutionary possibilities with a profound sense of aggrievement. Since the former conditions generally were not to be found in eighteenth-century Europe, we may surmise that vague notions of social meliorism, of abstract justice and natural equality, not to mention the more intangible concepts of intellectual and moral freedom, could hardly have begun to take root in a still essentially illiterate peasant population. Great peasant revolts like that of Pugachev in Russia seem less an act of expectation in the utopian line of the Levellers and Diggers than a violent gesture of desperation in the tradition of earlier European peasant uprisings like the Jacquerie and the German Peasants War.

The brief sketch we have drawn of usual peasant attitudes fits our knowledge of other agrarian societies. In such an environment, custom constitutes not only law but moral sanction as well. The traditional conservatism inherent in village life precludes almost by definition any linear view of historical evolution or of secular salvation in some historically conceived new order. In this regard we might note that in the great T'ai P'ing peasant uprising of mid-nineteenth century China, the messianic notions of a utopian society dimly formulated by Hung Hsiu-ch'üan had little direct impact on most of his following. But the noteworthy point is that Hung's grotesquely distorted "Christian" notions were in fact derived from his ephemeral contacts with Victorian missionaries and their history-minded, progress-conscious faith.

To return to eighteenth-century Europe, the very notion of a consistent mass opinion seems out of place. There existed as yet no mass consciousness, partly because there were only inadequate technological means for sustaining it except under extraordinary circumstances. Of course, there did exist common values to much of peasant society that resulted from the common experiences of peasant living and rural Christian rituals. These experiences seemed to focus on loyalty to certain established institutions, especially the Church and the consecrated monarch. Their common denominator was an emphasis on tradition but with little or no thought of an evolutionary history. Such seems to be the lesson of the popular suspicion and hostility that greeted Joseph II's well-intentioned but ill-fated reforms of the Hapsburg Empire. In general, the eighteenth-century elites viewed the peasant as a bumpkin or a lout because he was far removed from their polite society and because his primitive "superstition" stood in sharp contrast to their trust in reason and their growing faith in the future. Marie Antoinette stiltedly playing the shepherdess in the fake environs of the Little Trianon suggests a change in this fashion. After Rousseau, many romantics were to enlist the peasant's vaunted naturalness for the cause of their historical meliorism. But these considerations do not affect our general point about eighteenth-century peasant society, namely that it lay largely outside the current of apparent "progress" and hardly formulated any notion of transcendence through historical consciousness, which remained alien to the rural scene.

Let us note that if additions to our scant evidence should eventually refute this largely speculative analysis of the ahistoricity of eighteenth-century popular values, it would only strengthen our thesis. If we should have to conclude that unexpressed hopes of an historical "liberation" had wider currency and influence than we may presently suppose, we would only have emphasized further the swelling current of historical consciousness and the development in modern times of a sense of redemptive historicity. Let us then proceed cautiously by adopting the most plausible supposition and the one least favorable to our argument, and turn by way of illustration to the particular conditions in France.

There is a vast body of evidence on the conditions of living under the *ancien régime,* and even on states of mind and popular attitudes. The nation in which the Enlightenment had largely originated enjoyed, not surprisingly, the most prosperous and socially conscious peasant population of its day. To qualify this statement, one must note that rural conditions varied widely, ranging often within the compass of a small area from comparative comfort to great misery. But on the whole, they provided for a higher level of peasant life than that found elsewhere on the Continent. Of special concern to us is the impact of these circumstances on popular attitudes towards prospects for the future. For despite their comparative prosperity, most French peasants still endured an arduous life under the triple economic burden of landlord, Church and state. Eventually the conditions of peasant life generated grumbling and far-reaching protests, first against landlords and taxes, and eventually against the structure of society. Yet peasant protests and demands for economic reforms rarely developed into a philosophy of social equality or of political rights. Significantly, widespread discontent hardly ever took the form of an overall conception of history, as it did for intellectual reformers like Turgot. It is ironic that the French peasantry, with its essentially ahistorical outlook, was to play a key role in events whose effect was both to ground and to generalize the historicist faith within much of our culture.

Revealing evidence on the conditions of rural life is provided in the travel accounts of that itinerant English agricultural publicist, Arthur Young. On one hand, he shows that if there was any single quality which characterized the administration of the old regime, it was the arbitrariness of its various jurisdictions and their lack of rational order, from the famous distinctions of *pays d'élection* and *pays d'état* to overlapping local authorities. The conditions of existence consequently varied enormously from one village to the next, depending upon its accidental inheritance of traditional exemptions or long-standing charges, not to mention from one agricultural region to another such as between the rich plains of the Loire and the rugged farms of Brittany. That there were many areas of great poverty appears beyond doubt. Young further wonders at the remarkable failure to invest in improved productivity, and he describes the distress of much French farmland, though this was often but a surface poverty, consciously preserved to circumvent tax collectors.

> Pass Payrac, and meet many beggars, which we had not done before. All the country, girls and women, are without shoes or stockings; and the ploughmen at their work have neither sabots nor feet to their stockings. This is a poverty that strikes at the root of national prosperity; a large consumption among the poor being of more consequence than among the rich: the wealth of a nation lies in its circulation and consumption; and the case of poor people abstaining from the use of the manufactures of leather and wool ought to be considered as an evil of the first magnitude. It reminded me of the misery of Ireland. . . .[1]

It is a familiar theme that the accumulated burdens of tithes and church dues, of poll and land taxes, income taxes, salt taxes, rents to landlords, vestiges of archaic manorial obligations and the despised *corvée*, made the peasant's life a hard one. This judgment is sound not only by our standards but also by the more relevant standards of the contemporary leisured elites and urban middle class. Yet on the other hand, the French peasant did enjoy numerous comparative advantages. While the social and economic gulf separating him from the privileged estates remained huge, serfdom had long disappeared. He benefited from a personal freedom limited, to be sure, by the availability of few effective alternatives to his laborious routines. More significantly, he had come to live a step above the borderline of threatening starvation. Constant undernourishment and regular famines were no longer an integral part of his experience. In parts of France, peasants lived well, owning at least a portion of their land, eating meat with fair regularity and prospering in a way they dared not show for fear of the rapacious tax farmer. After all, the country had not been known as "la doulce France" for nothing. Arthur Young writes from Béarn (August 12, 1787):

> A succession of many well built, tight and COMFORT-ABLE farming cottages, built of stone and covered with tiles. . . . To every house belongs a farm, perfectly well enclosed, with grass borders mown and neatly kept around the corn fields. . . .

Comparing conditions there to those in England, he writes:

> . . . we have very little to what I have seen in this ride of twelve miles from Pau to Moneng. It is all in the hands of little proprietors, without the farms being so small as to occasion a vicious and miserable population. It is visible in their new built houses and stables. . . .[2]

And he adds: "A peasant does not think of rendering his pig comfortable if his own happiness hangs by the thread of a nine-year lease. . . ."

It was precisely the relative elevation of their position which eventually permitted some French peasants to take their minds off the business of surviving and to become conscious of their position in society. Then the fact that their lot still remained a depressingly hard one, afflicted by arbitrary vexations and irritating aristocratic privileges, such as the nobleman's right to hunt through planted fields and, of course, the privilege of his dispensation from many taxes, appeared increasingly galling. Once the peasant became conscious of his position and measured it in comparison to that of others, the question of change arose. Protest was rarely directed against the regime and its institutions, and certainly not against the monarchy which continued to benefit from the traditional veneration and loyalty. It was directed essentially against abuses, and to an increasing extent against noble landlords and their bailiffs. As such, it did not entail any general political consciousness or conception of human rights. It did, however, express a significant new consciousness of self and society, and an active sense of social grievance that was to break out in the drama of the Great Fear.

We find evidence of the detailed condition of the French countryside just before 1789, and insights into prevailing states of mind and levels of expectations, in the famed *cahiers* prepared for the Estates General. These documents furnish materials for an unparalleled assessment of an eighteenth-century European nation, from the national to the regional and local levels. They confirm our assumption that even in the advanced society of France, peasant concerns were primarily directed towards the removal of specific injustices rather than to an ideology of political freedom or universal historical meliorism. But these concerns did establish the background of resentments for a later revolutionary mass movement half-consciously serving the ideologies and programs developed by others. The parish *cahiers* furnish the context in which rising hopes, grounded in concrete economic demands and proposed social reforms, become converted into the revolutionary notion of the abolition of privilege and into the ideal of social justice. Turned primarily against conditions rather than against institutions, they nonetheless contributed the prerequisite raw materials for potential mass alienation from the existing society as evidenced by the peasant rebellions of 1789. For it was the explosion of peasant violence into a mass movement that put new revolutionary energies into gear. We may conclude that the French peasantry eventually provided the unwitting social and economic energy for transforming a small minority's trust in historical progress into a powerful historical force.

It is the bourgeoisie, we have long been told, that organized and led the French Revolution. Recent scholarship has considerably refined and changed this notion, giving an enhanced role to other social elements, notably the aristocracy whose combined truculence and class aspirations set the movement slowly going in the Assembly of Notables and the Parlement of Paris. The quiet origins of the Revolution are manifest not in radical demands, but rather in a momentary conservative reassertion of traditional rights and privileges. Significantly, the popular hero of the early revolutionary phase was the nobleman, the Marquis de Lafayette. Even the leaders of the Third Estate, like Sieyès and Mirabeau, came respectively from the two privileged orders, the clergy and the nobility. As for the bourgeoisie itself, it was anything but a homogeneous or consistent class. It ranged from small property holders on the edge of the growing ranks of a pre-industrial proletariat and of the large mass of paupers, to a few powerful merchants and bankers a step away from purchasing their patents of nobility and the tax exemptions that would accompany their new title. Its interests and ideas were as variegated and conflicting as its economic conditions and social status.

The resurgence of the aristocracy partly sealed off the avenues of social mobility through government service and the social ambitions of the educated or wealthy upper middle class. Traditionally a supporter of the crown against the nobility, the bourgeois now found himself increasingly thrust into intellectual and political opposition by his declining influence and prestige under Louis XV, and by the alliance of the monarchy with the aristocratic court and the privileged orders. This situation made the financial burdens and the near bankruptcy of the state, which bore heavily on the peasantry and much of the middle class, all the more galling. But it is virtually meaningless to generalize such negative considerations into the myth of the bourgeoisie constituting a self-conscious entity or advocating some well-defined, consistent bourgeois ideology. Its only common denominator was the great outcry against fiscal abuses, growing economic mismanagement and inordinate waste; its only common policy was the insistent demand for tax reform, sound economic management by the government and budgetary economy. These demands were not voiced by the bourgeoisie alone, nor did they constitute a program of utopian historicity.

But if the bourgeoisie as a whole did not launch and perhaps not even lead the early Revolution, certain bourgeois elements did animate it with their own "enlightened" aspirations and new historical ideals. The Enlightenment, it should be noted, had not been an inherently bourgeois phenomenon. Much of its impetus came from certain segments of the aristocracy, from men like Buffon, d'Alembert and Holbach. It was especially in vogue with the well-born leisured classes who had the time and taste for polite conversation and wit, and it drew its primary inspiration from the high society of the salons. Yet it was often men of the middle class like Diderot, Bayle, Turgot, Voltaire and the humbly born Rousseau who set their intellectual stamp upon it. In a society based largely on noble birth, how could the bourgeois assert his own worth better than by proclaiming the rationalist doctrine of the natural equality of men? Here ideology, the yearning for rational universal principles, and class interest all merged.

During the Revolution, Enlightenment ideals helped to draw aristocrats like Lafayette and Mirabeau to the cause of moderate political innovations, and later to make the Marquis de Condorcet a republican leader. It is important to note, however, that these men did not act within their own order. They joined themselves to the essentially bourgeois ranks of the Third Estate and seemed to corroborate Sieyès' famous remark that the Third Estate was everything. We may therefore say that despite the revolutionary role of other classes, it was nonetheless an educated segment largely drawn from the bourgeoisie that found in the National Assembly a new consciousness of its identity and of its ideology. It was primarily this group of upper bourgeois that came to stand for a progressivist and egalitarian doctrine of the historical liberation of humanity, and that propagated a secular revolutionary redemption of mankind.

We shall see that successive bourgeois groups organized the diffuse and even contradictory forces in the revolutionary movement. Through the accelerating succession of short-lived regimes, different bourgeois clubs and factions sought each time to present some new ideological focus of action and principle of unity in the name of a dominant revolutionary minority. Each of these chapters in the history of the Revolution saw new, abortive attempts to define a moral unity of purpose. Consequently, there were built upon the original demands for reform, which sank into the background, new sets of political ideals and moral values, all incarnated in historical expectations of a transcendent future.

Thus bourgeois elements were to play the key role, from our point of view, of taking concrete demands and often amorphous protests, and converting them into a general policy within an ideological framework. Bourgeois ideologues and their occasional aristocratic allies played the distinctive revolutionary role of turning economic and social grievances which had little general effect upon history into secular objectives that held out the promise of human liberation. Diffuse demands for piecemeal reforms were thereby harnessed to a central doctrine of political ideals and natural rights which transcended the existing order in its moral conception of the citizen, of civil liberties and of civic virtue. Instead of a patchwork addition to the inordinately confused administrative structure of France, there emerged, for both good and ill, a revolutionary program of apparent rationalistic cogency and above all, of transcendent historicity.

In sum, if we look back to the revolutionary roles of both the bourgeois movements and the peasant uprising, we find that in each case economic and social grievances supplied the motive force in developing new ideals. More than the abstract formulations of intellectuals, the actual conditions of life propagated new political demands. Economic and class questions had coalesced bourgeois opposition to the regime, to its decrepit finances, ruinous taxes and waste, and its privileged orders. Economic and class questions had generated peasant discontent against noble landlords, their tax privileges and vestigial feudal dues. The explosive resentment of the peasantry enabled the Third Estate to shake

the deeply entrenched resistance of the established order. Thereby
it prepared the ground for the proclamation of elusive bourgeois
aspirations and the redeeming vision of an ideal state. The new
ideologues offered their disciples a sense of vicarious transcendence of the human condition and their individual mortality
through their participation in the revolutionary liberation of mankind. Thus they eventually converted the historicist faith of certain
literate elites into a phenomenon of mass expectations.

We may conclude that the key to our understanding of late
eighteenth-century history is the fact that it produced a legacy of
mass consciousness of, and faith in, historical ideals. Of course, this
was not yet the age of regular mass movements. It remained for
the Industrial Revolution to provide the necessary technology to
make mass currents of opinion routine, and to raise mass wants
and hopes to continuing political significance. But the eighteenth
century was the time when secular historical objectives and aspirations were first used to organize mass movements in behalf of
worldly ideals that served a transcendent purpose. During the age
of Voltaire, the aristocratic elites and educated bourgeoisie still
dominated political life and sometimes responded to ideological claims. During the height of the Revolution, ruling factions
used patriotic appeals and egalitarian principles to build French
mass armies, evoke popular support and win the allegiance of the
urban populations to the revolutionary cause. Patriotism became
the agency of transcendent historicity. Amid the revolutionary
drama, ideologues and opportunists were to discover in the new
nationalist fervor the psychological device for harnessing popular
emotions and hopes to the republican cause. Later, a Corsican
adventurer would appropriate the same nationalist faith to secure
loyalty to his own person and power, under the guise of revolutionary principles.

2. Towards the First Republic of Hope

The new hope in history took the form primarily of political idealism and the glorification of nationalist sentiment. In the new historical consciousness, patriotism became the redeeming secular

value in that the patriotic act saved the individual from all his other sins. It permitted him to transcend his condition in life and his brief moment in time, and linked him to the national heroes of the past and the endless generations to come. It conferred upon him a feeling of immortality, partly through the memories of his compatriots, but above all in his identification with the eternal nation. Thus the vision of a glorious France standing above all Frenchmen constituted a form of individual historical purpose and redemption.

Paralleling the nationalist spirit, there was incarnate in much of the revolutionary ideology a supra-national ideal, namely the liberation of humanity. The new French regime would provide the model and the stimulus for the extension of libertarian ideals and civic virtues into a universal movement of justice and freedom. From Paris, the new formulations of human rights would radiate over other nations; natural rights were the property not just of Frenchmen but of all mankind. To France and her revolutionary partisans would belong the eternal glory of having caused the decisive breakthrough towards a new moral order expressed in political life. Thus a combination of intense patriotism and internationalist idealism characterized much of the official ideology of the newly emerging revolutionary elites. To show how the new historical idealism functioned among the masses, we must briefly consider the changing values of the Revolution and their relation to the interests and desires of the general populace, beginning with the liberalism that constituted a major portion of the Enlightenment's legacy. Liberal hopes were now cast in a political optimism that had implications of ethical salvation. In the new proclamations and manifestos, we find expression not only of principles derived from the *philosophes*, but of a pervasive belief that these principles would lead to a morally better world—a world of men liberated from the dehumanizing oppression of their present lot. At last history would achieve its destiny in the individual's right to be a free man:

> The representatives of the French people, organized in National Assembly, considering that ignorance, forgetfulness or contempt of the rights of man are the sole causes

of the public miseries and of the corruption of governments, have resolved to set forth in a solemn declaration
the natural, inalienable, and sacred rights of man, in order
that this declaration, being ever present to all the members
of the social body, may unceasingly remind them that the
demands of the citizens, grounded henceforth upon single
and incontestable principles, may always take the direction
of maintaining the constitution and the welfare of all. . . .[3]

In these introductory phrases of the famed Declaration of the
Rights of Man and the Citizen we see the influence of the American Declaration of Independence. Further on we find that of Montesquieu: "Any society in which the guarantee of rights is not
secured or the separation of powers not determined has no constitution at all." (Clause 16.) We hear the voice of Locke: "The aim
of every political association is the preservation of the natural and
imprescriptible rights of man. These rights are liberty, property,
security and resistance to oppression." (Clause 2.) And we find
especially the imprint of Rousseau:

> Men are born and remain free and equal in rights.
> Social distinctions can be based only upon public utility.
> (Clause 1.)
>
> The source of all sovereignty is essentially in the nation;
> no body, no individual can exercise authority that does not
> proceed from it, in plain terms. (Clause 3.)
>
> Law is the expression of the general will. All citizens have
> the right to take part personally or by their representatives
> in its formation. . . . (Clause 6.)

Finally comes the typical "envoi" of the Declaration's middle-
class authors: "Property being a sacred and inviolable right, . . ."[4]
It is above all the style and moral sentiments of the Declaration
that concern us. There is in its phraseology a tone of confidence;
the anticipation of ending public miseries and of maintaining the
freedom and welfare of all citizens constitutes not only an optimistic view of the future, but also a transcendent hope of human
freedom and virtue.

Practice rarely coincides with theory. When the Assembly

drew up its Constitution, it allowed its class interest to intrude
upon the egalitarian principles heralded in the Declaration. It be-
trayed its own ideals when it introduced the notorious distinction
between active and passive citizens. It repudiated its own historical vision when it distinguished property-holding citizens, who
could vote and hold office, from the poor who could not. The new
class structure, based on wealth rather than birth, could hardly be
reconciled with the proud affirmation of equal political rights
for all men. Yet the action of the legislators was not simply
hypocrisy. They saw in their policy a necessary expedient until the
time in the near future when all Frenchmen would share the quali-
fications of first-class citizenship. Discrimination, to them, was a
temporary necessity resulting from the inequities of past society; it
was not a principle for the permanent ordering of things. Here we
see their trust in history, which would eventually resolve the inescapable moral contradictions of the present. This faith of the
members of the Assembly appears to us a naïve justification of
their class bias. We recognize it as a thinly veiled rationalization
of their economic interests, and of their commitment to preserve
the sacred character of property rights. It is easy to promise equality for tomorrow and withhold it for today. Yet their argument,
for all its self-delusive quality, shows how history itself was expected to restore the ideal unity between the class Constitution and the universal Declaration, or in short, to redeem and
transcend the present condition of man.

By 1791, the revolution appeared to have run its course. It
had generally accomplished the basic reforms awaited in 1788,
and drawn up a constitution. It seemed to be settling down to a
calm political life as a responsible monarchy. Yet to subsequent
generations, the French Revolution had merely begun. Much of
the legacy it left to Europe of drama, aspirations, terror and hopes
came out of its later phases. During the ensuing years, the continuing revolutionary movement was radically to change its character,
before it finally fell back exhausted into the Thermidorean reaction. In the process, it was repeatedly to change its base of support
as well as its ideological commitments and historical pretensions.
To a significant degree, the issues and the clash of historical

values emerged from the encounter between revolutionary policies and the role of the Church. This confrontation had its roots in the character of the hierarchy and some of the religious orders during the *ancien régime,* and their collective identification with the structure of privilege and the inequities of society. But it arose also from the inherent hostility of men raised in the ideas of Enlightenment rationalism for the Church as an institution. They opposed what they saw as the Church's antagonism to science, reason, and philosophical and political innovations. Much of their resentment stemmed from the conflict between two radically different conceptions of the meaning of history and of man's prospects for building his own ideal world.

That reforms of clerical abuses were sorely needed was a point few sincere Catholics disputed. Seen from the perspective of the National Assembly, the desire to reform the Church in France was nothing but a logical counterpart to its reorganization of the French state at a time when church and state were customarily joined. Therefore it proceeded to rationalize Church structure and administration. It limited the worldly preoccupations of bishops who previously had spent much time and money in the Versailles court. It planned a symmetrical organization of the institution.

But the deeper suspicions between the Church and the National Assembly went far beyond administration and form. Deism was the fashion among bourgeois deputies. What sympathy could men who had enacted the Declaration of the Rights of Man under the auspices of Voltaire's Supreme Being feel for the spiritual claims of a religion which avowed mysticism and supernaturalism? What tact would men with a penchant for abstract universal order display towards the religious susceptibilities and traditions of the French people? In applying their rational pattern to religious affairs, they were bound to run into the absolute contradiction between philosophical deism and the spiritual claims of Christianity. In extending the principle of popular election from the civil authority to priests and bishops in accordance with their ideals, they confronted the irreducible conflict between rationalist ideas and the Church's view of the mystery of divine grace. Behind this conflict lay the Christian dogma of original sin, which precluded human perfectibility and unlimited historical progress in the secular world. In its orthodox interpretation, Christian teaching precluded any transcendence of the human condition and immortalization of the self except through the grace of God. It rejected any suggestions that man should presume to create his own moral values or claim to erect his own perfect state. Psychologically, such a position was wholly opposed to the historical aspirations and utopian pretensions of the radical ideologues who subsequently dominated the revolutionary movement.

It was the Civil Constitution of the Clergy that really divided France. It finally alienated much of the traditionally Catholic French peasantry. Already suspicious of the revolutionary government, many peasants were inclined to return to their native conservatism once their basic desire for land and the abolition of the class privileges of the old regime had been satisfied. Since the demands of the peasantry had been primarily social and economic, the religious and ideological realignment tended to throw many sections of it back to the defense of the new status quo. In consequence, the Revolution of the bourgeoisie was increasingly to separate itself from its rural base, or to find there but a grudging and sullen obedience. It tended to divorce itself from much of the agrarian population. The nature of the Revolution was thereby to change critically; it became increasingly a phenomenon of towns and cities, in the sense of an urban mass replacing rural masses, and of urban economic interests displacing rural economic interests. Of course, the urban element had been present in the popular revolution virtually since its beginning, but only sporadically. Now the role of the Parisian mass was to be more constant and its pressure more relentless. A key factor here is that where the economic position of the peasantry had improved and its social disabilities decreased through the August reforms, that of the city populace had not. The significance of this situation is that urban masses are more accessibly gathered in crowds, more easily influenced by tribunes like Marat, Desmoulins and Danton, and more readily subject to the continuing emotional waves of mob psychology. In the city, a reciprocal influence

occurred: greater pressure from the mass upon the revolutionary
leadership, and greater responsiveness of the mob to revolutionary
demagogues. Thus the increasing urbanization of the Revolution's
supporters brought on a decisive transformation in revolutionary
psychology and expectations, and of the transcendent image of
the future it presented.

The increasing momentum and radicalism of the movement
is exemplified by the dramatic events leading up to the Jacobins'
seizure of power. In 1792, the constitutional monarchy gave way
to the first republican phase under the rule of the Girondins. Their
historical hopes are familiar to us, for they were voiced by Condorcet. The Girondins raised French nationalism and revolutionary idealism to a new pitch. They nonchalantly invited war
with a coalition of European monarchs and launched a sort of
republican crusade. Theirs was a broad vision built on a narrow
social base. They were not consciously hypocritical; romantic
visionaries with a republican mission to the world, self-confident
in their leadership and enlightened values, they were emotionally
out of touch with the wants and passions of those who did not
share their fortunate security, complaisant learning or facile
utopianism. It was their vanity and smugness that defeated their
hopes, and the colorless abstractness of their ideal. Those who
would succeed in striking a popular response of dedication, zeal
and violent hatred in an age of revolutionary drama and tensions,
would be those able to create an historical mythology, more of
flesh . . . and blood.

3. Historical Transcendence and the Jacobin Ideal

The clubs of the Mountain had three priceless assets: discipline,
unity and passion. They knew what they wanted, a radical and
pure republic—not the anemic, compromised republic of the
Girondists. They sought moral unity in revolutionary idealism and
national patriotism. Their trinitarian creed of "liberty, equality,
fraternity" suggested a secular religion, a point borne out by the
absolute devotion and sacrifice required from disciples and followers. The key articles of dogma were the belief in human free-

dom and political equality, a republic of fraternity and justice, and the identification of revolutionary republican ideals with the national destiny of France, or rather with a purified French people.

Modern nationalism is a product of the Jacobin revolution. It owes its immediate origins to the outbreak of war in 1792. Patriotism and civic valor were the primary French resources in defense of the Republic at bay, invaded by a coalition of the major military powers of Europe. It is hardly surprising that the international situation, irresponsibly engaged upon by the Girondist war party, should soon come to cause grave anxiety, fear and even despair. No wonder that for the supporters of the Revolution, nationalism and republican sentiments soon converged.

Revolutionary patriotism did not preclude internationalism, or a romantic aspiration to universal human solidarity. The ideal of the fraternity of Frenchmen did not bar the ideal of the brotherhood of man. French republicans accepted foreign disciples in the midst of their own national legislature, and sent them indiscriminately to the guillotine. National exclusiveness was a sentiment generally reserved to the late nineteenth century. Of course, we must not confuse the emotional internationalism of revolutionary idealists with the cool cosmopolitanism of the eighteenth-century intellectual elites that had made French culture their spiritual home. Yet both sought a universal frame of reference for their moral and intellectual values. In the end, however, nationalism and the identification of revolutionary principles with republican France constituted the prime source of Jacobin enthusiasm, until passionate patriotism and revolutionism became one.

National sentiment functioned as the basis of the Revolution's mass appeal. It constituted the psychological bond of the new mass movement, significantly distinguishing the revolutionary currents of 1793 from the peasant movement of 1789. One Girondist paper bore the revealing title, *Patriote Français*. The climax of revolutionary patriotism came with the desperate call to the nation-in-arms, the famed *levée-en-masse*. More than just a step to conscript soldiers and organize labor for defense production, the levy involved a spiritual rallying of the people behind republican ideology, and its basic ethical principles. The ringing patriotic slogan, "liberty, equality, fraternity," evoked an ideal society attainable within man's secular horizons. Thus the doctrine of perfectibility, elicited from some of the ideas of the Enlightenment, was at last to be realized in the new nation-state of a liberated France.

The psychological quality of this transcendent secular utopianism was expressed in the patriotic rituals and symbolism that gave a distinctive stamp to the nationalistic Jacobin regime: the sacred emblems such as the tricolor, the revolutionary motto and the *Marseillaise*. We may note also the messianic tone of official proclamations and the evangelistic rituals of frequent republican ceremonies and festivities. The halls of the Jacobin clubs were decorated with the symbolic trappings of the new creed; the meetings of the club generally began with an invocation to the Spirit of Reason. The emotional power of the arts, frequently an accompaniment to fervent religious exercises, was enlisted. David, the "official" painter of the Republic, conveyed its classical mythology and propensity for the civic values of Greece and Rome and the puritan rigor of the Republic militant. Music, perhaps best suited to assist patriotic ceremonies by arousing emotions, was consecrated to the Jacobin cause by the new anthem and by such famed marching songs as *Ça ira*. Occasional concerts, intended as festive ceremonials, glorified revolutionary ideals. Radical pamphleteers and publicists—most notably Marat, with his sensationalist *L'Ami du Peuple*, Desmoulins, with his violent *Révolutions de France et de Brabant* and *Tribune des Patriotes*, and Hébert with his scurrilous *Père Duchesne*—mixed occasionally obscene denunciations with messianic oratory.

The patriotic spirit lent itself admirably to dramatic staging. Patriotic ceremonies provided a detailed orchestration of revolutionary sentiments and hopes. Old men were to spur youth to revolutionary acts of courage by reciting the tales of their own wounds and valor. Young women would fire their loved ones to patriotic heroism, while the children waved banners. The nationalistic routines of life of many of the poor city dwellers, the *sansculottes*, included the wearing of the revolutionary red bonnet with its tricolor cockade. The new forms of address—"*citoyen* Carnot" and *"ci-devant* Marquis de Condorcet"—marked the break with the past. It is generally such a change in the form of greeting that offers a revealing clue to the presence of a transcendent sense of history. Later examples, such as the use of "comrade," or the salutation "brother" in the labor movement, are the dessicated remains of a once evangelistic fraternal spirit. The infamous *Heil* was another barren testimony to an appeal to a transcending and immortalizing goal, in this instance the grotesque idea of German destiny embodied in the *Führer*. But to return to the French Revolution, perhaps the adoption of the revolutionary calendar offers the clearest symbolic evidence of the conception of a new world and a new civic morality, categorically differentiated from the previous condition of life. Thus the idea of man collectively reborn is signaled by the advent of the "new time" of republican freedom that marks off the new secular dispensation and salvation of humanity.

The living incarnation of the Jacobin ideal was the Incorruptible One, Maximilien Robespierre. In him there seemed to breathe the fervor of French patriotism, of uncompromising republicanism and of revolutionary unity. A less powerful figure than is often portrayed, and sometimes less a personal dictator than the head of a dictatorship, he nonetheless dominated the imaginations of many of his contemporaries, as he has dominated the subsequent images of the French Revolution. Perhaps we can picture the well-known contradictions in this man: the moderately successful lawyer from Arras, shocked by the notion of the death penalty, who became the hero of the Paris mob and the high priest of the Terror. Perhaps we can visualize the contrast in this fastidious gentleman of refined manners, continuing to dress in the upper-class fashion of wig and silk breeches when lesser persons of his party courted popular admiration in the more democratic costume of trousers and their natural hair. Let us think of the irony of Robespierre, contemptuously rejecting in the midst of a crowd the phrygian bonnet which had become *de rigueur* for popular patriots.

To Robespierre, the ideal state was the Republic of Reason and Virtue. Rejecting the atheism of the extremists, the *enragés,*

he envisaged a French people morally regenerated and purified
by their civic faith, and a France united in the worship of the
Supreme Deity of Reason. A dual triumph over atheist materialism and Christian irrationality! With much pomp, he staged a
celebration of the new religion to inspire the public. In a setting of
ponderous rituals borrowed from classical antiquity, the ceremony
sought to conjure up an historical continuity from the rationalist
humanism of Greek and Roman civilization to the values of the
new French Republic. The event consisted basically of a pseudo-
classical pageant, animated by allegorical figures clothed in flowing
white gowns and laurel crowns. It is precisely this mystic symbolism and patriotic romanticization of the Republic of Virtue that
characterize the transcendent quality of the mystique, and that
seek to lend an other-worldly luminescence to the ideal of reason.
Robespierre, who remained a mystic rationalist, accompanied his
Feast of the Supreme Being and the proclamation of a ruling Intellect with an affirmation of the immortality of the soul. But the
psychological purpose of the procession was to infuse the ultimately
historical values of patriotism and service to humanity with a
transcendent meaning. So trust in a redeeming historical destiny
and in a transcendent purpose to human life is finally reduced to
an allegory—a trite tableau serving as the new morality play!

In conclusion, let us note once again that the idea which has
concerned us in the French Revolution is the concept of transcendence through historical consciousness; it is neither the sentiment of nationalism nor the notion of progress, nor the idea of
utopia in itself. A man may sacrifice himself for his country out of
a sense of duty, without either seeing in it anything more than a
passing secular reality or endowing it with any supra-human life;
his transcendent objective may lie elsewhere, perhaps in his private religious beliefs. A liberal aristocrat might have envisaged
limited improvements and social reforms without either ideal
hopes or a sense of transcendent historicity; he may have lost faith
in any redeeming value. A utopianist may imagine his ideal state,
not as an historically meaningful goal but as something existing
permanently in another realm of being—a timeless "reality" paralleling the historical reality of our present existence. He would not

seek a transformation of present society out of a fellow-feeling for humanity, but rather yearn for a personal withdrawal to his own south-sea island. Such a perspective is ahistorical. Nor does the mere possibility of an ill-defined historical progress suffice for our purpose. The concept of the future must contain, as in the Jacobin case, either an attainable perfectibility, or a clearly infinite continuity of human aspirations and goodness. It must combine a utopian element with a linear view of the redeeming quality in man's development of moral self-consciousness, and with some intimation of eternity. It is the combination of qualities that is essential here. For only in this way can the sense of history appear to stand for self-transcendence and immortality through the unending ideal. Only in its capacity for *eternalizing* our alter ego, through our personal participation in some ostensibly ultimate historical destiny of man, can historical consciousness appear to provide a vicarious redemption of our present values.

4. The Terror: Contradictions of Secular Transcendence

The ideology of the Jacobin dictatorship, unlike that of previous regimes, was essentially democratic. That is to say, it directed its appeal not only to a minority of property holders but to the people. The Robespierreists especially received much of their support from the populace, notably from the poor people of Paris. Partly as a consequence of this fact, Jacobin social and economic policies came to be increasingly radical, or to have a less direct bourgeois class bias. Though their policies always reflected the interests of property holders, they involved less overt discrimination against the propertyless. In fact, the Robespierreists, who were themselves drawn largely from the bourgeoisie, shifted the balance in the revolutionary movement and the focus of the revolutionary appeal from the upper middle class to the lower middle class and urban laborer. They lost the support of much of the former element, which had been the backbone of most of the previous revolutionary movements. This situation in turn further accentuated their identification with the Paris populace against many of the wealthier merchants and especially the grain speculators. To characterize the change in direction, one may say that in 1793, the mass appeal of the republican government had been based primarily on revolutionary patriotism; by 1794, there had been added to that policy a wartime program of egalitarian social and economic legislation. Thus the revolutionary momentum, which had begun in the consciously restrictive class character of the Constitution of 1791, reached its natural fulfillment in the popular democratic ideology of the Robespierreist period. In the midst of dictatorship the impact of egalitarian democratic ideals rapidly reached a climax, and the legacy of revolutionary mass values was forged.

It was the press of events as much as the inherent dynamics of the Jacobin party that accounted for the crucial change in the impetus of the revolutionary movement and in the influence of revolutionary values upon subsequent European history. The desperate conditions of revolution, war and counterrevolution had led to severe food shortages in the poor quarters of the larger cities, particularly Paris, aggravated by the activities of grain speculators and by hoarding. The high price of bread and the threat of famine produced riots in Paris in 1793 and 1794, and thus intensified the social and economic pressure of urban mass movements upon the revolutionary government. Once again, it was essentially material factors that lay behind a new political development and that accounted for a new ideological turn. New legislation regulated grain prices and wages, restricted hoarding and threatened grain speculators with execution. Rationing was established to ensure a minimum distribution of food. The laws of maxima and minima were war measures intended to secure the desperate needs of the poor population of the capital, not expressions of economic principles. They were put into effect by a bourgeois government, not as deliberate acts of socialism but as emergency expedients in time of crisis. Yet they demonstrate a responsiveness to increased egalitarian demands and a willingness to undertake radical social reforms. The Jacobins, we have noted, never forsook their middle-class character or their sense of property rights. But the decree of Ventôse 1794 concerning confiscation of the possessions of disloyal citizens marks a new policy that foreshadows at least a partial redistribution of wealth.

Unintentionally, Robespierreist policy suggested a vague ideal of social and economic democracy to accompany the goal of political democracy and to give a new meaning of hope to the Revolution in the eyes of the populace. The climactic phases of the Jacobin regime produced a new conception of transcendence through history in the elaboration of a democratic mass ideology, suited psychologically to the urban population of nineteenth-century industrial Europe. While of non-socialist inspiration, it nonetheless offered a precedent for egalitarian and socialist values geared to the rising consciousness of mass identity in a proletarian society. From the Jacobin phase had emerged the implicit notion of permanent revolution—formulated over a century later by Leon Trotsky—in which the mystique of revolutionism itself becomes the guiding force. Revolution for its own sake, as a principle of movement and expression of iconoclasm, exhibits the desire to break out of the present human condition and to achieve, however elusively, some transcendent state of freedom and individual fulfillment. Hence revolutionary activity becomes psychologically attractive to the ideologue, regardless of its objective. It is the revolutionary's sense of redeeming anticipation that suffices as his motivation. This principle of revolution for its own sake which characterizes the climactic frenzy of Jacobin rule brings us to the critical transition from primitive violence to arbitrary yet systematic terror that is one of the essential traits of the totalitarian state.

The Terror was the consequence of both the internal contradictions of the regime and the deepening crisis of the revolutionary government. The Jacobin leaders had to face a desperate military situation after early republican reverses and the treason of the Girondist general, Dumouriez. As the revolutionary government in Paris increasingly alienated itself from much of the Catholic peasantry, it drove part of the latter towards the aristocrats and the non-juring priests. An incredibly bitter civil war broke out in parts of France, notably Brittany and the Vendée, marked by inordinate brutalities as each side was increasingly driven by its crusading zeal. As the Revolution tended to separate itself not only from the peasantry but also from much of the moderate and wealthier bourgeoisie, it became increasingly the prisoner of Paris and the Parisian radical element. Then, as revolutionary power came to be ever more centralized in the city, it was increasingly estranged from the provinces and from provincial towns such as Nantes and Lyon. After the Jacobins had driven the Girondins out of the Convention and executed those of their leaders and partisans who were unable to flee, a new bitter opposition arose in the Girondin strongholds. A regional conflict therefore was added to the other sources of tension and the growing desperation on all sides. The worsening economic situation and food shortages and the radical legislation of the government eventually added a further form of opposition as class conflict between property holders and the poor sharpened in several of the larger cities, especially in Paris. Thus the Jacobin leaders had to confront, besides the coalition of the major powers of Europe, a fourfold opposition on the home front. They had to fight against aristocrats and non-juring priests, against the peasants of several regions or provinces, against certain rebellious towns and against the prosperous bourgeoisie of the cities. The government had to cope with the problem of recruiting, organizing and equipping a new French army, with economic dislocation and an acute grain crisis, and with disorganized but numerous counterrevolutionary forces. That it responded with drastic punitive measures is not to be wondered at.

While Paris increasingly dominated the revolution, there arose in the capital itself overlapping and occasionally conflicting centers of power. The official authority of the republican government was vested in the Convention from which virtually all but the sympathizers of the Jacobins or the most cowed deputies had been purged. But the authority of the Convention had been largely preempted by its leading committees, especially the two key committees of General Security and of Public Safety. Furthermore, many of the critical decisions on policies were reached in the halls of the Jacobin Club where until 9 Thermidor of the Year II (July 27, 1794), Robespierre's influence prevailed, though not without bitter disputes. In addition to these various sources of power, the city government of Paris, the Commune, became increasingly demanding and influential in the later phase of the Jacobin regime as the movement of the Paris mobs and the riots charged the atmosphere in which the government worked. The Commune commanded the loyalties of much of the active populace in the Paris sections which were the ultimate source of support for Robespierre. With all this confusion added to the centralization of power in the Jacobin organization, it is natural that the arbitrariness of revolutionary violence increased.

We can see that there were many reasons in the dangerous situation confronting the Jacobin government, including those of their own making, that help to account for their resort to drastic punitive measures and intimidation, as well as to explain the psychological mood of the Terror. But the issue which really concerns us is the relation of the Terror to the internal dynamics of the revolutionary movement, especially to its ideology and to its secular-historical redemption. For the growing momentum of violence was as much a consequence of the internal characteristics of revolutionary psychology as of external circumstances. To the ideologue, the external challenges were a stimulus to his zeal. But internal divisions in the movement, corruption and factionalism, directly jeopardized his faith and threatened the possibility of attaining the transcendent revolutionary goal. Therefore the focus of the Terror shifted from privileged classes and apparent enemies of the Revolution, or those falsely accused, to the Jacobins' own ranks and leaders. The theme of the Revolution devouring her own children is a familiar metaphor. It exemplifies the self-contradiction, not of Jacobin ideology, but of its function of providing historical salvation to the true believer.

In Robespierre's view, the Republic must forge a Rousseau-styled moral bond among citizens. Consequently, factionalism and corruption are both to be seen not as political problems but as the worst moral offenses. In such a perspective, men like Danton who turn the pure ideal of republican virtue to their own interest and pleasure are the most guilty of sin. Factional divisions were no less a problem than corruption. Among the many subjects of discord on which opposing Jacobin groups or sects thrived, few loomed larger than conflicts over doctrine and over continuation of the Terror itself. As in most political conflicts, however, these considerations were mixed in with personal animosities and were often mere subterfuges for rivalries and power struggles. Soon partisan hostilities became bitter feuds and blood purges. Hébert and his followers wanted to push the secular ideology of the Revolution to its logical end, eliminate all vestiges of Christianity and establish a thoroughgoing atheism devoid of the mystic overtones of Robespierre's worship of reason. Danton, who had initiated the Terror, now wanted a lessening of violence and an end of mass executions. Robespierre purged each faction in turn and sent their leaders to the guillotine. In his view, continuation of the revolutionary tribunals was a necessity. To stop while enemies of the Republic were still dangerous would make a mockery of all the suffering France had endured. Was he proving to himself his incorruptibility by sacrificing close friends like Camille Desmoulins, guillotined on April 5, 1794? The elect are few, and the life of the puritan revolutionary is severe! At this stage, the Terror had become endemic and self-sustaining. From an occasional device of vengeance or fear it had become a policy of intimidation. From a deliberate policy it had become a form of purifying sacrifice, a public catharsis in honor of the new civic faith.

We must see the Terror of the revolutionary tribunals and the guillotine in the context of violence and bloodshed of the time. A larger number of victims were claimed by the atrocities of the civil war and by such barbaric punishments as Carrier's infamous drownings in Nantes and Collot's massacres in Lyon than were executed by the revolutionary courts. Psychopathic personalities like these men often gravitate to positions of power in revolutionary movements. But a court procedure that, under the infamous Prairial law, invites false denunciations, establishes mass tribunals with virtually no legal protection for the accused or examination of evidence, and is consequently organized to secure judicial murders, constitutes a distinct phenomenon of totalitarianism. The regime was literally consuming itself in its own violence. After his speech of 8 Thermidor affirming the need for uncompromising continuation of intimidation and purges, Robespierre is said to have remarked that his words had constituted his last will and testament and that he would "drink the hemlock"—even here, the historical allusion to antiquity remains. In its self-destruction,

Jacobinism had come to face its ultimate contradiction, namely the impossibility of achieving a transcendence-giving objective within its own history, or within its own time. It had engendered a totalitarian democracy in which despotic centralization and terror were the necessary agencies of brotherhood, justice and liberty.

What accounts for this appalling contradiction inherent in the Jacobin vision and its psychology? Why had the very sincerity of the ideal of freedom produced a far more tyrannical regime than the monarchy of Louis XVI? To Robespierre and his disciples, and to those who had supported the Terror until it threatened to turn upon them, the rationalization of the contradiction was ready at hand. Men are free—free to choose anything except slavery. But the Republic itself is freedom. Therefore the aim of free men can only be a Jacobin victory essential to the liberation of man. Those disloyal to the regime are traitors to their own liberty. Here we see the grotesque caricature of Rousseau's General Will. To the true believer, the totalitarian state was not an infringement of his real freedom. Totalitarian democracy was merely a political necessity that did not tarnish the ideal of liberty as an imminent and transcendent quality in history. The key to this enigma constitutes the essential point of our historical analysis. It is that despite the ahistoricity of the Jacobins' abstract universal model, they had fashioned a secularized and historicized vision of man's self-transcendence. For they had located man's moral redemption, and his breaking through the human condition, in his achievement of the ideal political state that will give historical "presence" to the ultimate value incarnate in the historical process.

Despite its apparent ahistoricity, the Jacobins' revolutionary ideology gave a decisive boost to our modern faith in history. The transcendent desire for liberation from the prison of our existence and for moral self-fulfillment was to be attained not by each individual withdrawing into some timeless state of consciousness, but within an historically defined condition in historical time. The transfigured state of human consciousness was not to be construed as a continuing timeless reality in some other realm of human experience, but as the outcome of a moving process or evolution to which a specific and unique date could be attached. Thus the initiation of a new calendar suggests a secular version of the Christian sense of time and of a day of deliverance. Emptied of its religious content, the Christian time sense had been preserved and its redeeming object grafted upon an historical objective. Here was the source of Jacobin psychology, of its millenarian and evangelistic style, namely that it had to capture transcendence fully within history. It had to give immediacy to an ideal requiring the transmutation of corrupt secular society. The impulse, not to reform the old order, but to annihilate it, created the totalitarian mystique. Referring to the execution of enemies of *la patrie* by the revolutionary tribunals, the Robespierreist Couthon is said to have remarked that it was less a matter of punishing them than of utterly destroying them. Totalitarianism, in other words, appears as the final price of secularizing the eschatology of salvation and the transcendent ideal. The burden of human salvation is too much for history to bear. Trying to make it do so produces the pathological convulsions brought about by the contradiction between totalitarian order and the ideal of human freedom.

What are we to conclude? We have devoted so much attention to the French Revolution and to material that is probably familiar to the reader because its utopian vision goes to the very heart of our subject: man's transcendence of his own mortality through commitment to the historical future and his contribution to an ideal historical condition. The essential point for us about the Revolution is that it constituted a secularized salvation because it converted libertarian theory into a concrete historical ideal. The point about the Jacobin period is that it converted the egalitarian historical ideal of a literate minority into the redeeming expectation of an urban mass.

It would be an error to see mass movements in the late eighteenth century as ordinary phenomena of political life. It still took an extraordinary combination of circumstances—war, bitter civil strife and fervent revolutionism—to coalesce a potential mass movement into a decisive historical force. The mob of Jacobin supporters in Paris were a small minority of the French people. They constituted an embryonic mass movement, not by their number, but by the character of their pre-proletarian following. Not until the Industrial Revolution would a mass identity become "normal" or constitute an on-going political reality. Yet the essential characteristics of modern mass movements were revealed in the Jacobin period. The Revolution had offered a preview of many of the distinctive attributes of popular political forces and of modern ideological values. It had set a precedent of ideals that would be essentially secular and historical. The Jacobins sought a moral goal that would define man's redemptive transcendence in terms of a revolutionary ideal of justice and liberty or of a patriotic identification with the nation-state. In short, the Revolution indicated that our modern popular ideals would tend to be historicist in that they would rest upon the conviction of a link between the past and man's creation of a transcendent state within his worldly future.

If the Revolution dissolved its contradictions in a totalitarian order, it also turned into concrete historical form its vision of human progress and freedom. It effected a remarkable shift from the earlier years of the century, marked by the lack of historical consciousness and even of ideological expectations among the illiterate strata of the population. During the eighteenth century, the intellectual rationalism of the elites of the salons was converted into a middle-class political utopianism. Then the Revolution converted the aristocratic Enlightenment of the Marquis de Condorcet, expressing the historicist outlook of the Girondist bourgeoisie, into the transcendent historical idealism of the bourgeois Jacobins, voicing the new historical expectations of the *sans-culottes* populace. In giving shape to the idea of progress through the dual forms of revolutionary values and patriotism, the Jacobin republic set the precedents for modern mass movements, and outlined their key characteristics of nationalism and egalitarian hopes. Here lies the impact of the French Revolution on our times, and specifically on the nature of our historical consciousness: it wrote into the actual events of our historical tradition a legacy of secularized purpose and of transcendent historicity.

A postscript: we have all heard that Napoleon's significance lay in spreading the ideals of the French Revolution to the nations of Europe. Historians have long wrestled with the question: was

Napoleon the true "heir" to the Revolution or not? They have
balanced on one side Bonaparte's plebiscitary dictatorship and on
the other his enshrining of revolutionary equality, fraternity and
patriotism. Our concern is only that in capitalizing on revolutionary slogans, in writing equality before the law into his Code, and
especially in promoting nationalism, Napoleon was but oppor-
tunistically attaching his own popular despotism and legend to the
psychological forces the Republic had left to him. When Napoleon
took over the tricolor, he inherited with it the outlook of the
Revolution it symbolized: faith in history.

PART III

PART II.

V

HISTORICAL IDEALS
AND FAUSTIAN STRIVING

1. Political Values in the Context of the Vienna Congress

In 1803, Beethoven began composing his E Flat Major Symphony in honor of Napoleon; in 1804, he changed the dedication and entitled the work the *Eroica* instead. His initial intent had been an offering to Bonaparte, embodiment of the French Revolution and of the people's cause Beethoven ardently loved. The symbolic crossing out of Napoleon's name on the great Third Symphony was testimony, in Beethoven's tempestuous populism, to Napoleon's betrayal of the liberal hopes with which he had previously sought to identify his career and to preserve his charismatic popularity. Many idealists who had once been Bonaparte's admirers eventually caught sight of the thinly veiled despotism beneath the veneer of republicanism. Yet the genuine enthusiasm with which Napoleon's successes were initially greeted evidenced the spreading influence of French revolutionary ideas. Napoleon's Grand Army and the French tricolor were the common instruments of nationalist liberal ideology. Meanwhile, the nations of the Continent had been prepared by their own native poetic traditions and national myths to respond to the Napoleonic influence. By the nineteenth century, the idea of nationality, if not yet that of nationalism, was deeply imbedded in the literature of distinctive European cultures. The French example and the apparent inspiration of early Bonapartism completed the conversion of cultural nationality into the political patriotism of liberals and students, especially in Italy and Germany. Thus the nationalism inspired by Schiller and Fichte culminated after the Napoleonic era in the patriotic passion found in Weber, Wagner and other romantics. The unifying impact of Dante's poetry and of later Italian literature stimulated the political vision of liberal Italian nationalism born of Napoleonic experience and expressed in the patriotic appeal of Mazzini and the *risorgimento*.

Eighteen fifteen: Napoleon's empire lay in ruins, partly defeated by the moral ideal of freedom and the emotion of patriotism he had helped to spread across the Continent. The historical forces and the history-centered values that had arisen during the preceding decade survived. But the new mood that now predominated in Europe was the reaction against Bonapartism and the liberal values of the French Revolution that ironically had become identified with his imperial despotism. Under the conservatism of Metternich and the mood of the Vienna Congress, a new historical outlook and a new function of historical consciousness arose. As national and republican principles were driven underground by the victorious coalition of European monarchs and their ministers, conservatism colored the prevailing historical perspective, just as in the preceding decade revolutionism had set the predominant historical tone. But a conservative view of history and a conservative frame of historical awareness were not new in 1815; they were as old as historical consciousness itself.

At the beginning of the revolutionary drama in France, an Anglo-Irish statesman, Edmund Burke, had formulated a distinctive perspective of history and of its relation to moral values that was to shape the conservative form of historicism and its legacy to our time. For Burke was to give to nineteenth-century conservatism its own sense of a meaning and purpose inherent in the historical process, and to attack radicalism on the charge that it ignored the essential historical characteristics of a nation's life. But the real issue between the conservative and liberal perspectives of history was that the conservative historicism of Burke did not constitute a transcendent doctrine. To him, there was no historical utopia or immanent ideal state, with its distinctive function of eternalizing our alter ego. While he laid heavy emphasis on the moral weight of historical traditions, of accumulated customs, practices and prejudices, he repudiated the role of history as an agent for the collective redemption of society. He did not antici- pate the achievement of a perfected or morally regenerated man- kind. Thus Burke left conservatism with an essentially non-tran- scendent view of history, as opposed to the revolutionary appeal to man's future liberation, and the liberal conception of a redemp- tory historical purpose. Burke's view proved a psychological dis- advantage in the currents of the age. It was especially unsuited to popular aspirations, so that later in the century conservatives were forced to adopt transcendent nationalism for their historical needs. Thereby they were eventually to develop their own tran- scendent sense of history, taking over the claim to the immortaliz- ing function of patriotic valor. But this development still lay in the future. For the moment, the conservative view of history to which Burke and others gave voice predominated; it stood opposed to the form of utopian historicity that had emerged from the French Revolution.

Looking at the world from the vantage point of English tradi- tionalism and constitutional liberties, Burke inveighed against Jacobin messianism, not in opposition to liberty, but in its de- fense. True freedom, he argued, could only be the outcome of historical traditions. Rights emerge from practices developed through the ages which have their own inherent reason that is not identified with the abstract rational categories Burke attributed to the *philosophes* and to their revolutionary followers. For him, liberty could become a meaningful reality only within the frame- work of an accumulated historical wisdom embedded in the col- lective intelligence and vision of each people. Appropriate institu- tions forged over generations could not be summarily disrupted without jeopardizing a nation's cultural balance, and indeed its whole life and identity. Burke saw the position of the Enlighten- ment, and of its Jacobin disciples, as fundamentally ahistorical. He rejected its abstract solutions which seemed to dispense with the varieties of human history, the singularity of particular na- tional circumstances and human experience itself.

The conservatism of Vienna, which was to dominate the official politics and ideology of most Continental monarchies in the first half of the nineteenth century, resembles the critiques of Burke in some significant respects, and differs vastly in others. Metternich and Burke, as unlike in personality and philosophy as one could imagine, are alike in that both reviled the ideological framework of revolutionary France, especially Jacobinism. But if Burke despised what he regarded as the false rational doctrine of rights of the Enlightenment, he did not propose to freeze the order of the old regime. Rather, he saw ancient custom as the root from which natural and gradual historical change would spring. It was through this historical continuity that real freedom would be preserved, as in the case of the traditional liberties of the American colonists which he tried to defend against the claims of some Tories. His opposition to a repressive policy against the American colonies was only an apparent contradiction to his subsequent strictures against the revolutionary principle in France—the former, indeed, appeared to him a movement in line with historical evolution, the latter against it. In short, Burke's view of history contained its own moral and religious framework that related man's historical acts and purpose to a transcendent Christian objective. But it was an objective that lay outside the historical future. Therefore it did not, like historicist ideals, place a mortgage on the achievement of specified redemptive goals of humanity, or impose upon historicism the burden of redeeming mankind.

With Metternich, conservatism became an attempted immobilism, devised as an *ad hoc* policy in defense of Hapsburg prerogatives. It served a political necessity in the minister's effort to preserve the dynasty's power, prestige and possessions, all of which were closely identified with the social and religious structure of the *ancien régime*. But it also represents a general principle of morality and history, namely the common conservative fear that a change in the established order will undo the mechanism and equilibrium of society. For in the conservative view of history, civilization is never far from the edge of chaos, due to the force of human greed and aggressiveness. As explained in the unsentimental conservatism of de Maistre, human nature is a dangerous element when it is unchecked by the restraints imposed in the social

order, including the necessary fear of the executioner. In less extreme arguments, the checks are primarily those of custom and
convention, of the established order and place of things, or in a
word, the wisdom built into the institutions and historical consciousness of a people. In practice, however, these aims also depend upon police powers, repression of dangerous movements and
ideas, censorship and severe punishment to defend a partially
resurrected political and social structure of Europe. Here conservatism is raised from a pragmatic consideration of class interests
and the preservation of personal privileges into a general historical
and philosophical principle. It proclaims that the inherent selfishness of human nature in the mass makes any notable change in the
order of society a threat to civilization rather than a hope of
liberty or utopia.

But Metternich entertained no romantic illusions about
ideologies, even the ideology of conservatism. It was rather ideology itself that constituted the danger, because of its apparent
ahistorical quality and the inevitable risk that it might find new
rational grounds upon which to attack the regime. In this sense,
even authoritarian ideology stood opposed to the inbred habit of
traditional response to authority. We find in the end that separating the world of Metternich from that of his liberal foes were their
respective psychological predispositions, which expressed themselves in the conflict between romantic hopes in the historical
regeneration of man, and resignation to the untranscendability of
human nature.

2. *Liberal and Conservative Attitudes Towards History*

The conflict between conservatism and liberalism dominated the
political and cultural history of Europe during the first half of the
nineteenth century, culminating in the revolutions of 1830 and
1848. In a general sense, the distinction between conservatism
and liberalism, seen as the difference between forces of "order"
and of "change," is as old as political consciousness itself. But in
a specific sense, liberal and conservative ideals were crystallized in
the legacies of the French Revolution, the Napoleonic Age and the

Vienna Congress. Each ideology represented not only political
values, but economic and social forces as well. Reduced to the
most popular explanations, the differences between them have
been generally described in terms of their opposing views on
individual rights, government powers and constitutional processes.
But from our point of view, the essential difference between them
lies in their distinctive perspectives of history, and especially in
their contrasting attitudes towards historical transcendence.

The Continental liberals of the early nineteenth century were
predominantly the middle-class inhabitants of towns and cities. In
a sense, they had inherited the Enlightenment perspective of the
eighteenth-century French bourgeois and of the cosmopolitan intelligentsia. But they were significantly to romanticize their inheritance and thus to transform its character. The key pillars of
their ideology were individualism and freedom—that is to say, the
concern with the individual's right to fulfill his personality and
capacities, his freedom to think and write, and to participate in
political life. The concrete manifestation of these ideals was primarily political, specifically in the achievement of parliamentary
and constitutional rights. With absolute monarchy or arbitrary
authority to be replaced by a constitutional regime, the other problems of social life would, in the liberal view, ultimately come to a
solution. Parliamentary responsibility was the key to civic progress. But if most nineteenth-century liberals fought for constitutional and parliamentary prerogatives, they were generally not
democrats. They rarely thought of granting every inhabitant a
vote, and they tended to regard political responsibilities as the
attribute of those who had a stake in society demonstrated by the
ownership of property and the payment of taxes. Here they be-
trayed, like their French forebears of 1791, their inherent class
bias, and the fact that their conception of freedom was clearly
limited to serve their class interest. Yet for all that, they did
develop the sense of liberty as a transcending ideal which many of
them defended with great unselfishness, and they did formulate a
wide vision of man's dignity, achieved in his individual historical
role.

The liberal perspective rested on a distinctive conception of history. Liberalism was essentially optimistic because it presupposed the perfectibility of man, which in turn rested upon the assumption of innate human goodness. We have, of course, encountered this attitude before in some of the currents of the Enlightenment, but its meaning was now subtly changed. Where goodness had meant to several of the *philosophes* man's perfectibility through reason and rational order, it tended in the nineteenth century to mean expectations predicated on human good will. Romantic liberal poets stressed man's innate kindness, benevolence and affection. The emotional quality of human sentiment, especially sympathy, became the basis of the new optimism about the evolution of society. Progress depended on the fulfillment of innate fellow-feeling rather than on the triumph of reason. In the literary culture of the age, man generally was presented, less as a thinking machine, in the sense of la Mettrie, than as a sentient, emotional being in the tradition of Rousseau. We should recall that Enlightenment thinkers like Diderot did not reject the man of feeling, and that romantics like Rousseau did not repudiate the ideal of reason. But the literary emphasis shifted from rational to sentimental values. The natural consequence of this tendency towards a relative irrationality was an emphasis on subjectivism. The romantic predisposition involved an introspectiveness about one's states of mind. It led to a concern with individuality, understood as distinctiveness of the person or ego, which characterized the prevailing romantic tone of the age.

It is easy to overplay the role of romantic humanitarian sentiments. One tends to forget that in a period of technological and industrial growth contrary currents existed. In an age of scientism and of the exploitation of labor, an inhumanitarian hardness was generally found in the practical behavior of self-interested men such as industrial entrepreneurs. It manifested itself in the bitter social strife and mercantile ruthlessness that marked a society of pragmatic material objectives and, for England, at least, of an often drab utilitarian philosophy. But it is significant that even this last doctrine participated in the general liberal assumption about human betterment and historical progress. Thus, despite Malthusian pessimism and the tangible misery of industrial cities, the

intimation of man's moral improvement and a humanitarian view
of historical progress grew. It is this quality which links modern
liberalism with that of previous periods: the presumption of the
potentially redeeming character of history. Hence, what truly defines liberalism is not any given set of policies or contextual attitudes, but a perspective of mankind. What distinguishes it is the
hope of transcending the human condition and of approaching
man's redemption through the historical process.

If we turn from the historicist presuppositions of liberalism
to an analysis of conservative historicism, we find that the contrast
is partly explained by the different social and economic elements
of the population from which each drew its strength and psychological characteristics. Where liberalism in the nineteenth century
was essentially an urban phenomenon, conservatism was primarily
strong in rural environments and villages, though it also attracted
the small citified aristocracy. This predominantly traditionalist
and provincial background expressed itself in the view that the
preservation of order was the primary necessity and object of civilized existence. Where liberalism emphasized individuality and
freedom, conservatism naturally stressed the value of the collective organism. It emphasized the maintenance of the hierarchy of
responsibility and authority without which civilization itself dissolves into chaos. The welfare of the collective entity was deemed
more important than the rights of the individual, because without
collective authority, no individual rights could exist. Since freedom can only be exercised where a consensus of cultural norms
prevails, the conservatives held, the preservation of traditional
culture becomes the necessary prerequisite to the presence of
liberty.

This perspective rested upon an image of history which assumed a pessimistic conception of human nature and of the historical prospects of mankind. The conservative's hope was not an
historical hope, nor did he anticipate transcendence in terms of
historical purpose, or the historical liberation of man. While
the historicism of romantic liberals was generally a corollary of their
semi-conscious predisposition towards the potential goodness in
humanity, conservative historicism was largely the expression of

conservatives' mistrust of human nature, at least in the mass. If, as they claimed, the natural tendency of the populace is towards disorder and tyranny as exemplified in the Terror, then the history of political life is at best a staving off of decay or, as Hume seemed to imply, a prospective reenactment of the decline of the Roman Empire. Authority must seek to preserve civilization, not to build an ideal city. The best that can be hoped of the future is that it will continue to reflect the values of the past, not that it will achieve some new ideal immanent within the historical process. Thus the liberal view of history is essentially evolutionary, the conservative view essentially recurrent. It is not a coincidence that those thinkers who formulated great cyclical patterns of history and politics, from Plato, Polybius and Thucydides to Spengler, tended to be both pessimistic and conservative. Nor is it a coincidence that those social philosophers who developed an evolutionary view of human history, from Herodotus to Condorcet, Comte and Marx, were essentially liberals in the broad sense of the term.

The conservatives tended to stress the traditional Christian conception of man, corrupted by original sin and consequently incapable of liberating himself from his baser instincts and lusts. It was generally conservatives who affirmed the Christian notion of man's guilt, as opposed to the liberals' thesis of unlimited perfectibility through history. It is not surprising that, quite apart from social and political interests, the Church generally found the attitude of conservatives more congenial to its view of life. In the Church's long-range perspective, the humane spirit of brotherhood pervading liberal romanticism was counterbalanced by the liberals' implicit pride in man's potential achievement and in the creation of his own ideal society. Liberals with their Pelagian approach often seemed to bypass the tragic sense of history or the inevitability, according to Christian teaching, of human guilt. In liberal Christianity, the forms and ethical precepts of Christian dogma were retained, but the theology of redemption was radically humanized and historicized.

To sum up the distinctions between the liberal and the conservative forms of Western historical consciousness, we may say

that where the archetypal myth of the former was either Promethean or Faustian, the archetypal model of the latter was essentially Biblical and Augustinian. In the conservative psychology, the
city of God and the city of man always remain distinct concepts
with reference to historical time. In the liberal psychology, they
form a temporal continuum; that is to say, they are joined in the
historical process through man's striving towards the ideal. In the
conservative view, history is essentially tradition. Conservatives
naturally emphasized stability against the sense of movement of
the liberal view of history. Conservatism, in other words, tended
to an image of order in the ideal relation between past, present
and future. In practice, it emphasized continuity amid evolution,
notably in preserving the social hierarchy of authority and status.
Liberalism, on the other hand, presented history as the inevitability of change, and emphasized evolution amid continuity. The
conservative sought in history the perpetuation of the past. The
liberal sought escape from the past and present human condition
into a novel and intelligible future. The latter conceived of history
as essentially an evolutionary pattern, the former as essentially a
traditional legacy; the one saw the temporal order as basically
cyclical, the other as basically linear.

Subsequently, the conservatives developed a sense of universal historical meaning that expressed an ultimate and suprahistorical purpose. Here appears the key distinction between
conservatism as a mystique and a merely conservative impulse or
opportune policy. Conservatives like Burke saw in history the
hand of Providence, which is what made its traditions valuable to
them. They could not deny an immanent purpose and value in
man's historical experience. But for the old-style conservative,
history itself was not transcendent, and therefore could not serve
to save mankind. For him, history might well teach a moral lesson
and thus illuminate the need for redemption. Yet even the presence of an immanent and higher providential value could not
make history as such transcendent, for the simple reason that to
the older conservatives, there could be no transcendence within
secular time or within the potentialities of man. Thus, even the
ultimate purpose of history cannot transform man's historical destiny into his personal salvation.

3. Nationalism and Romanticism

The dialectic of nineteenth-century liberalism and conservatism was complicated by the insistent theme of nationalism, the dominant political motif of the age. National sentiment was intimately wedded to early nineteenth-century liberalism. It animated the liberal conception of history and historical progress. It provided the passionate emotional drive behind liberal ideology. The liberal ideal, in turn, generally assumed the form of a transcending goal of national brotherhood and freedom. We have already seen the development of national patriotism into a basic moral value in the history of the French Revolution. We have seen how it became the expression of a secularized transcendence in history, because it offered the individual a purpose to life. It represented a vicarious extension of his identity in the collective nation-state, beyond his own ephemeral existence. Sacrifice for one's country became the central tenet of moral regeneration, and national heroes provided a new gallery of saints. Jules Michelet once referred to France as "God's soul on earth."

It is not necessary for us to go over the growth of national sentiments in nineteenth-century Europe, though we must consider the impact of nationalism on the values of liberal historicity. Our concern is that student organizations, such as the romantic German *Burschenschaften,* the currents of national poetry and legend, the patriotic societies like the *Carbonari* and the Young Italy, and national heroes like Kossuth, or Mazzini and Garibaldi, expressed the new transcendent value placed in the state. Nations developed their own bodies of patriotic *sacra scripta*—declarations of independence or of rights, constitutions, epic poems and the works of consecrated national poets like Dante and Schiller— as well as festivals, rituals and all the accoutrements of national mythologies.

Why did the mirabilia of patriotism become fused, for a time, with the symbolism of liberal dogmas? Why did liberalism and nationalism "marry" in the first half of the nineteenth century? There was nothing inherent in the nature of either to draw it irremediably to the other, as was amply demonstrated in subsequent events when the two ideals were to become separated and even opposed, with striking consequences for each. That they were so intimately tied together between 1815 and 1848 is largely explained by the genesis of their respective developments. For one thing, they both expressed the social and economic interest of the bourgeoisie. Each emerged from the storm of the Revolution and thus became categorized as part of the revolutionary impulse, both to its disciples and to its enemies. The position of Metternich in maintaining the Hapsburg possessions and power required him to check liberal aspirations along with nationalist currents that might dismember the multinational empire. Hatred of Metternich's system united liberal and patriotic emotions. This relationship meant that just as liberalism provided an individualizing counterweight to collective national goals, nationalism provided a moral bond for the community against the atomistic tendencies of self-centered liberal values.

After 1848, when these two movements were divorced in many countries, patriotism provided the new conservative clientele with a transcendent value. The statist tendency in nationalism, released from the counterweight of liberal individualism, increasingly followed its internal logic towards imperialist or racist doctrines. Thus patriotic dogmatism eventually constituted the conservatives' own brand of future-oriented historicity. Even social conservatism equipped itself with a transcendent political vision and an historicist frame of reference. In their continuing struggle with the popular emotional appeal of the liberal doctrine of progress, conservative movements ultimately used nationalist goals for their own version of historical destiny. Forced to compete with the optimistic forecasts of history of radicals and socialists, conservatism had to resort to a redemptive view of future historical objectives and purposes. The conservative proclamation of patriotic ideals offered the individual an alternative messianic sense. In fact, if we may project our concern for a moment out of the nineteenth century into more recent forms of right-wing nationalism, we find that in National Socialism, self-transcendence is to be achieved through devotion to the "party," ideally identified with the historical destiny of the "folk." Here we reach the crux of the modern impetus to historicity, ironically embodied in a

revolutionism of the right. But it is a vitiated historical consciousness, satanized by the relentlessness of an inherent contradiction:
to attain a transcendent state within a purely secular and historical
frame.

To return to the first half of the nineteenth century, liberal
national movements became the characteristic forms of bourgeois
political ideology. Occasionally liberal demands, such as Corn
Law repeal in England, evoked popular support, despite the fact
that the urban masses derived little benefit from bourgeois class
claims or political gains. But in enlarging the basis of suffrage,
liberal historicist idealism at least seemed to hold out to them a
hope of eventual liberation, whereas conservative historicism did
not. We need not go into the Paris Revolution of 1830, begun by
the bourgeoisie, though executed by the populace which, as usual,
manned the barricades. Delacroix has left us a famous painting of
revolutionary ardor that the ensuing regime of Louis-Philippe
hardly warranted—a romantic and dramatic piece, more in keeping, perhaps, with the spirit of '93, portraying "Liberty Leading the
People." The revolutionary wave which swept across Europe early
in 1848 was started in Paris. The new French Revolution marked
another bourgeois-led uprising for liberal political goals and
middle-class interests. But it ended in June 1848, with a part of the
populace of the French capital, swelled by an influx of impover-
ished peasants, engaged in a bitter social war. Here was a pre-
proletarian outbreak foreshadowing later working-class uprisings
against the middle-class order. The unemployed workers and
farm migrants in Paris depended upon the new public-works
system inspired by the socialist leader, Louis Blanc. They were
staunchly attached to these National Workshops. Suddenly, they
found themselves cornered by the more conservative rulers of the
Second French Republic who opposed the workshop program as a
dangerous threat to private property. In desperation, they launched
a fateful attempt to secure their livelihood, and in the process, to
recapture the revolutionary hopes and ideals which somehow had
always turned out to profit other classes.

The Paris "June days" mark an emergent form of revolutionary mass current and the popularization of a new conception of

historical utopianism that was to be economic and social rather than primarily political. In subsequent socialist ideologies, the primary emphasis on historical transcendence was to focus on a new definition of equality—a definition born of the character of industrial society and of the experience of industrial masses. Meanwhile, the conception of liberty was undergoing subtle change. The new liberals concerned themselves more with economic problems and social justice. They considered the variety of opportunities open to an individual who finds himself born into a largely predetermined social background, rather than purely formal political rights. But for all the bitterness between socialists and old-style liberals, and despite the fact that the former regarded the latter as their inveterate class enemies and oppressors while they in turn feared socialists as the wreckers of order and culture, it remains true that they both shared the same fundamental psychology of history. They shared the same basic historical sense, namely the expectation of change, progress and an end to man's alienation from society. In other words, the socialists inherited the liberals' expectation of historical transcendence and secularized redemption.

Romanticism provides a major clue to the values of the early nineteenth century and an underlying coherence amid the multiplicity of conflicting ideals. It was the romantic predisposition that formed the psychological bond of utopian historicity between liberalism and socialism, much as these respective "isms" bitterly opposed each other in their policies, objectives and sources of support. It was romanticism that provided the common denominator of democratic and utopian-socialist objectives, because it inspired the fundamental unspoken attitude towards individual and collective self-transcendence.

Romanticism was preeminently history-oriented. Romantic writers looked to the past, especially the glamorized legends of their own national background. The distinguishing mood of the romantic style is nostalgia, which can involve the collective memories of history as much as the personal memories of individual experiences. Romantic historical interests focused on the Middle Ages, depicted in the novels of Victor Hugo and Sir Walter

Scott. They were drawn to the Gothic culture of the thirteenth century which appealed to the romantics' Christian sensibility and mystic inclinations. The romanticized legend of Joan of Arc became a popular theme. To be sure, the resulting image of medieval life and civilization was a sentimentalized distortion whch may tell us more about romanticism than about the characteristics of the Gothic age; but it attests the romantics' consciousness of history and the pervasiveness of their historical interest.

Romantic poets gave voice to the feeling of fraternity that was an intrinsic part of the historicist outlook. They stimulated patriotic sentiments with their evocation of national cultural traditions and heroes. They glamorized the simplicity of "the people" and thereby enhanced the claims of those reformers who wanted to extend suffrage. It is true that romanticism could also serve a conservative outlook and the aristocratic ideal of benevolent paternalism. Factory-reform laws in Britain were often initiated by romantic conservatives, sometimes against the opposition of liberals. Chateaubriand in France and the young Disraeli in England attest the compatibility of conservative politics and the romantic style. Some romantics, glamorizing the Middle Ages' hierarchic society, anointed monarchs and code of chivalry, felt little sympathy for democratic movements or egalitarian ideals. But the predominant romantic impetus, epitomized in Byron's devotion to freedom, was directed towards political reforms such as were associated, until mid-century, with liberal policies.

The romantics praised liberty. Shelley passionately voiced the ideal of freedom in *Prometheus Unbound*. By and large, the romantic impulse and its psychological inclination fed the humanitarian instincts in both democratic and revolutionary ideals. In the well-known preface to *Hernani*, Victor Hugo wrote "Romanticism [is] liberalism in literature. . . . Liberalism in literature will not be less popular than in politics. Liberty in Art, liberty in Society: behold the double banner that rallies the intelligence. . . ."[1]

In sum, romanticism contributed to the essential historicity of nineteenth-century thought—the thought of a Fichte, a Goethe or a Michelet. In the romantic atmosphere, history increasingly impinged on the mathematical sciences as the organizing principle

of knowledge, evidenced in the new vogue of historical philosophies that characterized the period from Hegel to Marx. The forms
of historical consciousness which had gradually been built up over
the preceding centuries now dominated the age. The intimation of
moral transcendence which had figured notably in the enlightened
historicity of the eighteenth century and in the secular futurism
of the Jacobins now culminated in a new spiritualized transcendence identified with national historical objectives and the historical
liberation of mankind. In democratic and revolutionary ideals,
many romantics found a manifestation of their trust in the moral
goodness of men. The future, built upon the past, would release
them from the present condition of life and its dehumanizing artificiality. It would secure not only political rights, but man's full
individuality and existential freedom in living and dying. For
romantic feeling veiled an intense concern with death, seen as
the ultimate reality in our self-awareness. One of the main themes
of romantic art was the transcendence of mortality and presentness through the eternity of love, beauty and man's yearning for the moral ideal. Thus the great romantic, Goethe, related
the individual's mortality to his idealized eternity in the historical
continuum. Historicity becomes the form of human experience
best suited to the confrontation with death, as expressed in
Faustian striving. Here we reach the threshold of a total identification of historicity and transcendence. Beyond this point, history
absorbs all forms of being, and becomes synonymous with existence itself. Thus in Hegel, the dialectic of Being and non-Being is
encompassed in the central theme of an historicized Becoming.
The transfiguration of man's life then is manifest in a succession
of historical stages that evolve inexorably towards the Absolute
Idea.

4. Romantic Historicity and the Faust Archetype

Liberalism, nationalism, and occasional social protest constituted
the popular forces of the first half of the nineteenth century, and
occasionally amounted to mass movements. These popular currents, exemplified in the Revolutions of 1830 and 1848, produced

rational justifications that reflected the response of the elites, but that also became in themselves active historical forces. For they inspired men with a goal or vision, and incarnated its emotional power in the arts. During the romantic age, it was especially music and literature that conveyed the new attitudes and historical values. Perhaps these media were best suited to communicate the quality of movement in *Sturm und Drang*. In the other arts, the emotional and aesthetic impact must be captured and contained within the moment, or simply removed above time into a timeless realm. In a piece of literature or music, on the contrary, continuity of development in time constitutes an essential part of its aesthetic meaning, and its cumulative development. It thereby parallels historical consciousness, linking memory and anticipation.

Not that painting failed to participate in the romantic style; on the contrary, it contributed significantly to the romantic mood, notably in the depiction of nature as in the popular landscapes of the Corot group and the Barbizon School, or in the intense quality of Turner's scenes, and the drama of Delacroix's canvases. William Blake could translate his passionate mystic insight into romantic drawings as well as into verse. Later on, Dante Gabriel Rossetti was to develop a comparable versatility of media. Measured by the quantity of works decorating Victorian homes, painting is perhaps the most abundant of romantic products. But the fact remains that most of the great figures in the nineteenth century arts prior to impressionism—the men of romantic genius—were writers, composers and poets: Goethe, Byron and Wordsworth, Victor Hugo, Lamartine and Heine, Beethoven, Schubert and Mendelssohn, and eventually Schumann, Wagner and Brahms. Thus music, novels and verse embodied the semi-conscious forces of romanticism's innermost impulses. They captured its elusive yearning for a transcendent reality in that most intimate and introspective expression of a civilization, the poetic visions and myths that reveal its collective psyche.

In the late eighteenth century, Friedrich Schiller bequeathed his romantic impetus to German letters, and sanctified the ideals of German patriotism and freedom. The subjects of his plays attest his essentially historical caste of mind: Don Carlos, Maria

Stuart, the Wallenstein dramas, Wilhelm Tell, and Joan of Arc, to mention a few. Nor is it surprising that the national German poet-dramatist should have written a history of the Thirty Years' War and one on the Netherlands' Revolt, which he saw as a chapter in the rise of human liberty. In *Wilhelm Tell*, he voices the twin liberal ideals of freedom and of patriotism.

The historicity of Schiller's thought also appears in the *Sturm und Drang* of his verses. In many of his poems one finds the sense of progress and human evolution towards freedom, justice, loyalty and the neo-knightly code of the romantic patriot. Thus, in his poem, "The Walk," Schiller describes the advance of culture and society amid the eternal constancy of nature, in a vein that prefigures some of Tennyson's lines on evolution. In his most famous ballad, "The Bell," Schiller exalts "The Instinct of the Fatherland" as the most glorious of all social bonds and concludes, after the episodes of man's due suffering and travail, with an optimistic vision of concord and peace. That same hopeful note about the future of humanity is struck in the "Hymn to Joy," which Beethoven used as the triumphant climax to his own humanist affirmation of the destiny of man, in the choral movement of the Ninth Symphony. But perhaps it is in his long poem, "The Artists," that Schiller best summarizes his faith in progress, expressing his debt to the Enlightenment, and even more his trust in the yet higher virtue of human sentiment and aesthetic passion.

In music, it is primarily in Beethoven's works that we find the aesthetic form of man's historical striving expressed in the spirit of revolt and the appeal to liberty. We know that Beethoven was a democrat by temperament. In the opera, *Fidelio*, he voices his hope in freedom and progress. The driving power of his music suggests the Promethean struggle of man. Yet Beethoven expressed faith in the redeeming purpose of a Divine Providence manifest in history. Of all his works, it is the ending of the Ninth Symphony that best suggests his transcendent historical vision. For it proclaims the individual's liberation through involvement in the ideal of humanity. Here the brotherhood of man is not only a moral ideal, but also an historical goal. Where Bach found spiritual meaning in the majesty of his vision of the divine order, and in the emotional impact of the divine passion upon men, Beethoven found spirituality in a typically human surge of fellow-feeling. But because his humanity reaches towards the divine, it is preserved from a purely secularized historical illusion.

In the final analysis, it is still literature that contains the most explicit statement of historical idealism and of the quest for purpose in life through man's historical role. What Schiller began, his friend Goethe brought to fruition in his epic drama of *Faust*. Goethe was out of sympathy with the nationalism and political liberalism of his time. Yet he gave a philosophical expression to the historicist perspective and its ultimate form of self-transcendence. As scientist, he proposed an evolutionary and organic approach to nature that would release scientific knowledge from the grip of Newtonian mathematical thought. As philosopher-playwright, he reached in *Faust* the culmination of historical consciousness, in the sense of transcendence and immortalization achieved through the individual's historical presence and constant striving towards an historical ideal.

In Goethe's version, the Faust story becomes essentially the affirmation of man's dignity and of his relation to God through his historical striving to create an ideal. The genius of the human spirit and its true freedom are presented as the relentless effort in historical time to achieve a godlike ultimate work. Endless reaching for the historical realization of a perfect world provides the driving purpose in what constitutes the distinctive quality of man: his creative impulse. In the famous Part II of the drama, Goethe both opposes and joins the two basic modes in the Western tradition, the classic and the Christian creative drives. The Greek ideal stands out against modern Christian society's emphasis on movement. The ordered symmetry and balance of the classical world stand in a dialectical opposition to the storm and passion of Christian civilization's yearning and constant questing. The Apollonian and Dionysian modes are set off against one another in the two contrasting Walpurgisnight scenes, the classical and the Christian. But ultimately, it is the latter that prevails. Over and above the measured "completeness" of the Hellenic ideal, Goethe asserts the dynamism of modern man in his introspective personality and historical consciousness. In the classic drama, the redeeming value of the hero was his final acceptance of tragic destiny. In *Faust*, it is the hero's effort that constitutes man's salvation, because it is the only *free* instrument of individual redemption. The object striven for takes second place to the sheer fact of striving, the ideal city takes second place to the historical process of constructing it, and idealized Being is absorbed into a transcendent Becoming. Thus, finally, the ultimate moment is not the achievement of perfect bliss, but the blinding glimpse of our eternal reaching towards it.

In the conclusion of the drama, the last act of Part II, Faust —who has been granted by the Emperor in return for his services the privilege of building his own ideal city by literally wrenching it from the sea—reaches the climax of the historical impulse to transcendence. In his dying moment, he embodies the identification of transcendent immortality with historicity. Faust has achieved a succession of unsatisfying triumphs by committing himself to the devil. Now, in his final hallucination, all the evils of life beset him. He still sets his overseer, Mephistopheles, to the clearing of forests and the draining of marshes, in his frenzied vision of achieving at last the human ideal, the perfect society of work, reason and freedom. Therewith he comes ultimately to the prophetic insight, that only the constant yearning and effort for the ideal can exist, and that the ideal itself must remain unrealized. Every act is a state of suspension that can only resolve itself momentarily in the next. Only constant effort and conquest can ever remain. The moment of happiness is never attainable in itself. In Faust's final flash of revelation, it is precisely the continuity of this striving for a free humanity living in a free land that exhausts, and in the end transcends, his restless search. Nothing, he says, can ever destroy the fact that he, Faust, has existed and has created something, leaving his mark eternally upon the shape of things. It is thus through the historical realm of man's destiny that Faust achieves self-transcendence. Thereupon, in anticipating the ideal of a free society which can exist only in man's neverending struggle, he seemingly pronounces the fateful words of his initial compact with the devil: Let the moment linger![2]

Mephistopheles, patient so long, immediately forecloses his

mortgage on Faust's soul. Faust had apparently released him by the formula of ultimate satisfaction from further service, and has yielded at last to the time of his own death. The devil springs the trap—he has foreseen the moment, and the grave is ready—only to find his victim saved. Divine intervention and Margaret's supreme penance have snatched Faust's soul *in extremis*. Mephistopheles had missed a conditional subjunctive!

Indeed, Faust proclaims that he has now attained the highest moment. But he does not bid it endure except in a conditional sense. For its supreme quality consists precisely in his ultimate revelation of eternal movement and striving in which no moment could ever pause or could ever be the time of completed perfection. In other words, Faust had not bid the actual moment stay. He had only anticipated the beatific vision in which he would bid it pause and which now, in this last instant, he recognizes as the highest of the truly attainable forms of human satisfaction, namely the constant future expectation in which no moment can ever pause. The only fulfillment then comes in the recognition of his own ineffaceable contribution and presence, and of man constantly reconquering his freedom and dignity. Here no instant can ever be its own justification. It becomes meaningful only in relation to the future. The wish to have any single point in time endure would be self-defeating. This is the insight of eternal effort and incompleteness that constitutes Faust's supreme experience.

Faust had become reconciled with history and with the flow of time, not with the present. That is the great realization which Mephistopheles is unable to grasp and which he sneeringly dismisses when he muses that of all the glorious instants in Faust's experience, only this last, poorest and most general glimpse brought him contentment. Time, the devil remarks, had finally conquered Faust. In fact, it is historical time and the hope of eternal futuricity that had finally gotten the better of Mephistopheles. In the closing triumph of transcendence and redemption, in which Faust's pride in seeking to create his own ideal is forgiven him, the angel pronounces the saving phrase on Faust's soul, the magic formula of all historical transcendence: "Him who strives, I have the power to save."[3]

VI

TRANSCENDENCE AND
IDEALIST HISTORICITY

1. Historical Idealism

Beyond Faustian historical consciousness lies idealist historicity. Here the world is seen within the framework of an ideal meaning that constitutes the ultimate reality. The distinctive trait of historicist idealism is that all existence appears in a constant process of linear becoming, progressively unfolding the universal absolute. Thus being becomes fully historicized. Such is the general view expressed in the transcendent historical philosophy of Hegel.

To understand the rise of historical idealism, we must first consider the impact of Kantian philosophy on nineteenth-century thought, both as a direct influence on philosophical ideas and as a manifestation of certain historical currents in the modern Western outlook. The impact of Kant's fundamentally ahistorical philosophy upon our historical consciousness arises from three notable aspects of his work. First, he gave a distinctive, if qualified, formulation of the concept of historical progress toward universal peace. Secondly, he proposed an ethical philosophy that served to justify the belief that ideals of universal justice, equality and freedom, which animated much of nineteenth-century historical aspirations, are intrinsically right because they express the basic moral consciousness of rational man. Finally, his epistemology raised anew the old problem of the role of mind in the process of knowing, and hence of the relation of man's knowledge to reality. In doing so, it laid the essential groundwork for later idealist conceptions of history, and particularly for Hegel's historical approach to the meaning of being.

Kant's conception of history echoes the ideas of the Enlightenment, but it also sounds a new note and repudiates some of the key presuppositions attributed to the *philosophes*. Kant undermined the rationalist belief in our purely objective knowledge of external reality in its own terms, or of our ability to know the essence of things. Yet at the same time he raised human rationality to its highest point in his moral philosophy. He saw the rational mind not only as the necessary organizing agent of all consciousness of reality, but also as the universal legislator of the moral law. Thus Kant bridges the age of reason, with its trust in the objective advance of intelligence, and the introspective self-consciousness of modern thought. His conception of history and of the prospects of humanity consequently has a unique quality, though it is grounded in the enlightened teaching of the eighteenth century.

Kant argued that he was living in a period of enlightenment though not yet in an enlightened age. His major historical concern was how the latter age could be realized. Developing his conception of universal history, he set forth certain basic organizing premises. One was the Aristotelian idea that "all natural capacities of a creature are destined to evolve completely to their natural end."[1] Furthermore, he proclaimed that man's happiness must be the product of his own reason; therefore, man himself must solve the crucial problem of mankind, the organization of a universal civil society based on universal laws. Out of competitive interests must emerge a new rational world law to regulate the external relations among all states and ensure universal peace. A distinguishing point in Kant's conception of order is that he saw men's unsociability as inherent in their nature, and planned to base rational harmony on the indirect consequences of men's mutual antagonisms. He even regarded opposition and the competitive instinct as necessary to man, because it was such a competitive struggle which had permitted man to rise above the instinctual

condition of life to the creation of civilization and to his rational
state. There is a hint of subsequent social Darwinism in Kant's
attribution of human progress to the unsociable and antagonistic
drive in man. He argues that out of the very conditions of life and
of man's distinctive rational faculty, perpetual peace will ensue,
and that despite present wars and suffering, progress is a reality.

For Kant the evolution of humanity must be in accord with
the nature of man as a reasoning animal concerned with the future. This evolution is embodied, not in the progress of the individual but only of the human race in its totality. Indeed, the
conditions of personal satisfaction and of the advance of mankind often conflict. The perfection of reason, which opposes man's
animal nature, may be accompanied by great strain. In the
individual case, suffering may result. But in the aggregate, progress occurs through the more rational arrangement of the whole.

Certain hopeful conclusions emerge from Kant's conception
of a general history of mankind. One conclusion is that there is a
rational meaning in the evolution of human society. In the tradition of his age, Kant asserts the conviction of enlightened progress
in the advance of peace and reason. He projects the gradual fulfillment of the natural potentialities of the human race—though
with the critical consciousness that the idea of a Golden Age must
always remain a mere yearning, an inherently unattainable historical illusion.

The second aspect of Kant's influence on historical consciousness lies in his development of a distinctive rational moral
order. In his critical work on *The Metaphysical Groundwork of
Morals*, Kant states his basic principle concerning all behavior
that has moral significance, the "categorical imperative" always to
act in such a way that one's action can become a universal principle of conduct. In so doing, the individual participates in establishing the moral law, of which every reasoning individual is *ipso
facto* a "legislator." From this key principle, Kant deduced his
essential humanist postulate, namely that every individual must
always be treated as an end in himself, never as a means, for
treating someone as means to an end could not be turned into a
universal rule without thereby including oneself as merely the

means to someone else's purpose—something no rational being would willingly do.

The notion of the individual as the absolute and inviolable moral unit had a profound significance for modern Western historicity. It echoed the Christian concept of the soul's irreducible worth within the Providence of God. Kant attributed to the individual a new function by raising him to a transcendent ethical role insofar as he participates, through his rational capacity, in the universality of reason and of moral law.

Kant's idea of regarding every good action as an instance of universal rational morality and of treating each individual as an end in himself has a philosophically democratic quality. The basic tenet of any anti-egalitarian moral order, whether Plato's or Nietzsche's, is that lesser individuals are to be used as means to something. Kant's principle, on the contrary, implies a state of ethical equality among rational beings, even if not an ideal of social egalitarianism. Politically, Kant was not a democrat. The behavior of ordinary men was far removed from his high moral purpose. He mistrusted sentimental popular emotions that bore little relation to his rational ethical principle. In Kant's ethics, men carry out their obligations for the sole reason that it is their duty. Here the only meaningful moral impulse is neither compassion nor charity, but a dispassionate compulsion of mind to what is right in itself. Such an ideal seemed far removed from ordinary mass consciousness and behavior. Like many thinkers of the Enlightenment who were educated in a refined intellectual atmosphere, Kant remained skeptical of the populace. Yet for all his reserve about popular democracy, Kant was in many key respects a libertarian idealist. The sense of moral equality of rational men, each of whom legislates the moral law, fitted Kant's sympathy with the liberal ideology of the French Revolution and his admiration for Rousseau. In his ideal schema for securing perpetual peace, Kant stipulated that the only proper constitution for free states is that of a republic.

Kant expressed the general nineteenth-century desire for a transcendent moral order in history, though the form he gave it was peculiarly his own. He further stipulated an historical process that would lead to peace. Kant's moral philosophy, it should be noted, was essentially ahistorical; that is, its rational principles were unrelated to time or historical circumstances. The practical consequences of action were irrelevant to the moral value of the act, which was self-validating. Yet Kant's moral philosophy had historicist implications in another sense. Its transcendent ethic provided an historical goal of rational order, which Kant believed would be approached in the advance of human reason. Kant's moral law provided a new metaphysical inspiration for the attainment of an enlightened ethical and political ideal. It related the individual to the continuity of the ethical law in which he participates as a rational being. For Kant, immortality meant the eternal life of the soul. But there was also implicit a transcendent eternity in our identification with the absolute moral order of God. Kant's philosophy was not "historical" and would belie enlistment in the current of Western historicity. But it had significant consequences for subsequent idealist philosophies of historical thinkers. It established a metaphysical groundwork for an emergent historical idealism, based on the claim of an absolute rational moral order.

The third aspect of Kant's influence on historical consciousness comes about indirectly through his treatment of the problem of knowledge and reality. It was in part in responding critically to Kantian metaphysics that Hegel was led to historical idealism and came to construe history as the process of self-manifestation of the transcending absolute, and that another idealist, Fichte, saw history as the development of what he termed the universal ego. In the new post-Kantian frame, history was to be understood not as the process of an external reality but as the inner development of man's consciousness, manifesting the ultimate idea in the unfolding of our rational self-awareness. All the elements of thought and being could then be redefined in the perspective of the linear evolution of mind and a transcendent historical idealism.

For Kant, the fundamental epistemological problem resolved itself in the categories through which the mind is capable of knowing, and in the forms it therefore imposes upon sensory experience. He concluded that the nature of knowledge is fully determined by the characteristics of mind, and all the knowledge rational beings can ever achieve is defined by the necessary forms of consciousness. Since it is impossible to cross from inside our mind to any reality outside it except through the mental categories, it follows that the objects in themselves must remain inherently undeterminable. Thus in Kant's philosophy, there exists a solid barrier between the process of knowing, which concerns itself with phenomena, and the essence of Being, which is a matter of noumena. The latter, the so-called *Ding an Sich*, upon which the mind cannot impose its modalities of thought, is by definition precluded from our awareness. Against this view, Fichte, at first a disciple of Kant, argued that the very notion of a noumenal reality already infringed upon the alleged exclusion of noumena from the realm of knowledge, and implied some form of connection between them. For how could we conceive that there was a noumenal reality without admitting it into our consciousness? Thus in Fichte's radical idealism, there is no *Ding an Sich* outside of consciousness itself, no reality beyond the reality of mind in the infinity of the Absolute Ego.

But it was primarily Hegel who sought to bridge the Kantian polarity of Being-in-itself and knowledge by denying that there was anything at all "behind" the knowable forms. He asserts that the thing perceived is the reality, in the sense that the actual is "the essence manifesting itself." He writes: "Essence must appear. It appears as *existence*. Essence does not exist outside, or apart of, or behind, or beyond its existential experience. . . . Existence is a *being in and for itself.* . . ." And he adds:

> Physical appearance of life is life itself in the form of given externality. Only life can thus appear to itself. There is nothing in the appearance of life that does not manifest its essential existence, likewise there is no essential existence that does not manifest itself to others. Life is *self-manifestation.* . . .[2]

Thus Hegel wished to reintegrate the two basic problems of classic idealist philosophy, namely ontology and epistemology. It was Hegel who sought to unite the questions of being and knowing, or metaphysics and phenomenology, and the logic of mind. He attempted to do this specifically through historicity, that is to say, by resolving the question of existence in the antithesis of Being and Nothing through the unity of Becoming. For Hegel, history served as the key to the definition of reality, understood as part of the evolutionary process towards the Absolute Ideal. He saw this evolution going from "Pure Being"—sheer materiality and irrational existence—to absolute self-consciousness or ideality: "*The Absolute is Spirit*—this is its ultimate definition." Original Being is therefore the opposite of ultimate existence, which is fully rational because it is aware of itself. In *The Encyclopedia of Philosophy*, he writes:

> Philosophy is the *Science* (Wissenschaft) of *Comprehensiveness* (Vernunft) wherein the totality of Being becomes aware of itself; Being is identical with its own comprehensiveness.[3]

Here even ontology, the essence of Being, is historicized, because Being expresses itself in dialectical movement. Historical time becomes the single dimension of the rational reality and of human knowledge, the unique vehicle of evolution towards ultimate Existence and the Absolute Idea, which are one:

> Pure *Being* is simply what it is; it is at the same time pure thought, identity. The self-sameness of Being is the beginning definition of the Absolute; Being begins, beginning is.[4]

For Hegel, history is transcendent because it is precisely through the historical process that the absolute is revealed, or rather that the divine essence achieves definition and completes itself—in a word, that it becomes real. Universal history, in fact, is the transcendent *par excellence*. Hegel writes that it "belongs to the realm of Spirit." In the beginning of the evolutionary process, the ultimate is an unfilled category, an empty potentiality. It comes into actual being and forms itself only through the course of history, which is therefore the course of the divine. History, then, is the scene on which the transcendent becomes immanent; it follows an order which accomplishes the divine destiny through man. It is the "exhibition of Spirit in the process of working out the knowledge of that which it is potentially." As the seed already carries in itself "the whole nature of the tree" and the shape and flavor of its fruits, "so do the first traces of Spirit virtually contain the whole of history."[5] Hegel believed he had succeeded in preserving the essence of Christianity, and yet in reconciling Providence with humanity's cumulative experience.

But historicity applied not only to the evolution of mankind. It applied also to that of the cosmos, and to the dialectical nature of Being itself. In contrast to Augustine's theology, which had presented secular history as the evanescent world of man—it was the heavenly city alone which mattered—the new historicism was to identify history as the divine force itself, working out its own fulfillment through time:

> That the History of the World, with all the changing scenes which its annals present, is this process of development and the realization of Spirit—this is the true *Theodicoea*, the justification of God in History. Only *this* insight can reconcile Spirit with the History of the World —viz., that what has happened and is happening every day, is not only not 'without God,' but is essentially His Work.[6]

The time element here becomes of the essence not just to philosophy but to man's basic experience of reality, seen in an essentially historical perspective. Being appears more clearly as Being-in-time, and "History in general is therefore the development of Spirit in *Time*, as Nature is the development of the Idea in *Space*."[7] Where previous idealist philosophers had been bent, in the Platonic tradition, upon isolating the absolute from the temporal, where they had sought to distinguish that which was within time and subject to the rule of impermanence and change from the ultimate that was outside time, or where they had characterized temporal historical events as mere shadows of the fixed ideal reality, Hegel boldly combined the question of Being with the problem of temporality, ontology with historicity. For him, the primary philosophical fact was the process of Becoming through the dialectic of opposite ideas. To be sure, the logical opposition of categories, like positive and negative, is not a relationship in time. Contradiction, like all formal logic, is clearly atemporal. But the *resolution* of particular contradictions could only take place through a temporal process. Thus Hegel formulated his famed dialectical sequence of thesis, antithesis and synthesis in which each idea can be traced back to the first dynamic equation, and through which one can reconstruct all the categories of existence and of thought within one continuous logical becoming. As he states it: "Becoming is the first concrete thought, and therefore the first notion: whereas Being and Nought are empty abstractions."[8]

Even for individuals unconcerned with philosophies, the historical perspective became the new conceptual framework. They began to apprehend the world as an evolutionary process of conflicting historical forces—not in the abstract terms of Spirit, perhaps, but in their own more mundane values and concrete ideals. For Hegel, historicity involved a form of relativity. At least it appeared relative insofar as it showed that the objectives people held to be absolute at one moment were often discarded the next. But this relativism still remained tied to certain universal precepts, and therefore did not necessarily imply the pessimistic rejection of all ideals that has so often accompanied relativity in our own day. During the early nineteenth century, relative ideas still tended to function within an absolute frame, namely the nature of the evolutionary process itself, seen as a form of universal order in history. This frame gave a purpose to transitory historical values. If it is true that all ideals are relative to their particular phase of history and destined to give way to others in the movement of the dialectic, it could nonetheless be argued that inasmuch as each one is an integral part of the historical process, it participates cumulatively in the fulfillment of the Absolute. Each ideal then contributes to the ultimate, of which it contains a particle only seemingly in contradiction with other particles. "To refute a philosophy is to exhibit the dialectical movement in its principle, and thus reduce it to a constituent member of a higher concrete form of the Idea."[9] It is the contribution of values to the Absolute Ideal that, for all their historical relativity, gives values meaning. It relates them to a rational yet transcendent objective. In turn, this objective comes into being only through the inevitable process of history.

The Enlightenment impulse to find unity in things and to see history as a progression of dominant ideas was still manifest in the historical expectations of the nineteenth century. Despite the retreat of romantics from the emphasis on ultimate reason, the conception of a rational historical process continued to dominate much of the intellectual and the new popular sense of history. It characterized the Marxist viewpoint which emphatically asserts the rational order of historical development. As for historicist idealism, one of its most revealing concepts is contained in Hegel's famous dictum *"What is rational is actual and what is actual is rational,"*[10] meaning that a being that actualizes its essence in its existence (as for example a doctor realizes the essence of his profession only when he cures a patient) is in accord with the rational quality of the Absolute. Hegel, we should note, was not asserting that all reality is rational—indeed, such an assertion would belie his fundamentally historical tenet that the rational is in process of realizing itself. Nor, as is frequently alleged, was he defending the supposed rationality of all existing political institutions. He was proclaiming that a being manifests rationality to the extent that it synthesizes its essence with its existence (as a doctor would exemplify perfect rationality if he cured *all* his patients). History is to be understood as a rational process only in that it exhibits the dialectical movement towards the unity of being and essence. Such an abstract conception of history was immeasurably far removed from popular notions, but even people who had no interest in difficult idealist philosophies could find a recognizable reflection of their own intuitive sense that to have meaning, history must be intelligible to rational men, in these words of Hegel:

> The only Thought which Philosophy brings with it to the contemplation of History, is the simple conception of *Reason;* that Reason is the Sovereign of the World; that the history of the world, therefore presents us with a rational process.[11]

In the end, nineteenth-century historicism generally wound up as absolutism. Expressive of the aspirations of its time for historical certitude, the dialectic emerged as the new unchanging truth. It established a fixed order of linear movement in which the process was rigorously determined and the transcendent goal was absolute. The appearance of each relative idea in the rational sequence of evolution was considered an historical necessity contained within the dialectic itself. The ridigity of much of nineteenth century historicism inheres specifically in concluding to the rational inevitability of every idea in its time, once the logical structure of historical synthesis is granted. Whatever is, must be— is the popular phrasing of the notion of historical necessity. If this principle can lead to a rigid conservatism in its implicit emphasis on the inevitability of present conditions, it can serve equally well to justify the irresistibility of a no less rigid pattern of revolutionary change. A Hegelianism of the left could confront a Hegelianism of the right. The determinism of Marxist revolutionary ideology and the preeminence of the authoritarian state could be derived from the Hegelian dialectic. The noteworthy fact is that while the dialectical view boosted the historical relativism of ideas and values, it simultaneously promoted an absolute historicity. It encased historical relativism within a transcendent frame.

What philosophers and historians sought to accomplish at one level, many popular historical notions claimed to achieve at another. Each sought in its own way to combine historicity with a sense of certainty and the expectation of transcendent purpose. During the nineteenth century, popular belief in some redeeming historical goal was expressed in numerous versions of a patriotic or a revolutionary "Manifest Destiny," and in the conviction of its eventual historical realization. The sense of an inherent logic in the historical process, or an inherent force and direction in historical movement, was by no means limited to the esoteric constructs of idealist historical philosophers. Popular movements often shared the view of history unfolding itself according to an ordered plan that is real, and that manifests itself in necessary phases of cultural growth. Idealist historicity was essentially a philosophical abstraction of the widely prevalent view that a transcendent idea, such as "national glory," or the attainment of universal democracy, constitutes the ultimate reality behind man's rational historical development.

2. Idealism and the Historical Process

The notion of an objective and rational process in history was not a new discovery of the age. It crystallized over many centuries and appeared in several successive guises. But in the first half of the nineteenth century, a new quality was added, and a significant new perspective changed its psychological character. Before the nineteenth century, the objective of historical order and determinism had been applied to society. Now the meaning of historical change was rather to be located within man, in the changing quality of his self-consciousness and individuality. Here history emerges less as the scene of human actions and of objective external events—although that meaning is not precluded—then as the temporal reality through which the ego acquires its identity and self-awareness. For where history is seen as an ongoing drama of men's ideas, the past appears as a succession of life forms of human mentality. "The history of mind is its own act. . . . Mind is only what it does," and what it does is "to make itself the object of its own consciousness."[12]

Historicity serves as the essential instrument through which consciousness takes root, because it is only through the sense of time in the recollection of past experiences that man becomes aware of his ego's identity and distinctiveness. History then appears as the successive stages in the mind's apprehension of itself, up to full self-realization. Our individual minds are seen as part of the universal mind. Thus in Fichte's idealist view, for example, the absolute ego contains the whole world in its conscious will. In Hegel's idealist historicism, the unfolding of our thought reflects the self-development of the rational idea. When this self-realization reaches completion at one stage of consciousness, the time has come for the dialectical repudiation of that stage, and for the historical transition to a higher one. History thus shows the transcendence from one level of consciousness to another, and presents the on-going formation of a new cultural chrysalis for the next transcendent metamorphosis of rational mind.

History as the unfolding self-revelation of consciousness becomes actual only in the history of specific ideas, for it is in the process of rational thought that the mind is presumed to realize itself. All other considerations then are seen as means to an end, influencing history by virtue of their contribution to its rational development. To Hegel, history is therefore identified with the evolution of successive forms of thought, each of which in turn has dominated a phase of civilization. Such an outlook, we should note, is not entirely new with him or with nineteenth-century idealism; in fact, it is based on one of the established conventions of our modern understanding of history. For example, Voltaire's analysis of the great ages of man is built upon the rise of rational thinking, and Condorcet's vision rests upon the succeeding forms of increasingly rational human knowledge. But what is essentially new with Hegel is the shift in emphasis from man's understanding of the external world to his full rational awareness of his own being (an idea Voltaire had in effect rejected by affirming the continuing irrational element in human nature), and the logical order of the dialectical framework. Hegel conceived of every age as characterized by a dominant thesis that imposed its unique stamp upon the period, and that remained qualitatively distinct from both the preceding and succeeding levels of human consciousness. Particular events somehow manifested the dominant idea, and were essential to the process by which it worked itself out historically. This conception fitted remarkably into an age of conflicting ideologies, and gave a rational frame to the opposing political ideals of the nineteenth century. It had significant practical applications in turning historical consciousness into the sense of a continuing intellectual contest, played out at all levels of life and thought and yet permeated with the essential historical unity of a transcending rational purpose.

If history is a drama of conflicting ideas, the question arises: By what means are these ideas actualized, or given presence, in human affairs? Hegel's answer is: Through the actions of particular nations and individual heroes, each charged in his time with the unwitting furtherance of the historical process. These nations and heroes are "animated by their particular determinate principle," which finds expression in their constitutions as well as in "the whole range of their life and condition." An essential concept like freedom, for example, manifests itself in the acts of persons,

unaware of their own historical destiny, who serve to incarnate
and carry forward the successive ideological stages of history.
Their thoughts and actions may appear limited to their immediate
considerations, and they remain preoccupied with their own
worldly concerns, yet they are constantly the unknowing instrument and agent of the "world mind at work within them." Thus
the absolute spirit becomes the transcendent idea of history; the
forms that it takes pass away, "while the absolute mind prepares
and works out its transition to the next higher phase."[13]

In his conception of the hero's role, Hegel was again echoing
in his own distinctive way a time-honored Western view. Our
historical literature and popular myths have traditionally focused
on the actions of supposedly great men, usually conquerors. Our
histories used to be written largely in terms of the actions of
leaders, especially generals and kings, who were portrayed as the
makers of their age and their country. Popular historical myths
fastened upon the folklore of a Joan of Arc, the legends of a
Charlemagne, a Henry Barbarossa or a King Richard; conventional historical treatments identified mysticism with St. Francis,
the Reformation with Luther and exploration with Columbus.
Carlyle, who was notorious for his glorification of heroes, saw in
Cromwell and Frederick the Great men who rose above the conditions of their times and imposed their own creative wills upon
circumstances. Thus Hegel was merely giving his formulation of
a well-known attitude when he claimed that the "world-historical"
spirit functions through figures like Alexander, Caesar and Napoleon who have molded history by their creative will and power. If
a great man is never a hero to his butler, he remarked, the fault
lies with the butler, not the man. Hegel was following a well-
known fashion when he wrote that in the historical process
leaders inevitably arise, "by chance and in accord with the particular needs of the hour," so that "everything done and everything
actual is inaugurated and brought to completion by the single
decisive act of a leader."[14] "All actions," he asserted, "including
world-historical actions, culminate with individuals as subjects
giving actuality to the substantial."[15]

In effect, the new historicist outlook only reflected one of the central currents we have found imbedded at the core of Western historical consciousness and historistic values, namely the emphasis on the individual's personality and his creative action—though significantly restricted in Hegel to the few world-historical figures. In this perspective, the individual achieves meaningfulness by means of his distinctive contribution to the historical teleology of which he makes himself the tool. A liberal visionary like Condorcet saw himself as the champion of an ideal which he believed it to be the destiny of history to fulfill. A Marxist, working zealously for the classless society that he simultaneously conceives to be inevitable, seeks his prospect of redemptive transcendence and vicarious eternity through his moral-historical role. Nineteenth-century German historicity added a new element, by defining the process of history in terms of the self-realization of the world-mind, reflected in the growing self-consciousness of man. It thus introduced into historical consciousness an existentialist note that was to have great significance for the twentieth century. But history as the form of man's self-knowledge was presented from an absolutist spiritual point of view, and in an idealist frame, that have made it seem irrelevant to our condition.

With Hegel's conception of individuals as agents of the world-historical spirit we reach the great dilemma of idealist historicity, namely are men's historical acts determined or free? The dilemma is that transcendence through man's historical role rests upon his freedom of action, while the logical order of an inevitable historical development reduces him to a cog. This contradiction will appear in sharper focus in Hegel's attempt to resolve the conflict of freedom and necessity. For the moment we may note that if Hegel's great man fashions the times, he is also the product of their inevitable historical movement. He conquers Asia, and thereby diffuses Greek civilization over the ancient Near East. He conquers Europe and thereby spreads the ideals of the French Revolution. Hegel writes that world-historical figures are "the living instruments of what is in substance the deed of the world-mind and they are therefore at one with that deed though it is concealed from them and is not their aim and object." Because their motivations remain personal and mundane, their ob-

jectives specific rather than universal, they "receive no honour
or thanks from their contemporaries or from public opinion in
later years." Yet there is still room for the hope of vicarious
eternity in history inasmuch as Hegel adds, "all that is vouchsafed
to them by such opinion is undying fame in respect of the subjective form of their acts."[16]

Perhaps the moral problem of determinism in nineteenth-
century historicity has become too remote to engage our sentiments. Perhaps it appears meaningless in an age that has come to
live with the indeterminacy and uncertainty of everything, except
the basic anxiety of living (although behaviorists may have done
no more than to shift the question of determinism from history to
psychology, and to hide it under the body-mind problem). The
dilemmas of a philosophy which begins with the claim that the
essence of being is rational appear to be out of style in an age
accustomed to explaining most human experience in terms of the
unconscious, or the irrationality of existence. Today only some
theologians, an occasional theological historian like Toynbee, or a
neglected philosopher like Jaspers, consider a universal meaning
in history. Yet this is to beg the question: Why did the transcendent vision—specifically the historical vision—collapse? The
answer is that it failed. Perhaps, if we may be old-fashioned his-
toricists for a moment, we may say that it was bound to do so,
because it bore the seed of its own destruction, specifically, the
moral burden it placed on our historical consciousness to transcend the issue of freedom and determinism, and thereby resolve
the problem of evil. This is the issue we must now explain—the
critical paradox of our historical ideals.

3. *The Moral Burden of Historicity*

Did the abstract considerations of idealist history have any significant impact on the mainstreams of Western thought and the predominant focus of our culture? Have they had any bearing upon
ordinary men's values or behavior, notably in influencing popular
expectations and the way men seek a meaning in historical ideals?
To answer these questions, we must show how Hegel's historicism

reflected certain popular values, notably in regard to nationalist aspirations and the glorification of the state. We must show how the esoteric expressions of the idealist conception of history provided the psychological groundwork for later movements of mass consciousness, so that more down-to-earth objectives subsequently came to reflect the same categorical structure. But above all, we must show how the idealist conception of history provided a novel explanation of the meaning of the past, and built upon it worldly expectations that proved to be self-contradictory.

The great drama of nineteenth-century historical values was that of fate and freedom, which appeared in its political form under the guise of reason of state versus individual liberty. In liberal movements, the two principles sometimes tended to complement one another, but in their philosophical implications and psychological tendencies they confronted each other in categorically opposite terms. This opposition manifested itself during the late 1800's in the growing conflict between loyalty to the moral value of the nation and devotion to the moral ideal of personal freedom. Much like the consequences of Rousseau's General Will, the political implications of Hegelian historicity were to transform the meaning of freedom in such a way as to sacrifice the idea of liberty to the claim of statism.

In an age when national heroes were venerated as heralds of the higher moral destiny of their people, Hegel constructed his historical dialectic upon the concept of the emergent state. His glorification of it as a secular god stimulated the mass currents of our time. For many historical idealists, the nation-state became a living entity, endowed with a soul and personality of its own. It appeared as a transcendent reality greater than the sum of its citizens because it continued over generations, binding the living to their ancestors and descendants, and establishing their spiritual identity. This view has remained popular through much of the twentieth century. It has appeared in different forms in the thought of Mussolini and de Gaulle. To Hegel, it was the destiny of certain nation-states to embody for a while the world-historical idea. One nation after another occupied the stage to establish in its turn an intellectual and cultural hegemony over civilization.

Hegel added, "It is only once that it can make its hour strike." Thus nationalism was turned into an unrestrained idolization of the state as the highest embodiment of moral value, the agent of historical inevitability and the manifestation of the divine world-mind. In *The Philosophy of Right*, Hegel begins the key section on "The State" with the words: "The State is the actuality of the ethical idea," and in *The Philosophy of History* he remarks: "The State is the Idea of Spirit in the external manifestation of human Will and its Freedom," adding categorically: "The State is the Divine Idea as it exists on earth."[17]

Hegel felt that his own era was Germany's turn to establish its definitive claim to historic glory: "The Germanic Spirit is the Spirit of the new World." This age was not, however, to be just another ephemeral phase of history. Proclaiming a notion that was to have a satanic career in the twentieth century, Hegel asserted that it was nothing less that the whole dialectic of history which was due to reach its destiny in the German state. The universal function of the Germanic spirit was to achieve "the realization of absolute truth as the unlimited self-determination of Freedom—*that* Freedom which has its own absolute form itself as its purport." To this prophecy Hegel added the final touch: "The destiny of the German peoples is to be the bearers of the Christian principle," which sums up the meaning of history "for the Christian world is the world of completion; the grand principle of being is realized, consequently the end of days is fully come."[18]

Here, surely, was a remarkable conclusion to the rational idea of history! Even William Miller scarcely exhibited greater self-assurance in announcing the imminent end of the world! But did Hegel in fact mean to predict the completion of the dialectical process and the fulfillment of human destiny?[19] More likely, he was only indicating the culmination of the form of history that had characterized man's past, and the conclusion of the decisive moral conflicts that had dominated his previous experience. It would be seriously misleading to dismiss Hegel's historical philosophy on the pretext that it leads to an expectation of the fulfillment of all life in the German state. But in any case, the achievement of German destiny and the embodiment of the Christian principle in the Germanic spirit do mark for Hegel a decisive historical realization, more than the completion of just another step in the historical process. For the role of the German nation-state is to transcend the dialectic of opposing philosophical principles, namely to synthesize freedom and necessity; that is why the German state comes closest to realizing the divine idea on earth.

Freedom versus necessity! Moral choice versus historical inevitability! At last we have reached the end of our historicist *Himmelsfahrt.* We have come to the heart of all historical consciousness, the ultimately inescapable encounter in every form of historicity. History must be meaningful, and therefore ordered, if it is to provide us with the security and salvation of a transcendent release. Yet it must also be "open" and freely responsive to our initiatives if we are to achieve purpose and redemption through our historical, or Faustian, striving. That is the contradiction which the nineteenth-century forms of historical consciousness could not successfully overcome.

But the problem was not merely a matter of intellectual contradictions. The dilemma was also experienced as a concrete barrier which, in the end, frustrated popular empirical attempts to fashion reliable personal goals from historical hopes. Often history confronted the individual, moved by the urge to make his mark upon the historical process, with the imperviousness of apparently blind forces beyond his control. The individual then came to face the fallacy of seeking eternalization within a secular, temporal objective, and of looking for infinity in the finite historical realm.

For Hegel, history begins and ends as the process of self-realization of freedom: *"The final cause of the World at large,* we allege to be the *consciousness* of its own freedom on the part of Spirit, and *ipso facto,* the *reality* of that freedom." It is the Idea of Freedom that defines the organization and periodization of history. It establishes the distinctions between Oriental peoples, who know only the freedom of one, the Ancient World, which knew the freedom of some, and the Modern World which realizes the freedom of all—"that all men absolutely (man as *man*) are free."[20] But how do we reconcile this quality with the claim of universal historical order? For if history has rational unity, it is only insofar as events are not a matter of mere chance or of the accident of personality:

> The inquiry into the *essential destiny* of Reason—as far as it is considered in reference to the World—is identical with the question, *what is the ultimate design of the World?* And the expression implies that that design is destined to be realized.[21]

How can such a view be harmonized with the ideal of the liberty of the individual person and with the affirmation of his independence from the relentlessness of a predetermined fate?

The solution is to proclaim a new dialectical synthesis of freedom with necessity. Each of these polar opposites would then cease to be the apparent contradiction of the other. Liberty is redefined; it is no longer to be understood as the escape from inevitability into an irrational and arbitrary will, but is rather to be seen as the recognition of, and conscious acquiescence in, rational law. Necessity here is necessary to freedom, because the only alternative to law is chaos, in which men are slaves to chance: ". . . a limitation of caprice and self-will is regarded as a fettering of Freedom. We should on the contrary look upon such limitation as the indispensable proviso of emancipation."[22] He is free, then, who understands the inevitability of law; he is free because it no longer overwhelms him as a blind compulsion, but enlists his knowledgeable assent to its rational determinism. For if man and historical necessity are both rational, then man can be free only in knowingly assenting to its inevitablity. Otherwise he affirms a capricious choice that would belie his rationality. Man becomes master of his own acts to the extent that he comes to comprehend the law of necessity in accordance with which he must rationally choose to act. "Necessity is blind," Hegel writes, "only so long as it is not understood." He consequently dismisses "the charge of blind fatalism made against the Philosophy of History when it takes for its problem to understand the necessity of every event." And he concludes: "The philosophy of history rightly understood takes the rank of a *Theodicée*; and those who fancy they honour

Divine Providence by excluding necessity from it, are really de-
grading it by this exclusiveness to a blind and irrational caprice."[23] In effect, he removed the notion of liberty from his
definition of freedom.

Such was the capstone to the new historical philosophy. It
suggests the general failure of nineteenth-century historical
thought to find a systematic solution to the moral dilemma of
historicity. For Hegel, the task of providing the new synthesis of
freedom and historical inevitability in acknowledging the determinism of rational law was the *raison d'être* of the state. It constituted the critical function that would justify the state's claim to
be the moral-historical expression of transcendent spirit. For
the state is both the manifestation of historical necessity, and the
true meaning of rational freedom. Hegel writes that "society and
the state are the very conditions in which freedom is realized."[24]
Thus he eventually dissolved the creative will of the common
citizen—the proud claim that in modern times man as *man* is
free—in a state absolutism and in the elitism of a few world-
historical figures. Revealingly, the man who once welcomed the
revolutionary troops of Napoleonic France dismisses the sovereignty of the people as a most confused notion because "without
its monarch and the articulation of the whole which is the indispensable and direct concomitant of monarchy, the people is a
formless mass and no longer a state."[25] He sees sovereignty as
reposing in the idea of the single, individual ruler who expresses
the state's essential unity.

Hegel had conceived of a definition of freedom, made con-
sonant with historical determinism and absorbed into nationalism,
that has obvious totalitarian implications. Even more than Rousseau's ideal democratic community, Hegel's monarchical state en-
tailed an implicit political absolutism:

> The state is the actuality of concrete freedom. But con-
> crete freedom consists in this, that personal individuality
> and its particular interests not only achieve their complete
> development and gain explicit recognition for their right . . .
> but, for one thing, they also pass over of their own accord
> into the interest of the universal, and, for another thing,

they know and will the universal; they even recognize it as
their own substantive mind; they take it as their end and
aim and are active in its pursuit.[26]

Even more than Rousseau's ideal republic, Hegel's monolithic
nation-state denatured the liberty it claimed to espouse. Like
Rousseau, Hegel was trapped in the logic of his antithesis which
he could resolve only, while still maintaining the order of his
structure, by dialectically subverting the usual conception of one
of its terms into its opposite. That was because, for Hegel, the
state acted as an already secularized vehicle to transcendence. Just
in investing it with a spiritual role, Hegel made the state serve as
the instrument of man's moral transfiguration towards the absolute, and bear a burden of redemption beyond its power, except in
a demonic distortion.

In sum, the new historicism proclaimed the historical process
to be both rational and transcendent. In the dialectic, everything
became historicized: ideas, being, and even the divine absolute
spirit which defined itself through an inexorable evolution. Providence, then, is not merely an immanent, external cause of historical events, moving them but existing quite apart from them;
rather, it achieves its reality only in them. Consequently in historicist idealism, eschatology and historicity become synonymous.
Here, at last, the concept of historical transcendence has become
total.

Perhaps it is just by becoming total that it also becomes
totalitarian, that its very spirituality, in an ironic twist, fed a secular historical perspective on man's ideal vision of a transfigured
state of being. In any case, the absorption of eschatology into
history brings us back to an increasing secularism, such as we
encountered in another form in the Enlightenment, but with this
difference: for the first time, history becomes the *only* way of
transcending man's mortality in a worldview where *all* existence
has been historicized. The distinction between transcendence
"through" and "in" history is erased. The glorification of the state
as the agent of moral transfiguration, though fitted out with a
radically "spiritual" view of nationalism and of history, already
hints at the subsequent secularization of romantic ideals. State . . .

or class: are they not both, stripped of their romanticized mysticism, worldly objectives? Yet each in its way was popularly made to bear the whole weight of transcendent aspirations. In this respect more than in others, Hegel's historical idealism feeds the utopian materialism of Marx.

VII

TRANSCENDENCE THROUGH MATERIALIST IDEALS

1. *The Transcendent Value of Empirical Progress*

Dedicating the Crystal Palace Exhibition of 1851, Prince Albert spoke of it as a testimony to the unprecedented progress man had achieved in the previous century by means of the advance of technology and industry. Yet it is a matter of common knowledge that early industrialization produced the tragic squalor of midland industrial slums and a Dickensian world of exploited child labor amid appalling scenes of human misery. Perhaps a more significant indication of progress was the spread of a humanitarian revulsion against the misery of the poor, which had traditionally been regarded as the natural state of things, and the indignant conviction that now something must be done about it. Thus, if Ricardo and Malthus provided the entrepreneur with a ready rationalization of his profits and of his factory employees' inevitable poverty, Henry George was to point out, later in the century, the ironic tragedy of a civilization which had at last achieved, technologically, man's age-old dream of eliminating famine and want, only to find its new productive capacity adding to the sum of human misery.

Before midcentury, industrial workers in England had made repeated abortive attempts to break out of the economic and social grip of factory life. The Luddite riots against the introduction of machinery, the Peterloo massacre, Robert Owen's model community, trade unionism, Chartism, attempts at organizing socialist movements, were all early, frustrated efforts to relieve the oppressive conditions of industrial life. In a different but complementary vein, the protests of romantics expressed a more pervasive pessimism over industry and the consequences of an artificialized urban existence in general:

> The World is too much with us; late and soon
> Getting and spending, we lay waste our powers:
> Little we see in Nature that is ours. . . .[1]

But after the 1820's, another view of society, technology and industry gradually developed, vividly expressed in the confident tone of the 1851 Exhibition, and in the growing faith that a new era of industry would achieve a height of civilization and human happiness never before dreamt of. Perhaps the "new idea" of hope Saint-Just had seen in the Enlightenment, and which had abortively taken shape in the political objectives of the French Revolution, could become a reality in the rising social and economic expectations of a future age of industrial plenty. Because these hopes contrasted sharply with existing conditions, they constituted a transcendent aspiration which could endow sacrifices for social justice and a vision of the ideal with a transcendent quality. Perhaps social and economic change, rather than abstract political ideologies, could convert technical progress into an aspiration to human redemption.

Thus, trade-union organization and Chartism expressed not only revulsion against prevailing economic realities and parliamentary limitations, but also an optimistic faith in the possibility of reform and progress. Liberalism, for all of its bias in favor of the enterpreneur and in opposition to popular democracy, subscribed to an optimistic perspective of history. Adam Smith, who provided the capitalist with his central political tenet of free trade, anticipated that from the "invisible hand" regulating an open market would result the most efficient possible allocation of resources. This in turn would bring about the maximization of both productivity and profits, and hence lead to the best prospects for all-around economic well-being. The utilitarianism of Bentham and James Mill, for all its moral drabness, was a pragmatic philosophy that was instrumental in achieving judicial reform. In fact, from 1832 on, England became the stage for a century of gradual political and social evolution. Reform made her over, liberalizing and ultimately democratizing Parliament and local government, and changing the fabric of political life and values—all this under the patronage of a socially responsible governing class and the preservation of historical tradition. The initially "radical" program of the Chartist campaigns in due course was translated into accepted reforms of parliamentary procedures and suffrage.

Even conditions of labor, the most sensitive economic issue for the new class of industrial capitalists, gradually improved. After midcentury, a rise in real wages took place and attenuated the dramatic tensions of 1848. Thus conditions in the factories, the use of child labor, the interminable hours of colliery and mill employment were gradually mitigated through factory legislation. The Conservatives, under the influence of Lord Shaftesbury and Richard Oalster, pushed for social reforms which many Liberals had violently opposed as government intervention and infringement of the sacrosanct principle of "freedom of contract." These reforms gave added impetus to changing economic forces which worked against the worst abuses of industrial wage slavery. All of these changes gave some substance to a more encouraging view of the potential social consequences of industrialization, and explain, in part, the optimism that greeted Prince Albert's inaugural dedication of the industrial fair of 1851.

Industrial communications and the spread of literacy contributed to the generalization of the expectation of progress from elite circles to the strata of skilled workers. While the objectives and values of individuals and classes still conflicted as much as before, the antagonistic aims of these groups unwittingly participated in a common psychological impulse. They shared the faith in optimism, or in the romanticized rationalism of human betterment. But beyond the hope in progress, it was the semi-conscious faith in a new moral order that characterized the highest aspirations of labor and revolutionary movements, and that gave its distinctive quality to their historical objectives. The metaphysical historicity of German idealists and the cosmological historicity of French *philosophes* was paralleled by the new mass expectations, in the form of more tangible historical goals.

Hope at the popular level was expressed, in part, by a pragmatic trust in the benefits of machinery and in the increase of material things. This development should not surprise us. If there was any realm in which the case for cumulative progress seemed incontrovertible, it was in that of scientific knowledge and its application to technology. Those for whom the substantive needs of life still presented a daily challenge were naturally more inclined to construe meliorism or utopianism largely in terms of anticipated material benefits. The predominant scientific note of the age was man's apparently increasing mastery of his natural environment, as articulated by Henry Buckle. He found the distinctive trait of Western civilization in its development of control over the natural order, and contrasted this characteristic with the Asian tradition of man adapting himself to nature, or insuring himself against it. Modern Western man, Buckle argued, was liberating himself technologically from the limits of his natural condition, learning to control and dominate it by understanding its laws. Thus science applied in a new way to redemptive historicity. It seemed to place man in the position of Faust, acting in an historical context to refashion his natural environment. By means of his knowledge of scientific laws, man ostensibly could strive to recreate his world in accordance with his changing needs and moral predisposition. The scientific approach to history would enable him to seek transcendence in a rational order that was to liberate mankind from the present human condition.

The moral and historical response of nineteenth-century society to industrialization was ambivalent. Where romantics and mystic souls bemoaned man's alienation from his own nature in the fragmentation of specialized skills and the deluge of material things, or sought to recover the "wholeness" of the person outside a technological society, "practical men," on the contrary, welcomed the ingenuity of human inventiveness. They found in the victories of the new technology their best justification for confidence in material progress and its moral implications. In place of the aristocratic trust in abstract science stood the "plebeian" interest in the practical results consequent upon industrial development and in the tangible prospects of human happiness.

In sum, the key point to material expectations was the presupposition that technology would solve not only economic problems but social, and even moral, issues as well. This trust meant that the sense of progress in "things" and of the resolution of the problem of material want could be presumed, however dimly, to intimate an ethical transvaluation of society. In this sense, material goals often became in themselves transcendent, or rather, fulfilled a transcendent function. They signified less a specific worldly objective than the transformation of character man would undergo in achieving it. Like Faust, the individual would help build concrete things: a new world, through which he would create his own morally transformed reality, and which would ultimately save him. The vision of Goethe, for all its abstraction and dated romanticism, had captured one of the pulsebeats of its century. A new dignity in human labor was expected to give a transcendent quality to work, and to the world of objects it produced. Once man ceased to be alienated from the material realm, he would find moral purpose in the producing of goods, and see his labor contributing to the welfare and happiness of all mankind. In the vision of freedom of a humanity at last liberated from oppression, suffering and hunger, even menial factory work would be endowed with a transcendent purpose, in that it established the individual worker's moral participation in the universal solidarity of mankind. Then labor could recapture the spiritual quality it had lost with industrialization. Thus, the charge of materialism so often leveled against the new society failed to convey the distinctive nature of that materialism. It failed to show how material success had come to constitute a moral value, and to present an altruistic principle of human redemption through man's liberation from want and misery. In this perspective, the material-historical world was momentarily spiritualized.

In Britain, the momentum of reform, gradually changing the character of both major political parties and contributing to the eventual launching of the Labour Party, carried the hope of material progress into the new century. In the 1850's, Christian socialists like Frederick Denison Maurice and Charles Kingsley voiced an optimism in keeping with the mood of Victorian humanitarianism. Half a century later, the socialist Fabian Society proposed gradual empirical reforms motivated in part by a comparable moral impulse. In significant measure, it was the legacy of social Christian sentiment that inspired English protest movements to seek material advances in the condition of the poor.

It was probably Gladstone who in the late nineteenth century best reflected the Protestant reform impulse in politics. Gladstone was committed to the faith that the evolution towards parliamentary and democratic values constituted a moral obligation and provided a Christian reward. With these high principles, he combined a knack for political opportunism that some of his friends regarded as verging on hypocrisy. Yet even in his switch from Tory to Liberal, and in his often shifting policies, Gladstone was never a cynic. He always maintained a belief in Christian moral and humanitarian ideals as the ultimate aim of political action. When his policies failed, it was frequently on the side of sentimentality. Perhaps we can visualize him for a moment as the Great Liberal, figure of Victorian moralism, embodying the best humanitarian sentiments of his era. He seemed typical, even in his striking blindness to the fate of contemporary trade unionism, of that patrician consensus of parliamentary values which he shared with some of his most convinced political foes. Perhaps we can see him defending the secret ballot, civil service reform, or home rule, in the popular conviction of his day that politics should rest on a fundamental appeal to human decency and sympathy. In commemoration of him, with room, no doubt, for the usual discount of posthumous tributes, the Conservative leader, Lord Salisbury, said:

> What he sought were the attainments of great ideals, and, whether they were based on sound convictions or not, they could have issued from nothing but the greatest and purest moral aspirations; and he is honoured by his countrymen, because through so many years, across so many vicissitudes

and conflicts, they had recognized this one characteristic of his action, which has never ceased to be felt. . . . He will leave behind him the memory of a great Christian statesman . . . he will long be remembered not so much for the causes in which he was engaged or the political projects which he favoured, but as a great example, to which history hardly furnishes a parallel, of a great Christian man.[2]

In Gladstone's parliamentary career we find the model of liberal historicity. He represents its empirical objectives and pragmatic reforms, its compromises and hypocrisies, combined with transcendent moral ends. But the empiricism of liberal policies and the utilitarian character of much of Gladstone's piecemeal democratization express the redeeming moral purpose with which he infused his political goals and opportunist policies. It was a similar psychological quality, minus the talent for expediency, that was to mark the political evangelism of President Wilson. That is why each of these men saw himself with a world mission, to the occasional neglect, perhaps, of immediate problems closer to home. Gladstone was accused of greater sensitivity to the fate of Armenian Christians than to the dire plight of English workingmen. Wilson seemed more preoccupied in his later years with world problems than with Congressional matters. But both men imbued their practical political objectives with a redemptive historical inspiration.

Gladstone's Christian faith involved the belief in a personal afterlife. For many other nineteenth-century idealists swept up in the current of secularism, historicist eternalization had to take the place of immortality of the soul. But whether he performs his moral duty to God or to humanity, a person can identify himself through history with the everlasting ideals of justice and freedom. In striving towards historical goals rather than confining himself to individual acts of charity devoid of general social consequences, he leaves a permanent mark behind him. As he perceives it, he leaves a part of himself in the ineffaceable legacy of political actions and meliorist efforts, contained in the cumulative process of human advance in which he has participated.

But intellectual currents other than progressive historicity were rising in England and on the Continent in the late nineteenth century. A new hardness and pessimism colored much of European thought and politics. Bismarck was identified with the unromantic power diplomacy of *Realpolitik*. He coolly used German nationalism, for which he had little emotional attachment, to counter the popular historicity of liberal, and later of socialist ideals. Here was a concrete illustration of transcendent historical consciousness for mass consumption, in the form of patriotic sentiment, serving as the prime psychological instrument of social and political conservatism. In England, and subsequently on much of the Continent, the new nationalism increasingly emerged in aggressive imperialism, combining the evocation of Christian and patriotic feelings with the claim of national economic interests. William II found an imperial "destiny" for Germany—typically the language of transcendent aspirations. The mystique of Cecil Rhodes' African dreams and the adventurous romance of Kiplingism contributed to the popularization of the imperialist policy launched by Benjamin Disraeli. Surprisingly, the progressive liberalism and accompanying ethical presuppositions of Disraeli's great rival, Gladstone, appeared identified with the passing order of the nineteenth century. Disraeli's more aggressive policies fitted the changing climate of the prewar period. He proclaimed the responsibility of the elites and of the state for the welfare of the working classes. His enlistment of patriotism and imperial pageantry to arouse a new mass fervor belong to a matured industrial society in which some form of lower-middle-class consciousness has been widely achieved. When the lower-middle-classes' historicist yearnings remain unfulfilled, a militant nationalist movement is likely to arise.

The significant point is that up to the Second World War, more aggressive nationalisms were increasingly to win over certain mass audiences and to function as the operative forms of historical transcendence. Post-romantic nationalism remained one of the few surviving historistic values in the twentieth century. It became all the more frenzied because of the expectations people anticipated, and which seemed to have misfired with distressing psychological consequences.

In the intellectual currents of the second half of the nineteenth century, the name of Charles Darwin looms large. His ideas, or those mistakenly attributed to him, affected many of the attitudes and social values of the prewar era. The influence of his work had an especially notable effect on the changing character of historical consciousness, particularly among the literate public. The evolutionist perspective to which he gave great scientific prestige became remarkably popular, at least in certain circles. It was soon applied to social and political ideas, and to the justification of both old and new historical objectives. Social Darwinism provided a convenient rationalization of the new aggressive scale of values. In one sense, progress seemed implicit in the Darwinian notion of human evolution to ever more perfected organisms. Yet beneath this apparent optimism lay the law of the jungle, with all the pessimistic echoes of Malthus and Hobbes. For Hobbes, there had been some escape from fear into civil society and the despotic order of the *Leviathan*. In the struggle for survival of the fittest, there seemed to be no prospect of escape from what Tennyson suggested in his "Nature, red in tooth and claw."[3] Humanity was thus imprisoned in a natural law that had a radically different quality from the confident nature of Rousseau. It seemed to preclude man's liberating himself from the human condition. In short, the quest for meaning in life was trapped by a biological progress which led nowhere.

The irony is that Darwin brought historical consciousness to a new culmination by absorbing organic science into an evolutionary frame where time becomes the essential factor. He provided a new, empirical basis for the philosophical historicity of Hegelian inspiration. Yet he contributed decisively to the undermining of the faith in historical redemption. This development is not part of our present story; it belongs in the chapter on decline. For the moment, suffice it to note that Darwin seemed to justify, with all the apparatus of his painstaking science, the hardness of life, and thus to preempt the prospect of any form of historical utopia or transcendent moral order. But what if a doctrine should appear which could merge this toughness with the previous historicist faith? What might be the consequence of an ideal which could bring together the old romantic sentiment of optimistic historicity with the new unromantic "realism" of a scientifically determined social evolution based on class war? In the historical setting of the late nineteenth century, what power of emotional compulsion would be engendered by a worldview inheriting the two opposing historical themes: natural conflict, and the optimism of the future? Here was a key to the psychological force of a movement that took over the liberal ideal of historical progress while crystallizing proletarian hostility to bourgeois society and used liberal historicity to attack bitterly the specific objectives of a fading liberal world. This combination of conflict and hope largely explains the appeal in a mass society of a new worldview that seemed to offer, in its secular objective, a religious quality of certitude and of self-transcending purpose. It proclaimed a scientific determinism of historical progress. Yet it also provided a moral vision of secular redemption through history, an ideal communist state in which the present alienation of man from his true self would be resolved.

2. The Moral Sources of Socialist Historicity

The wellsprings of the socialist tradition in Europe are moral and religious. In fact, the tradition has been particularly related to the altruistic impulse in Christianity. Or at least it has emerged from the repressed undercurrent of revolutionary interpretations of Christian social ethics, specifically from the moral injunction to charity, justice and brotherhood. Early manifestations of collective social ideals and of the abolition of the property system were generally the consequence of radical Christian inspiration. They exhibited a fundamentalist desire to emulate the communistic quality of the initial Christian communities, and sometimes attested a humanitarian indignation over social injustice. In many cases, such as the Spiritual Franciscans and the radical Protestant groups like the followers of Jakob Boehme, Thomas Münzer or John of Leiden, communistic organization of the community of the elect represented the evangelical ideal of a sect but not a general social ideal intended for all mankind. In other cases, however, the evangelical impulse and social ethics of Christianity were joined into a general ideal of Christian social life. As long as property remained primarily agricultural and peasant uprisings or agrarian revolts constituted the most desperate form of popular revolutionary movements, Christian socialists advocated an egalitarian redistribution of land, as in the familiar case of Lilburne's "Levelers" or Winstanley's "Diggers." But such radical Puritan movements, viewed suspiciously by Protestant authorities, or branded as heresies, remained only fascinating historical curiosities. They were tangential to the mainstream of social teaching of both Lutheranism and Calvinism, and outside of Catholic church life.

Gradually, with the advance of the Enlightenment, the basis of socialist utopianism changed. The achievement of a rational organization of society, a more coherent economy and the scientific control of productivity became the new objectives of several "socialist" thinkers of the eighteenth century. Such considerations inspired Fourier and St. Simon. The new line of socialist idealism was essentially an intellectual movement, appealing both to the desire for symmetry and to the yearning for justice. Its intended clientele was the educated groups of enlightened bourgeois and aristocrats who might respond to the historical hope of organizing a perfected socialist society on the basis of rational order. Fourierism inspired the founding of a few idealist cooperative communities. St. Simonism became a movement that for a short time attracted sympathizers among the middle and upper classes, and influenced later French socialist ideas. But prior to the advent of industry, these various socialist schemes did not go effectively beyond the realm of ideas, or become major social forces. In this sense they earned Marx's jibe of "utopian."

It was industrialization which changed the nature and role of socialist ideals. It provided new audiences for programs of social protest. It appealed not only to the masses of workers, but also to a new type of militant Continental intellectual. The avant-garde of the intelligentsia found itself increasingly alienated from the ethical aridity of its aging capitalist bourgeois society, and from the increasing social irrelevance of the latter's simple optimistic faith.

Consequently, the post-industrial forms of socialism tended to differ radically from the pre-industrial ones in terms of psychological center of gravity. Eighteenth-century socialism appealed to the intelligentsia on the grounds of reason and moral duty. Utopian socialists like St. Simon had called for revolutions from above. In some cases, their ideal society was hierarchical and elitist. Post-industrial socialism, on the contrary, aimed its appeal at the grievances of an exploited class and naturally constituted an egalitarian movement. It was still ethical in inspiration. It still signified a moral indignation against the callousness of a bourgeois philosophy which depicted man as an economic animal, basing his actions on "enlightened egoism" and the principle of maximizing profits. But it had also acquired a new, unromantic cutting edge.

Socialist protest, to be sure, retained its flavor of a moral protest. It was a reaction, not just to the conditions of industrial life, but to the calloused rationalizations of classical capitalist economic principles. In effect, Adam Smith had reduced labor, and thus indirectly the working man himself, to a marketable commodity. He saw labor undifferentiatedly subject to the workings of supply and demand, and hence deserving the same economic consideration. The view of man as a materialistically motivated organism is a capitalist, not a socialist, legacy. In Smith's perspective, the outcome of his value theory was optimistic. But in the analysis of Malthus and Ricardo, capitalist economic "laws" led to the rational justification of hunger, want and subsistence wages. This conclusion conveniently excused the entrepreneur from moral guilt about the misery of workers. Small wonder that there was room here for an offended sense of social justice, and for morally outraged socialist protests in the name of restoring man to his proper moral dignity. In the career of Robert Owen, we find such protests forced to take on a more militant form. Owen abandoned futile appeals to England's political and industrial leaders, and turned instead to organizing working men. Egalitarianism took the road of conscious class appeal to industrial laborers. In the process it became more radical.

The uneasy sense that force rather than good example would

be necessary to change the unjust social order and the degradation of human beings in industrial towns was not a new notion. Apart from agrarian socialism of Puritan or millenarian inspiration, and besides the intellectual socialism of eighteenth-century rationalists, there was also a current of radical labor agitation among industrial workers and the urban poor. Its antecedents went back to the protests of journeymen against capitalist guildmasters. During the time of the Directory, "Gracchus" Babeuf—his name was a plebeian manifesto—had set a precedent for class war "from below" in his "Conspiracy of Equals." The erratic Luddite riots had evidenced labor unrest in industrial England. In France, pre-proletarian worker uprisings, notably in Lyon in 1834, marked the social history of the Restoration period. Here Auguste Blanqui agitated for revolution and formulated a new class-conscious socialist policy appealing directly to the militant worker.

While we can trace back the revolutionary socialism of class protest and mass action, we can also trace forward the old ethical appeal inherited from Christian radical movements and from the Enlightenment. It appeared in English Methodist socialism of midcentury. In France, it appears in the legacy of St. Simon, but more especially in the ethical impulse of Louis Blanc and Pierre-Joseph Proudhon. In this regard, the change from pre- to post-industrial socialism is primarily a matter of shifting emphasis between "ideal" and "class" appeals. But the change in character from utopian to class objectives involved a significant historical transition because it evoked a quite different political psychology. The new militancy was the by-product of a drastically altered economic structure that affected the nature of socialism and determined much of its historical consequences. The new socialism was a response to industrial mass society. Socialist ideas became historically significant only when large-scale industrial development occurred. Factory life provided socialism directly with a mass public of workers and indirectly with a literate audience aggrieved by the conditions of labor. Industrialization converted socialism from a marginal intellectual phenomenon into a major world force. It made of socialist idealism a new mass movement, incarnating a messianic historicity much as Jacobinism had done, and embodying the modern urge to historical transcendence in a new ideology. Upon this development rests a worldview that has given a decisively new cast to world-historical values and to redemptive historicity—Marxism.

3. Dialectical Materialism and Secularized Eschatology

Marxist socialism marked the final realization of a secularized world-historical perspective. Hegel's spirituality made history the vehicle of man's transcendence, and characterized the spirit of the state as the world-embodiment of the transcendent idea. In Marx's Hegelian outlook, the process of Becoming remains the essential quality of existence and contains the transcendent within itself, despite his apparent repudiation of all world-transcending ideals. In Marx, Hegel's notion of spirit is simply absorbed into the secular goal itself. That is to say, the distinctive attributes of spirit— order, direction, design—are attributed to the historical dialectic of the material world.

The key elements of Marxist thought are direct expressions of nineteenth-century historicity. For historical mindedness characterizes Marx's secularization of the Hegelian ideal, converted into dialectical materialism. Historicism appears in Marx's emphasis on the cumulative and vectorial process of social development. It is evident in his view of dynamic and qualitative change in the modes of production which, according to economic determinism, constitute the underlying factor in the growth and character of civilization. Engels derives Marxism not only from English materialism and capitalist economic theory, and the science-oriented atheism of the French Enlightenment, but also from the historicism of German idealist philosophy. In our time, Marxist historical analysis has become part of the contemporary language of social thought, and one of the major elements of our historical consciousness. Its critical ideas have become essential to much of our thinking, even on the part of many individuals who reject Marxism as a system or oppose Marx's political and moral conclusions. For the past century, these ideas have been thoroughly studied and debated. We shall therefore not review or discuss the themes of Marxism per se, but shall refer only to those of his ideas that are essential to our perspective.

It is a familiar point to recognize Marx as a religious prophet of the industrial age. Marxist socialism is now regularly described as a secular faith in an industrial society captivated by scientific rationalism. It has become a truism to recognize it as a secularized eschatology. That Marx's appeal is psychologically a moral and messianic one is evidenced by the ethic of the ideal communist state. Could there be a more obvious derivation from our Judeo-Christian heritage than the moving slogan which summarizes the tradition of egalitarian justice: "From each according to his ability, to each according to his needs"?

Marxist idealism appealed simultaneously to a romantic utopian *élan* and to the convincing rationality of scientific explanations. In this respect the *Communist Manifesto* is highly revealing. Its direct message to the worker touches the industrial wage earner in his most immediately sensitive spot, the desire for material satisfactions. At the same time, it offers a rational historical account—compelling in its simplicity—of the present state of affairs and, above all, prescribes a social remedy. It holds out the hope, indeed the certainty, of achieving equality and social justice. It arouses the powerful sentiment of destiny, the feeling that "history is with us," by claiming a scientific explanation of the historical process. It feeds upon the rationalism inherited from the *philosophes* and the romantic striving towards a humanitarian social order. To the intellectual, it offers the satisfaction of apparently enabling him to understand the process of history through a simple yet universal tool of rational analysis: the dialectic, which could encompass, relate and explain all social phenomena. It also offers the apparent power of prediction, and perhaps of control. The future is to be an open book to him who accepts economic determinism as the key to history. The once-magic power of knowing the future is available to all, by scientific means. Furthermore, that future will be morally good in the sense that it will bring a classless society and end man's estrangement from his fellowman. Here was a psychological triumph of historicity.

To the masses, Marxism offered a material objective as a

substitute for transcendent ideal value. The communist society that was to complete the next, socialist phase of history would not only change the lot of the proletariat, but would liberate the individual. It would end his self-alienation and bring him into a world in which he could achieve the full development of his personality. While Marxism undoubtedly appealed to Continental workers as a basic bread-and-butter issue and an expression of protest, it won its place as the dominant revolutionary ideology by converting these material objectives into an ideal of social justice. Socialist objectives proclaimed an end to false bourgeois morality, and socialist movements offered workers a share in transcendent aspirations that had long seemed a luxury of the prosperous. Thus, the rise of Marx's communism responded above all to specifically historical expectations. It arose from the historical aspirations which the new technology of communications and the growing literacy had spread during the nineteenth century to urban proletarian masses. Marxist historical values provided the essential mechanism of secular immortalization through the vision they offered of transcending the present condition of society and of achieving a redeeming humanist social ethic.

Thus, despite Marx's bitter criticism of utopian socialists and moralizers, his philosophy evidently contains a transcendent quality. Marxism took over from Hegel the key metaphysical proposition of the dialectic, namely that quantitative changes built up bit by bit transmute themselves into qualitative distinctions. Hence the movement of the dialectic involves categorical cultural innovations. The chapters of history constitute phases which are essentially differentiated by major transformations in the forms of human life, though they remain within the logic and scientific continuity of the historical process. Each successive historical age presents not merely an apparently "different" social order but rather an economic, political and intellectual world transcendent to the previous one. For Marx, the transcendence of nineteenth-century bourgeois society would come with the socialist revolution, and its final redemptory fulfillment in the communist ideal.

The quality of Marxism as an historicist faith providing the true believer with an apparently scientific, rational certitude of human salvation, rests upon Marx's analysis of history and his economic-historical prediction of the future. In the Preface to *A Contribution to the Critique of Political Economy* and in *The German Ideology*, he begins by asserting that ideas arise out of men's real existence, out of the actual material and social realities of their experience. Life is not determined by consciousness, he remarks, but consciousness by life. The social conditions and needs of living determine the general forms of our thought. From this initial premise, Marx concludes that the essential factor in history is the way in which a people secure their needs and wants. They must develop an appropriate form of social organization, resting upon the division of labor. This is the basis of "economic determinism." The particular method of production defines the whole life of a culture—its political system, moral values, religious beliefs, art forms, structure of knowledge and philosophy. These in turn, Marx and Engels argued, react upon the economic forces and consequently become themselves important elements of historical change. They both emphatically rejected the naïve determinism which would deny all but economic factors, and they asserted categorically the historical importance of political and ideological considerations. Nonetheless, they termed the latter ultimately derivatives of the forces of production; in the final analysis, they are only a superstructure on the economic base. Thus directly, or indirectly through the active political forces it engenders, and which acquire a momentum of their own, economics remains the key. To Marx, the fundamental fact of life and the basic reality of history remained the satisfaction of man's physical needs.

From the primacy of the mode of production, Marx developed his philosophy of historical change, or specifically what he called "dialectical materialism." He and Engels agreed with earlier materialist philosophers that the world is fundamentally matter and motion, and that thought, or spirit, must be derivative from material realities. But they both argued that classical materialism, particularly that of the Enlightenment, mistakenly assumed a static reality, a mechanistic world order. Marx, on the contrary, recognized the inherently historical-evolutionary character of life. It was precisely this Hegelian historicity of Marxism that constituted its key role in shaping the mass forms of historical consciousness and of transcendent aspirations.

Dialectical materialism was Marx's basic analysis of the pattern of historical change. Approached scientifically, history would divulge its meaning and reveal a structural unity in the process of movement. To Marx, each distinctive mode of production was tied to a particular form of wealth and property, inherent within the productive relationships, and to a particular technology. Each method of production involved a distinctive form of cooperation, or a social stage. The forms of property, in turn, determined the division of labor and defined the distinctions of class between those who own the means of production and those who do not. The latter are forced into dependence upon the former, and into an inevitable condition of exploitation. Such a situation engenders a basic antagonism between classes as one group tries to hold on to its property and power and the other seeks to wrest these from it. Marx had generalized Blanqui's specific insight into class conflict into the universal tension moving historical events, around which the other aspects of history gravitate, not without effect. History becomes an arena in which one exploited class after another is forced to wage an unequal war upon the successive dominant groups controlling property, wealth and power.

But history is more than the arena, it is also the product of this rivalry. In each successive stage of class conflict, it is a new mode of production, involving a different form of social intercourse, that leads to the emergence of a distinct phase of culture. By seemingly making all social phenomena and values relative to this relationship, Marx contributed greatly to the secularization of historical ideals. Partly inadvertently and partly by choice, he made the notion of secular historical transcendence into a theme specifically tailored to industrial mass consumption and the intellectual vanguard in a scientific, technological age. By claiming a scientific way of predicting the future, Marx had made historical knowledge serviceable for mass action and for mass redemption.

4. *The Science of Economics and the Transcendent Goal of History*

In order to understand the force of Marx's historical predictions and their appeal to numerous intellectuals, we must examine his critique of capitalism which describes the apparently scientific basis for his ideological position. The powerful attraction of his thought is largely a result of the impression of rationality given by his analysis of capitalist industrial economy. For the sense of certainty in Marx's vision of the classless society (the more certain to the degree the outlines of the communist state remain extremely vague) rests upon his explanation of the malfunction of the capitalist system.

For Marx, class division had until now determined the historical process by the successive attempts of each dominant class to win control over political authority. Thereby it not only extended its economic power over all realms of social life, but also formulated a world order of its own whose institutions and attitudes were but rationalizations or reflections of its class interest. Thus, modern Western concepts of family and religion were products of a particular type of commercial society. Similarly, the transition from chivalric ideals to mercantile values should be understood as the consequence of the shift in power from the landholding nobility to the bourgeoisie. All these ideas and institutions, all their philosophical defenses and religious sanctions, existed simply to buttress the existing social order. They provided the cultural imprimatur that the dominant class inevitably imposes upon its world. Even science developed within the frame of relative class concerns. Above all, it was the State that consummated capitalist power and bourgeois culture. The proletarian revolution would not only overthrow the government and the property system, but would sweep away the whole superstructure of middle-class society: its churches, laws, class values and morality. Marx differentiated between ideology that is necessarily relative to class interest and partisan, and his own scientific thought. Marxism, he claimed, though occurring like all other phenomena within the subjective time-frame and the dialectic of history, remained objectively in touch with historical reality. It was on this basis that he distinguished between mere historical hopes or ideals and the objective inevitability of socialism.

But, one may ask, why does each dominant group, after establishing its form of social organization, continue to live according to the frame of values of another group? Why does the new dominant economic group seek to climb the social ladder of a declining elite? Why, for example, did the bourgeoisie in nineteenth-century England emulate the aristocracy and seek admission to its ranks, while the lower classes paid deference to their "social betters"? This is a point of significance in Engels' analysis of history. When a new group first gains economic power, it finds itself in a world where authority, custom and status are attuned to the previous form of property and class interest. These institutions resist change and partly absorb some of the new families of wealth into the old elite's social order. The process by which the new dominant group liberates itself from that legacy and molds its own institutions and sacrosanct beliefs has in the past taken several generations, or even centuries. But it is here, in the long development of a new class order, extending control over authority, both religious and political, and fashioning new forces of social life, that, according to the Marxist perspective, the real drama of history takes place.

Marx's prophecy of revolution rested on two interrelated ideas: class conflict, and the self-destruction of the capitalist system. He saw the basis of capitalist economy in a set of interdependent characteristics and principles which, in the final analysis, are incompatible with one another. In capitalist society, according to Marx, various groups must always pursue inherently impossible objectives. The worker strives to raise his wages to the point where they will equal the market value of the goods he has made, not realizing that his aim is in contradiction with the system. The increase in the productive forces of the bourgeoisie only drives his wages down further. The individual capitalist seeks to maximize his profits, not realizing that for all except a few powerful entrepreneurs, short-term gains in productivity lead to intensified competition and eventual proletarization. Each capitalist seeks to accumulate profits by increasing his rate of returns on the variable capital he must spend for labor power. In the process, he must undertake policies which, when generalized among his competitors, only accentuate the contradictions between the interests of each individual and those of the system as a whole. Thus, according to Marx, capitalism produces its own gravediggers.

Marx finds the self-contradictions of capitalism in the competitive basis of capitalist life, which constantly drives marginal elements of the property-owning classes into the ranks of the proletariat, and in the ever-worsening crises of overproduction, that result in part from the relation of wage levels to what Marx termed "surplus value." The motivating economic impulse of the entrepreneur, Marx argued, is capital accumulation. The inevitable predisposition of the capitalist is to maximize profit. The key to profit, and hence to the whole capitalist economy, is the relative difference between the wage level labor receives and the exchange value of the commodities it manufactures. This difference is "surplus value," described in *Das Kapital*. The source of exploitation of the proletariat is the inevitable effort of competing capitalists to raise surplus value at the expense of wages. Among several ways of achieving this end, one is to increase productivity and thus reduce the proportionate level of labor costs. The result of these combined policies is to depress further the condition of life of the proletariat. Eventually, this procedure culminates in the individual worker's consciousness that exploitation is a class phenomenon binding him to unity with other workers. He generalizes his own bitter grievances into an overall revolutionary perspective and historical awareness. Here we can see how the phenomenon of class solidarity, which has ethical consequences, arises for Marx out of rational economic developments.

While the preceding processes are at work undermining the capitalist system, a related source of contradictions manifests itself in the mechanisms of capitalist competition. The growing productivity of industry aggravates the dilemma of capitalist production and profits, as each competing entrepreneur is forced to introduce more labor-saving machinery in order to keep labor costs down. The general consequence of these individual policies

—besides deepening the workers' misery—is to generate a relentless series of economic crises. These recurrent commercial upheavals throw the capitalist economy into chaos. The desperate attempts of individual entrepreneurs to escape from such conditions, for example by extending the range of capitalist enterprise into new markets, only succeed in aggravating subsequent contradictions. They convert the internal crisis of capitalism into a world-historical problem.

One consequence of crisis and competition is the ruin of many businesses and increased unemployment. A second is shrinkage of the circle of surviving capitalists and ever greater concentration of wealth. This increasing capital accumulation accompanies the changing technological requirements of industrial development. For Marx, the central factor in the pattern of bourgeois degeneration is intrinsic to the nature of capitalist industry *per se*. A machine functions as a substitute for human labor. Capitalist industrialization is essentially the introduction of labor-saving machinery in order to economize on wages. Thus technological innovation, which permits the application of constantly new labor-saving devices, is the core of Marx's analysis of the modern profit system. It causes the accumulated labor value that machines embody to be used for reducing labor's share in the exchange value of manufactured goods. In effect, labor is made to work against itself by indirectly providing the means for a direct depression of the wage level. Its accumulated effort is used against its present wage-power. Through labor-saving technology, the capitalist urge to profit maximization increases the reserve army of unemployed, necessary to keeping down labor costs. In short, technological change is the common denominator to the many contradictions of the capitalist mode of production that inevitably point the way to the future realization of socialism.

The need capitalists face to raise productivity and introduce new technology leads to ever greater concentrations of capital and machinery. The combination of unemployment and continuing depletion of entrepreneurial ranks produces a contracting circle in which ever more powerful industrialists pursue their self-interest with increasing abandon. Their number declines but their wealth grows, while the masses of the proletariat swell and their misery deepens. Eventually the scales tip. The rotted structure of capitalist economy topples, largely of its own weight. The advent of the classless society is at hand.

Marx had seen the tendency to concentration of industrial capitalism, but did not anticipate that capitalist society might develop political remedies for some of these problems, if only out of a sense of self-preservation. For Marx, the conception of the inevitability of economic processes precluded any alternative; the logical conclusion of the dynamics of capitalism could only be the virtual monopolization of the whole economic structure, culminating in its cataclysmic fall.

The self-destructiveness of capitalist economic organization does not mean, however, that the conscious actions of men are unnecessary to bring about the overthrow and transcendence of the class order. Economic determinism only means that history is pregnant with men's intentional behavior, taken in the mass. Like Hegel, Engels sees the individual as the agent of historical forces. He sees him as someone whose real freedom consists in the conscious recognition of the rational process of dialectical necessity. Still, the individual must choose—he must either stand with or against history—and he must act. It is specifically the function of socialist activity to prepare the proletariat's seizure of power. It must get ready for the day when the working class will capture the state and its coercive machinery. In the meantime, it must replace the ideology of nationalism with the international loyalty of the worker to his class. Marx characterized his philosophy as *praxis*: a philosophy of revolutionary activism where thought translates itself into, and is justified by, applied activity.

The idea of *praxis* qualified Marx's determinism with the necessity of individual participation. Expressing his scorn of bourgeois philosophy as an isolation from social responsibility, it stressed the active involvement of socialists in changing the human condition. It suggested a Promethean vision: Marx bringing to man the knowledge of a classless social order which will liberate humanity from the tyranny of the Olympian lords of industry. Above all, *praxis* tied in with the Faustian impulse, namely man's urge to create his own moral order in his own ideal world, and the glorification of striving towards historical perfectibility.

There is little doubt that Marxism derived much of its strength from the fact that, while it repudiated middle-class ideology and institutions, it expressed the psychology of historical progress which it had taken over from the old bourgeois liberal and democratic values. For many an intellectual, and for large segments of the working population, socialism answered the meliorist expectations of world-historical redemption they had become conditioned to feel but for which they found little outlet in the existing society.

In the last analysis, Marxist historicity fulfills a psychological function of idealization and self-transcendence. But its historical perspective has been detranscendentalized. Thereby the sense of history creates an inherent psychological contradiction between its social function and its objective—a contradiction that remains hidden so long as the material goal appears sufficiently remote to constitute a transcendent moral value to the existing social order. The transcendent role of history in Marxist expectations lies in the ultimate transformation by which society will liberate itself from its past. For that crucial change is expected to occur only through the dialectical process that is inherent in, and determined by, man's previous historical development. In other words, the utopian quality of Marxism appears in the conviction that history will provide the transcendence of the age-old framework of self-centered and aggressive life. The future social order is expected to achieve man's final liberation from the whole historical process of class conflict, and thus to go beyond the historical reality of class itself. In effect, the human community would be "reborn."

While the transition to socialism is to occur unromantically, through the economic contradictions of capitalism, its essential quality and appeal lie in the fact that the consequences of the change would be largely psychological and moral. Marxism represents one of the last and most typical expressions of the ideal of historical progress, at a time when disillusionment was undermining other forms of faith in history. Economic determinism, we may say, was less an inversion of German idealism than an attempt to capture ideality within the historical "substance." For what could be more rigidly idealistic than a worldview which invested the very natural forces of society supposedly governing history with a vectorial quality—with conformity to a pattern, an idea? What is more "idealistic" than finding in history a direction which would lead "objectively" to the ethically desirable state of socialism? Is this not a counterpart to Condorcet's view that egalitarianism and human freedom are implicit in the process of nature? What could more fittingly represent a culmination to historical transcendence than a "scientific" analysis in which history "contains" the movement towards an ideal human condition—a state where the self-alienation of man would be ended?

5. The Marxist Movement and the Psychology of Transcendent Values

During the prewar decades, socialist movements grew significantly in Europe. Large socialist and labor parties arose in Western countries. No doubt, many people adhered to Marxism and other causes out of conscious choice and an emotional receptivity to their ideological goals. It seems especially likely that many of those who joined socialist movements from the ranks of the upper-middle class and the intelligentsia did so partly out of a yearning for its humanitarian objectives, as well as out of a feeling of hostility to their own class society. But did most workers join out of ideological commitment? This question can hardly be answered with certainty. The reasons why a person sympathizes with a movement involve a host of intangibles. According to Marx's own view, it was primarily factors of social background and economic interest that in the aggregate would determine people's values. The prevailing tendency of thought today is to recognize that conscious ideological motivation plays a very minor role in most people's behavior and political outlook. Generally speaking, it serves as a refuge or a rationalization for more immediate and selfish reasons. Or it simply covers an habitual response, unconsciously adopted from one's peers. Ideological commitment seems especially marginal to the mass currents of proletarian movements.

Even if ideological concerns rarely cause a person to join a movement or deliberately to adopt its values, it does not necessarily follow that such considerations play no role in his subsequent attitudes or behavior. The reasons why a person initially comes to participate in a value-centered group may have nothing to do with the nature and motives of his later actions. An individual who joins a movement out of social reflexes or for purely contingent reasons, may come eventually to internalize its values. But the party's transcendence-giving quality need not be related, in the experience of most of its members, to its formal doctrines and ideology. Many a militant socialist worker may have given little thought to the ultimate objective of a classless society, and used Marxist slogans merely as a matter of ritual conformity. He was likely, however, to be greatly influenced by his feeling of solidarity with his comrades. It was the moral comfort he derived from his sense of unity and fellowship in "the cause," not the analysis of capitalist contradictions, that gave his actions self-transcending value and meaning. The unity of a movement that went beyond his own existence provided him with an intimation of higher purpose and of a kind of redemption for his unsatisfying life.

It is the psychology of the revolutionary movement in itself that marked the appeal of the new mass forces, far more than did their specific objectives or doctrinal content. Marx served as a prophet in providing the redeeming appeal of revolutionism *per se,* not in furnishing a theoretical analysis of bourgeois culture. The haziness of ultimate communist society was an essential asset to its transcendent role. The conviction that such an objective existed somewhere was more relevant to socialist experience than was the explanation of its characteristics. The Christian's image of heaven remains generally vague. Thus we find that the transcendent attribute of Marxist ideals inhered in the bond of fellow-feeling and participation in a moral community, not in the official dogma. It was this moral quality that defined the eternalizing function of the cause, and constituted its real strength. For it responded to one of the most significant elements of self-interest properly understood, namely the psychological need for an immortal identity and place.

We may conclude that one of the main cultural consequences of Marxism upon Western civilization, and later upon the world, was its influence on historicity. Much of its importance lay in the distinctive psychological form it gave to the mass consciousness of history in modern times. During the years before the First World War, new proletarian movements arose. Anarchism and syndicalism appeared, rivaling the appeal of Marxist organizations in certain countries and even in the First International. Meanwhile, Marxism developed along two generally different lines, reformist and orthodox, sometimes held together uneasily in the structure of a single party. Feuds on doctrine arose on such matters as participation in democratic bourgeois governments, and on the more fundamental question of an evolutionary versus a revolutionary interpretation of class conflict. The old ethical inspiration partially reemerged from beneath the hard economic approach, at least among reformist socialists. Fabians in England and Social Democrats on the Continent reaffirmed the moral basis of their social protests and ideals. They professed a humanitarian mission in history which assured a form of eternal legacy to those who participated in the good cause and in the militant comradeship of the party.

Let us end by evoking briefly the figure of the great French socialist tribune, Jean Jaurès. Perhaps better than anyone he represented the moral impulse and humanitarian sentiment behind the socialist movement. Its transcendent view of history animated his political battles, from the Dreyfus case to the building of the Socialist Party. It is not a coincidence that Jaurès was also a noted historian of the French Revolution, for it was largely his sense of history and of historical transcendence that gave a distinctive quality to his political faith. It helped him formulate a social vision for an industrial age still moved by democratic aspirations. But it was also this faith that in the end rendered illusory the noble efforts of democrats and socialists to find transcendent purpose in their historical perspective. Its fallacy was the effort to achieve the redemption of humanity within history. What defeated social democratic hopes was the vain attempt to invest the secular historical world with the task of providing a transcendent immortality for the individual and a redeeming eternity for the community. These were the self-contradictory aspirations that would soon give way to our modern pessimism of the future and our despair of history. Perhaps Jaurès was among the last of the old prophetic breed before the world of Verdun and of historical disillusionment swallowed us.

VIII

TRANSCENDENCE AND
HISTORICAL CONSCIOUSNESS—
SUMMARY

"The future is ours"—how often in our culture has not this consoling and invigorating thought spurred social change and the pursuit of new ideals? How often in modern times has not this implicit faith mitigated the uncertainties of the present? Both the
relentless impatience of totalitarian movements and the confident,
active anticipation of liberals and social democrats attest the effect
of the historical ideal of salvation. Belief in historical redemption
supports the dynamism and constant change that is the distinctive
trait of our Western civilization, though non-Westerners may see it
rather as a sign of restless instability.

The sense of historical transcendence has been essentially a
Western phenomenon, rooted in the redemptive perspective of history. Other civilizations, of course, have developed their own
modes of transcendence, for the attempt to go beyond one's own
ego and escape annihilation is of one man's basic psychological
impulses. Certain civilizations, such as China and Islam, developed
historical consciousness. But it was only the West that sought to
merge man's consciousness of history with his desire for transcendence and immortality. Only the West came to view life in a
clearly historical redemptive perspective, based on its linear time

sense and on its transcendentalization of historical goals. Perhaps the key quality in our modern sense of historical value has been the secularization of the transcendent objective. The consequence has been the tendency to make the historical realm not only the *vehicle* of our immortalizing aspirations, but their *object* as well.

In non-historical forms of transcendence, release may be sought through the dissolution of the ego in a timeless One, or approached through the merger of the self with the spirit of one's ancestors. In either case, the key step to transfiguration is the loss of individual identity. The ego seeks self-transcendence through passive receptivity to the natural or spiritual forces around it, or by recognizing the illusory nature of Being. In transcendent historicity, on the other hand, the search for eternalization takes a different form, characterized by activism and individualism. It emphasizes striving as a redemptive quality in itself, and it stresses the ego's self-conscious will. Transcendence then takes the form of the individual's vicarious survival in the secular historical ideal with which he has identified his name.

The hope of historical redemption is built upon the distinctiveness of the individual's contribution and Faustian "doing," through which he creates his own moral order. It depends on a creative originality in which "immortality" is represented by the survival of the individual's accomplishment and legacy. Eternalization is found in the perhaps unrecognized but irrevocable contribution he feels proud to have made in behalf of his ideal society. Consequently a man's aim should be to achieve immortality by impressing his personality and presence on the march of events —to make even a small contribution in the cumulative development of mankind. Men of genius can attach their names to a work of art, a scientific discovery or some other remarkable achievement. For the vast majority, historical transcendence could mean little more than the knowledge of a small, unrecorded contribution to the well-being of their fellowmen, an anonymous but ineffaceable legacy to future generations. In all these various aspects of immortalization, the predisposition to value individualism, creative action and originality characterizes our self-affirmation and historical striving.

The Enlightenment formulated a secular perspective of transcendence through science and reason. According to the views of some of the more optimistic *philosophes*, not necessarily representative of their time, man would learn to apply the mathematical symmetry of nature to the organization of society. He would model the future state on the perfect rationality of the natural order. Thus a linear sense of history marked by progress was grafted upon the ahistorical ideal of an absolute world order mirrored in the new physical sciences.

In its extreme form, the faith in history amounts to utopian trust in the immanent perfectibility of man. In less extreme form, it is the hope of continuing progress. Most *philosophes* entertained serious reservations about utopianizing the future. Some of the best known among them ridiculed the expectation of human perfection and goodness, or the hope of transforming human nature. Several of them viewed the destiny of man with foreboding. But in Condorcet, the redemptive hope of the Enlightenment came into its own. Then the ideal of reason seemed to culminate in the moral and historical philosophy of Kant. Despite his repudiation of rationalism in epistemology and of utopianism in history, Kant anticipated further progress of the human mind and the attainment of universal peace. He proposed an ideal of rational ethical order. Meanwhile, socialist theoreticians like St. Simon and Fourier applied the ideal of reason to plans for collective utopian life based on a technological and cooperative organization of society and of production. From our point of view, it is significant that the Enlightenment produced its own forms of historical consciousness. Condorcet and others developed a transcendent view of the future, *not because they postulated the idea of progress but because they came to anticipate a moral change in social life and in the nature of man.*

An exemplification of such a perspective came in mid-nineteenth century with the positivistic philosophy of history of Auguste Comte. Basing his sociological analysis partly on the legacy of St. Simon and Condorcet, Comte envisaged a humanitarian reform of society, and a secular religion of man. In line with the well-established tradition of historiography, he presented

history according to a linear development of three successive
stages of consciousness: the age of theology, of metaphysics and of
positive science. Pushing further the ideas of Buckle, Comte saw
these stages as descriptive of the ways in which man approached
his environment. Man progressed from the time he sought the
explanation of things in irrational beliefs to the period when he
found it in rational speculation that remained, however, still abstract and philosophical. Now he has finally come to find positive
understanding in empirical knowledge and in the objective sciences. The latter, in turn, are cumulative, progressing from the
theoretical and universal order of mathematics and physics to the
ultimate concrete science of society. The new sociology, built
upon the other sciences, permits the projection of a rationally
organized community, a positivist utopia of social harmony and
humanist ethics.

Comte not only formulated a conception of historical
progress; he even ascribed to his positivist ideal a religious function and quality exemplified in a rationalist priesthood, a puritan
and utilitarian ethic, and a theatrical ritual outdoing Robespierre's
Feast of Reason:

> These festivals, then, should be of two kinds, correspond-
> ing to the two essential aspects of Humanity . . . the love
> of Order, namely, and the love of Progress.

> As the static festivals represent Morality, so the dynamic
> festivals, those of Progress, will represent History. In these
> the worship of Humanity assumes a more concrete and ani-
> mated form: as it will consist principally in rendering
> honour to the noblest types of each phase of human de-
> velopment . . . [and] to the celebration of the Future, the
> normal state to which all these phases have been tending.[1]

Despite its unscientific pageantry, Comte's worship of Humanity reveals an important aspect of late nineteenth-century science and history. His sociology suggests the transition from the
dominance of physical science over philosophical and historical
thinking to the prevalence of historical consciousness even in scientific thought. In the age of Darwin and Wallace, evolutionism

became the essence of the new scientific outlook in geology and biology, and in the emerging science of society. Much as Newton's mechanics set the pattern of thinking of the eighteenth century, the biologism of Spencer and Bergson set new intellectual styles in the pre-World War I era. For science now meant organic as well as mechanical order; it meant biology as well as astronomy, chemistry and physics. Even natural science was partially historicized.

Distinct from the social scientist's trust in positivist knowledge and empirical data is the philosophical notion that historical reality is an idea, specifically *an idea in process*. Though Hegel's absolute idealism appeared radical in its thoroughgoing historicity, it was in a sense only a manifestation of the deep-rooted historical consciousness woven into the fabric of Western culture. Hegel's dialectic presupposes that history is determined by a rational spirit, and that this spirit forms itself through history. For Hegel, the absolute idea was the logical culmination of the historical process. Transcendence is a function of that historical process and of its central spiritual reality, embodied for modern man in the state. The Hegelian impact on historicity can be summed up in two key themes. The first is that the rational order of Becoming encompasses *all* reality in its dialectical chain. The second is that the meaning of transcendence through time is manifest in *qualitative* changes in the historical world. From here it was but a step to the secularization of the historical teleology in Marxism, a materialist teleology that was to preserve every attribute of the ideal, except that it claimed to discard ideality.

Contrasting with the idea of historical redemption through science or rational idealism stands a third category: transcendence through romantic historicity. Its theme is liberation by means of fellow-feeling and love. Victor Hugo and Heinrich Heine, for example, sought an ideal of future brotherhood in romantic visions of historical purpose. The religion of humanity elaborated by Comte and affirmed by such divergent personalities as George Eliot and Jean Jaurès appealed no less to an ardent romantic patriot and social idealist like Mazzini, who wrote:

> Your first duties—first as regards importance—are, as I have already told you, towards Humanity. You are *men*

before you are either citizens or fathers. If you do not bear
witness to your belief in the Unity of that family, consequent upon the Unity of God, and in that fraternity among
the peoples which is destined to reduce that unity of action;
if . . . [you are not ready] for the redemption of the be-
trayed or oppressed[,] you violate your law of life, you
comprehend not that Religion which will be the guide and
blessing of the future.[2]

In England, Dickens' novels depicting the sufferings of the poor
and the oppressed, and expressing a sentimental trust in human
good will, helped nurture the humanitarian impulse of the reform
movement. Tennyson voiced a hesitant but nonetheless real hope
in the rising prospects of humanity. In much of the literature of
the period, the idea of progress translated itself into the expectation of an ethical regeneration of man. Thus midcentury literature
and art fed the currents of political and social philosophies seeking the redemption of humanity in the ideal state of the future.
They shared the intrinsic historicity of evolutionist thought and
the sense of emotional transcendence of the romantic age.

The historical consciousness of romanticism is intimately
connected with the romantics' aesthetic impulse. Immortalization
through art and eternalization through history have long constituted parallel yet interacting themes, if only because art forms
relate directly to their historical setting. In the romantic concern
with the past, poetry and history were closely joined through the
sentiment of nostalgia. Tradition took precedence over abstract
reason. While this attitude could obviously serve a "conservative"
purpose, as in the case of Chateaubriand, it led primarily to liberalism. In fact, romanticism often projected a sentimental vision
of the future. It is noteworthy that the popular literary figures of
the Victorian age, romantics like Hugo, Heine and Lamartine,
combined literary fervor with a sense of history and liberal ideals.
A romantic historian, Michelet, was among the foremost historical
dramatists, imbued with an heroic vision of the past and the future. He saw history in the perspectives and expectations of a
popular democrat who has faith in the populace and anticipates
man's freedom. Significantly he termed history a "resurrection."

A prevalent romantic assumption was the idea that man is not evil by nature. Such an outlook fitted a form of historical consciousness in which redemption was to be won through good will. For some romantics, the ideal was approached in history by a few heroes and creative personalities. For others, it was the consequence of the fundamental goodness of "the people." Self-transcendence depended upon the individual's moral participation in humanitarian political ideals, and upon his mystic, quasi-religious identification with a spiritual tradition transcending the present.

One of the major forms of historical transcendence has been the faith in libertarian and egalitarian values. The expectation of human salvation appeared in the successive ideologies of revolutionary liberals, democrats and socialists. Underlying all of these movements was a common predisposition to see redemption in terms of political movement towards the good society. In its earlier form it meant the achievement of constitutional government, then of parliamentary democracy, and finally of the classless state. Liberalism was primarily expressive of middle-class values, but it left a legacy of historicist faith to socialism and proletarian mass movements. For the libertarian and egalitarian vision offered the individual an historical goal beyond his own condition and limits, and a confidence of overcoming vicariously his own mortality and time. Thus it added to an often drab existence a purpose-giving aim in contributing to the universal liberation of humanity.

Christianity was affected by the Pelagian predisposition of liberal historicity. Certain forms of Protestantism responded to the popular notions of the goodness of man and of the improvability of society. In several instances they emphasized the dynamic political consequences of Christian social teachings against the prevalent conservatism of the religious institutions. They opposed, psychologically, the doctrine of passive acceptance of the established social order espoused by most national church bodies, and generally supported in Catholic policies. For some groups, the Christian social ethic and the ideal of economic justice became the primary expression of Christian spiritual values. The new appeal to social conscience even affected official Church doctrines, as in the case of Leo XIII's famed encyclical, "Rerum Novarum," though both Catholicism and conservative Protestantism steadfastly rejected the idea of human perfectibility. In other instances, more radical notions of Christian democracy and Christian socialism appeared. Small but active Protestant movements and occasional Catholic figures, like Marcel Sangnier and Charles Péguy, proclaimed not only social justice for the worker but also moral and political freedom for the individual. While conservatism remained deeply entrenched in many church institutions, the liberal perspective influenced Christian attitudes, particularly in England and the United States. The consequence was a more humanistic and also more secularized approach to redemption through historical consciousness.

During the late nineteenth century, progressive political and social changes were gradually achieved in parts of Europe, especially in England. In Germany, the autocratic Bismarck pioneered a paternalist system of social security and welfare benefits for labor. In France, despite bitter social frictions, union organization and parliamentary agitation gradually lessened some of the worst sufferings of the working man. But in general, such change occurred with insufficient consistency or speed to end the alienation of many workers and intellectuals from society. Therefore the demands of revolutionary movements kept ahead of social and political gains. Liberalism changed; in Britain, a segment of the Liberal Party was influenced by new ideals that abandoned the old laissez-faire mentality. The idea that the government had some responsibility for the welfare of its citizens took root. A new liberal policy was advocated by T. H. Green. John Stuart Mill seemed to bridge the ideological gap between the old liberalism and the new socialism. Although the French Radical Party endorsed a social ideal of human solidarity largely to cover its own opportunist goals, solidarism provided a secular moral value of sorts. Gradually, however, the hopes of bourgeois reformers lost ground on two fronts, due both to their successes and to their failures. On one side, democratic conservatism offered a renewed challenge to liberal expectations and policies. On the other hand, new mass movements shifted the center of gravity of political life.

Proletarian militancy and intellectual alienation strengthened the appeal of socialist values and hopes.

Under both the continuing influence of the French Revolution and the spread of industrialization, the ideal of transcendent historicity became a mass phenomenon. In factory towns and large cities, the material conditions of industrial life accentuated resentments, but also generated revolutionary hopes for the future. The mystique of Jacobinism stimulated mass historical consciousness. The development of industrial civilization changed the urban revolutionary movement from an exceptional phenomenon into a latent feature of the class structure.

As the conception of a redeeming historical future spread throughout the urban masses, it manifested itself in an increasing variety of political and ideological forms. Accompanying the general growth of literacy in Western countries, a new force of mass historicity appeared. Aspirations to expansionist nationalism pulled mass opinion in one direction. Proletarian organization, workingmen's movements and socialist ideals pulled it another. But all these forces shared the common quality of translating public sentiments into historical values and futurist hopes. While non-ideological concerns generally motivated the individual's enlistment in a revolutionary cause, it was the eternal life of the movement and the self-transcendent solidarity of the group that invigorated his social action. From Chartism in England to the general strike of syndicalists, mass demonstrations occurred with increasing frequency. For Europe, the current of egalitarian mass movements culminated in the ill-fated promise of the Russian Revolution. The new century is often referred to as the Age of the Common Man. The difficulty with this phrase lies not in the definition, but in the implication of romantic idealism that was naïvely attached to it before the period of concentration camps and of total war.

The sense of profound social oppression reflected in the current of unrest was a consequence of changing standards more than of changing conditions. A standard of life that is accepted as normal under one form of culture may be felt to be intolerable under another. The critical question is not the condition itself, but the way it is evaluated. It seems unlikely, for example, that the London of Hogarth was less full of social misery than the London of Marx. The novelty of the nineteenth century was that large parts of the urban masses and of the elites aspired to improve social conditions. These aspirations generally began as demands for material reforms, but eventually expressed themselves in the sense of social justice, and in redemptive historical hopes.

The belief in self-transcendence through history exists on several distinct levels of experience and ideology. At the most basic level, it appears in the aspiration to a better life for one's children; at another level, in the hope of participating in some great national destiny, or the destiny of a class. At its broadest level, self-transcendence manifests itself in consciousness of humanity and faith in a universal ideal. Its most frequent expression is in the hope of change in the material conditions of life, through a revolutionary reorganization of labor and society. Thus material progress becomes a moral objective, and serves as a form of ethical liberation. Material objectives often appear to take on a moral quality of their own, and to function in a transcendent capacity. As long as such objectives remained far removed from the existing conditions of life, they could serve as an apparently transcendent end. But they contained within them the eventual self-contradiction of their transcendent function and their basically detranscendentalized nature.

A different type of messianic historicity—one that has played a particularly significant political role—is that of transcendence through patriotic idealism. We have followed the growing momentum of nationalism as the agency of transcendent aspirations in the writings of Rousseau and Hegel. The former saddled the state with a moral quality. The latter burdened it with a spiritual function, or rather, he burdened spirituality with statism. In Rousseau, state absolutism was partly vindicated by the moral bond consented to by its citizens. In Hegel, it was the expression of necessity.

Jacobin patriotism converted nationalism into a radical revolutionary tradition. In historical literature, the romantic expression of nationalism and popular democracy came to a climax in

Michelet's *History of France*. But he was only the foremost of a host of other patriot-historians in various countries, such as George Bancroft in the United States. The national heroes of the age, like Mazzini and Garibaldi, attested the charismatic role of the patriotic leaders and the messianic quality of nationalist movements.

The popularization of national consciousness, long established in England and France, eventually took root in Germany. To the concept of nation, German historicism added the concept of the *Volk*, with its collective soul. The mysticism of a *Volksgeist* and the "living spirit" of the state invigorated the psychology of manifest destiny. Applicable specifically to the United States in its westward march, this term also serves in a more general way to characterize European nationalism, especially after 1848. Thus, it became the manifest destiny of Italy to re-create the glory of the Roman Empire, and of Britain, to maintain the new "pax Brittanica." France was to diffuse a civilizing mission. Russia, long intimidated by Western culture, was to develop pan-Slavism. The function of defending orthodox Christian values against the false secularism and liberalism emanating from the West became her manifest destiny. The new German Empire was to find greatness in the triumph of Germanic philosophy, science and industry—and later in William II's call to Germany's "world mission." The first stanza of *Deutschland Über Alles* conveys its aggressively self-transcending appeal. From these passionate national feelings, it was an easy transition to imperialism as the inevitable duty of patriotic citizens, and as the avenue to immortal fame. The acquisition of colonies was largely grounded in economic circumstances and in the competition of capitalist industrial states for new fields of investment. But imperialism manifested a psychological impulse, expressed in the form of ardent nationalism that led to the subsequent worship of the superstate.

Militant patriotism eventually provided a form of historical transcendence for conservatives. After 1848, nationalism tended increasingly to become the ideal through which conservative movements sought to win popular support. As the former combination of patriotic and liberal sentiments waned, the inherent attributes of nationalism tended towards an unrestrained statism. An expansionist aggressiveness provided conservative groups with an ideal vision of an "integral nation" or of an empire. This version of historical transcendence, however, did not presuppose progress or human perfectibility. It did not involve utopianism or faith, either in the potential benevolence of man, or in the attainability of a rational social order. Transcendent historicity had been alien to the conservative perspective. Conservative thinkers such as Burke had generally repudiated the notion that history could contain an ideal society born of the mind of man. They repudiated messianic fervor directed towards purely historical goals. Thus the conservative use of nationalist psychology to develop a mass appeal was an important novelty in Western thought.

The new redemptive function of conservative historicity revealed the radical distinction between the conception of historical self-transcendence and the idea of progress, which had previously seemed interchangeable. For the notion of progress could not serve as a redeeming goal for conservatives who viewed the ideal social dynamic as mimesis and saw the proper model of life as preservation of traditional values. It was irrelevant to a totalitarianism that glorified a return to barbarism and primitive violence, and that scorned the progressive achievements of culture. But the sense of transcendent historicity could serve conservative movements and totalitarian regimes. Service for the sake of history itself functioned as a redemptive value. History offered the intimation of an eternal future, for example in the nationalistic form of world dominance. In other words, the objective of identification with an "everlasting" empire, a racist movement or an ideal of power, provided a form of secular immortalization in situations where the concept of progress could not arise. Historicity thus made possible a vitiated type of secularized immortality beyond the spectrum of utopianism or perfectibility, that ultimately came to reveal its own inherent self-contradiction.

The conservative use of nationalist historical consciousness spread across Europe, from England and France to Germany and Russia. Hegel's legacy seemed to be a blessing for both German nationalism and the Prussian monarchy. Bismarck skillfully used nationalist sentiments for his own ends, and Treitschke provided a passionate historical argument for the Prussian state and the German Empire. William II embodied the transcendent appeal of German imperialism in his theatrical glorification of German destiny. In England, Disraeli reversed the "Little-Englander" policy of midcentury. Combining colonialism with a paternal appeal to protect the welfare of the laboring class, he made Victorian imperialism the expression of patriotic glory. In France, the Dreyfus case crystallized the new identification of transcendent nationalism with the political right—a relation exemplified also in Italian irridentism. In Russia, Nicholas II used the psychological appeal of Slavophilia to give impetus to a pan-Slav policy and to clothe his own historical objectives in the transcendent purpose of propagating Orthodox Christianity. Significantly, it was primarily militant nationalism that survived into the twentieth century as an active form of historical ideal. After liberalism, democracy and reformist socialism successively lost their mass appeal, militant nationalism remained to embody a sense of historical meaning and purpose. Even conservative nationalist movements, proclaiming their ties to tradition, sometimes adopted the "radical" role of advocating political and social change, as in the case of Gaullism in France. Against the feeling of a disintegrating civilization and the futility of history, a frenzied form of nationalism still asserted a redemptive view of the future, generally in perverted, totalitarian movements. The same nationalist psychology could be applied to one's class as well as to one's race or state. In each case, the agency of historical redemption was the revolutionary party. Thus authoritarian ideologies often served a revolutionary purpose. It is one of the ironies of history that in our time, transcendence through historical consciousness has been embodied in movements of the extreme right and in totalitarian regimes such as those of Stalin and Hitler.

PART IV

PART IV

IX

THE DECLINE OF
HISTORICAL TRANSCENDENCE

1. *Science, and the Pessimism of the Future*

Untranscendability and the finality of death—these are recurrent themes of twentieth-century disillusionment and pessimism. A fear of the immutability of the human condition has produced growing reverberations in modern arts and thought, and even in modern mass movements. Sometimes the feeling has spread that man's condition is indeed changing, but only in the direction of greater frustrations and misery. When the assets and liabilities of modern civilization are added up, the balance, it is often said, is increasingly unfavorable to contemporary man. In any case, the sense of futility, so pervasive in aesthetic and intellectual currents since the First World War, rests upon the anxiety that there may be no way out of the human predicament. It expresses the fear that there is no escape from present reality and no liberation from the finite limitations of our existence.

The notable fact about this modern anxiety is that it signifies specifically our disillusionment with historical transcendence. The present moral dilemma in Western culture appears implicitly as a crisis of faith in the meaning of history. Its source lies in the growing doubt of the sense of unity and purpose which historical aspirations provided. For we have seen that the expectations of a redemptive future state became the common denominator of most of the prevalent Western values—liberal Christianity, secular scientism, patriotism, democracy, socialism and other humanitarian ideals. All of these hopes were predicated on the notion of a transcendent meaning in life through historical destiny. Each of them found in its teleological goal an eternal identity and a vicarious immortality for the individual ego. The more the values of our modern civilization converged upon the central mechanism of historical consciousness as the way out of the individual's finiteness, the more the new sense of historical futility created a psychological void. Because the West mortgaged its values to its linear view of time and destiny, the default of history was devastating: the measure of previous hopes became the measure of present despair.

There have been many crises of values in Western civilization. What makes the present dilemma different is that it involves no mere failure of one particular system for the cure of souls, but the intimation that such a cure can never be found, and that any future redemptive ideal we may seek will eventually prove as illusory as our previous convictions. The futility of one illusion becomes the futility of all moral aspirations. The unending lot of man as sufferer, which in Judaism and Christianity had held out the hope of individual salvation, thus leads to stoic resignation. The new absolutism asserts the ultimate meaninglessness of existence. Man can no longer presume to transcend his mortality through redemptive action. He is faced with the annihilation of the self in the absolute finality of death.

Despair and futility have no date of origin in history; in human experience, pessimism has been the constant counterpart to faith. Until the recent past, the hardship of living had given little encouragement to an optimistic view of man's future except to a small elite. Even in the eighteenth and nineteenth centuries, the rising expressions of hope were accompanied by counter-currents of pessimism and world weariness—from the ideas of Schopenhauer to the *Weltschmerz* of the romantics and the *mal de siècle* of the turn of the century. While optimistic national historians looked to the future liberation of man and the glorious destiny of their own people, Jakob Burckhardt, with remarkable prophetic insight, voiced anxious forebodings concerning the prospects of Western civilization. But the rising sense of futility of much of twentieth-century thought represents something different, namely a radical nihilism that is the outgrowth of the failure of historical hopes. Thus while contemporary expressions of alienation have their roots deep in past human experience, they constitute a distinctively modern psychological phenomenon. Ironically, it is the very elements on which the previous currents of historical faith had been based—notably science—that now served to engender disillusionment. Against the rationalism and balanced natural order of Newtonian thought, there arose with Darwinism the view of nature, already suggested by Hobbes, as a competitive jungle.

Several nineteenth-century scientific developments had a direct impact on historical thought. In a certain sense, Darwinism and the social sciences constituted the new disciplines of the age, much as Newtonian physics had been the dominant science of the seventeenth and eighteenth centuries. Through Marx, Comte and Darwin, the new rationalism became essentially evolutionary and historicist; much of the new scientific work concerned the explanation of Becoming in cultural and organic terms. Philosophy anticipated and responded to the new intellectual development. Historicist philosophies accompanied and reflected the new historical sciences. Just as the seventeenth and eighteenth centuries had produced scientific philosophers, such as Descartes, Locke, Hume and Kant, the nineteenth century produced historical philosophers, such as Hegel, Marx, Spencer and Dilthey.

But subsequent scientific and philosophical currents rising in the late eighteen hundreds were to turn away from the evolutionary and historical perspective, as well as from the sense of transcendent liberation that had been explicit in Hegel and implicit in Marx. The relation of these new scientific and philosophical ideas to historical consciousness, and especially to a transcending historicity, was indirect and diffuse. Thus to understand the collapse of our trust in historical consciousness, we must investigate fields of science and philosophy that at first glance may seem irrelevant to our topic, because it is precisely this increasing irrelevance that

constitutes our concern. We must consider the dehistoricizing and
detranscendentalizing aspects of modern thought, beginning with
scientific and philosophical notions, that are to be found throughout the *Gestalt* of contemporary culture.

The legacy of eighteenth-century science was a sense of
mathematical equilibrium and scientific determinism. There was
comfort in the apparent certainty of physical knowledge and confidence in the absolute nature of truth. But in the late nineteenth
century, cracks began to appear in the Newtonian mechanism and
its certitudes. Problems arose in both physics and astronomy. The
famed Second Law of Thermodynamics stated that without the
intervention of an outside agent, heat could flow only from a body
of higher temperature to one of lower temperature. This meant an
irreversible pattern of diffusion of energy within a system. Such a
law appeared to violate the symmetry of classical physics and of
its philosophical presumptions. Lifted by non-scientists from the
realm of thermodynamics and applied analogically to the cosmos
as a whole, the asymmetry of the Second Law was taken to imply
a lineal devolution of our universe through time. This new view of
irreversible cosmic change had grave consequences upon non-
scientific thought. Reduced to its basic meaning, it suggested to
many intellectuals that the universe was running down. Through
the dissipation of energy and the accompanying increase of
entropy, or disorder, the world would burn itself out, and devolve
into a state of utter inertia.

Obviously, the prospect of such an absolute mortality had
dire psychological implications for the whole idea of historical
redemption. Why sacrifice oneself for the future if that too was
doomed? If the whole universe was gradually but relentlessly
grinding to a halt, of what significance was trivial progress? The
essence of transcendence through historicity, we know, is the
sense of immortalization which logically rests upon the possibility
of eternal existence. But if the ultimate teleological resolution of
the historical future was to be an endlessly inert, dead cosmos,
what was the purpose of striving for a vicarious personal transcendence? So disarming is this concept that in Marxism—where
the sense of secular redemption is, of course, essential—it has

been charged that the physical concept of entropy is a bourgeois plot, an evidence of the class character of bourgeois physics, to undermine the proletariat's sense of socialist liberation and ultimate purposefulness.

During the closing decades of the century, other fields of physics contributed to the growing awareness of discrepancies in the Newtonian order, and gave rise to further doubts as to the certainty of established scientific precepts. The new attitude is revealed in the philosophy of science of Ernst Mach, who hinted at the relativism and subjectivism of later years. By casting doubt on the previous conviction of certitude in science, the revolution in physics also undermined indirectly the trust in the objectivity of historical understanding. Thereby it implicitly vitiated the projection of "positive" historical laws, as in Buckle, Comte or Marx, upon a progressive future. No wonder Lenin subsequently felt compelled to defend socialist materialism against the philosophical idealism suggested by the new scientific theories. For the cumulative changes in the physical sciences seemed to jeopardize, derivatively, the trust in a rational historical process supposedly in harmony with the order of nature.

Then Henri Becquerel and the Curies discovered an element with the remarkable property of emitting light and heat, that is to say of releasing energy and of "losing" mass. The discovery of radioactivity upset the older conception of matter and undermined the accompanying popular cosmology. Furthermore radiation disintegration, by which radioactive elements continuously burn themselves out at a known rate until they reach the inert state of lead, suggested a parallel to the larger cosmic process of dissipation of energy inferred from the Second Law of Thermodynamics. Finally, out of the work of Thomson, Rutherford, Böhr and others came a new conception of the atom. No longer was it an indivisible, solid mass of substance, but rather a complex agglomeration of energized particles. The fractioning of the basic unit of matter prepared the way for a new structure of physics, but not until after it had shattered the old billiard-balls notion of the physical world and the conception of material reality that went with it. As science cast doubt on all the old concepts of natural law and order, the achievement of an ideal society based on natural law became increasingly remote. A sense of ultimate relativism communicated itself to other areas of thought and was translated into uncertainty about other kinds of knowledge, for science had been the basic source of our self-confidence in the achievements of the human mind. Various forms of transcendent historicity, including Marxism, thus appeared to rest on increasingly uncertain grounds.

2. Estrangement and the Artist

Indeterminacy found cultural expression in the arts three-quarters of a century before it became a formal scientific principle. The scientific studies of light had a direct bearing upon the aesthetic objectives of the impressionist and post-impressionist painters of the last half of the century. Their attempt to translate new physical concepts into visual aesthetic forms involved the breakdown of what had been regarded as absolute bases of painting technique and indivisible entities of form and light. Iconoclastic in its approach and immediate objectives, impressionism in painting and music, it is true, remained clearly an outgrowth of the romanticism it set out to replace; it is the impressionistic quality in Turner's romantic scenes that Santayana characterized as manifesting a new indeterminacy of time and form. Still, in rebelling against nineteenth-century academicism, the impressionist painters did launch an innovation of style and time sense—a momentary timelessness in the suspension of finite duration—which implicitly challenged the notion of a definite historical time. Thus impressionism revealed a new indifference of the artist towards history through the depiction of the atemporality of human experience.

Perhaps Debussy renders this atemporal quality most clearly. His music is marked by a sense of suspension in time, nostalgic sentiment and dreamlike images. Timelessness characterizes the haunting mood and subjective imagery of his opera, Pelléas and Mélisande, in which neither past nor future has any reality. Similarly, his tone poem The Afternoon of a Faun seems to evoke an indefinite, lingering moment. By focusing on the "presentness" or immediacy of all experience, impressionism minimized concern with historical developments and objectives, and avoided social criticism or involvement in political and moral ideals. It differs in this respect from the preceding romanticism and especially from the later *art engagé* of socialism. By concerning itself with the artist's perception of his subject rather than with the subject itself, the impressionist movement contributed to the relativistic currents of modern culture and their ahistorical consequences, namely the confinement of the individual within his contemporary age, his subjective world, and himself.

But if impressionist art is atemporal and subjective, it is certaintly not anti-transcendent, in that it does not express the inherent untranscendability of man's condition; nor does it exemplify the individual's radical alienation from the world and from his own nature, or the inescapable force of guilt, suffering and despair. Impressionism had little of the sense of tragedy and of man's isolation in the universe that characterizes later painting and literature. It did not emphasize the individual's aloneness that was suggested in some of the contemporary pre-symbolist poets like Baudelaire and Rimbaud, in Nietzsche and the nihilistic undercurrent in philosophy, or in the muffled rumbling of a "transvaluation of values."

After 1870, colonial expansion confronted European society with a new challenge to its values and its confidence in its own history at the very moment when its world influence reached a climax. The new wave of imperialism brought Europe into more direct and intensive contact with the non-Western world, particularly with high Asian civilizations and primitive cultures. The greatest popular response to colonialism came from Britain, in Kiplingesque literature and Royal Academy paintings depicting acts of valor in exotic settings. The popular arts reflected self-confidence in the West's superiority over all other civilizations, as well as the glamor of imperialist pageantry, and the romantic thrill of the discovery of new worlds.

Imperialism and colonialism revived historical sentiments by enhancing the role of patriotic values and national traditions. By implicitly comparing the achievements of European nations with those of more primitive societies, writers such as Kipling drew

attention to the historical progress of the West. Imperialist literature thus reinforced historical traditions and the new nationalist
conservatism, and implied a redemptive historical goal in the new
world significance of the nation-state. Participation in imperial
development gave new self-transcending meaning to the old nationalist sentiment, since the future of the empire was regarded as
virtually "eternal."

But there was another artistic response to the rediscovery of
primitive societies, which expressed a quite different view of the
balance between advanced civilizations and tribal cultures. Limited in appeal to small *avant-garde* groups, this second reaction to
the non-Western world nonetheless revealed significant undertones
within Western consciousness. In Conrad's novels, the "native"
setting serves as the stage on which to challenge Western ideals
and presumptions. The art movement launched, and best exemplified, by Gauguin expounded an even more radical theme: the
glorification of primitive life and the repudiation of the values of
civilization.

The return-to-nature theme, evoking a Rousseau-like romanticism, constituted the prevalent aesthetic tradition of mid-nine-
teenth-century art. The primitivism of Gauguin, however, involved
a significantly different interpretation of the theme from that of
the romantics and of the impressionists. For in Gauguin's canvases of Tahitian life, there is not only a revolutionary use of
colors and forms, but a new expression of alienation. Ganguin was
not using primitivism as a critique of specific abuses or injustices
in Western civilization as Tacitus had used the Germanic tribes or
as the intellectuals of the Enlightenment, from Montesquieu and
Diderot to Rousseau, had used the essentially fictitious noble
savage. For the art of Gauguin was not intended as a form of
social satire; it was not an inverted expression of hope in progress
or support for political reform. It was an attack, not on specific
social ills but on civilization itself. In Gauguin's interpretation
of the encounter between civilized and primitive man it is
the latter who emerges as superior—superior in the sense of
an existence closer to man's natural feelings and instincts, and
therefore more authentically human. The childlike simplicity and

naturalness of unspoiled peoples were a repudiation of the values of civilization. Thus did the artist express, in a manner quite different from sentimental landscapes hanging in London drawing rooms, his estrangement from European society, and his indifference to its historical prospects.

With the primitivism of Henri Rousseau, the theme of escape from reality went even further into a dream world of exotic fantasies and symbols, leading straight into the unconscious, irrational realm of Freud or Jung. Limited as his art was in its appeal, it remains expressive, in the historian's view, of certain undercurrents of Western sensibility which had a powerful impact upon the next generation. The rejection of Western aesthetic tradition leaves a style of art that is essentially, if not yet consciously, ahistorical. No wonder the *fauves* seemed shocking to the critics of their day, and artists suffered an isolation from society quite in contrast with their predecessors of the Renaissance or the eighteenth century. The *avant garde* became more clearly cut off as its sense of the futility of civilization and of the irrationality of life contrasted with the common-sense view of Western culture and historical experience still prevalent in mass tastes and reflected in popular arts.

Meanwhile a few literary figures accentuated the strangeness of the new currents by serving as sensitive indicators of tremors deep inside the psychic strata of their society. Some poets functioned unwittingly as prophets of historical despair by proclaiming the inherent "brokenness" and suffering of human existence. Baudelaire, for example, spent much of his life in self-inflicted torment, leaving a single major work, *The Flowers of Evil.* It remains a landmark in the passion for the morbid and the beauty of ugliness. It exhibits the mystic intensity of life that escapes the gentility of more polite arts. In psychological terms, it is the anality of Baudelaire's imagery that is revealing of the intense sensuality and id-character of his vision. Rimbaud quit writing poetry after his celebrated quarrel with Verlaine in his twentieth year. By then, his most influential work, *Le Bateau ivre*, had already exhibited iconoclastic qualities of mystic, irrational dreams in a world of often despondent fantasies. In a few of his pages is suggested the hellish view of life so prevalent in the arts of our day. As for Verlaine, his alternating moods of despairing self-hatred and fervent religious symbolism, of Christian triumph and degradation, accentuate the prophetic insight of the symbolists' pre-existentialist theme, namely the accursedness of man's solitary being.

The quality most generally attributed to these poets was decadence. From a twentieth-century perspective, they were wrestling with violent Dionysian impulses deep in the psyche. We can find in them a prophetic current of radical subjectivism and a bitter rejection of the optimism of progress. Their themes of irrationality, sensuality and the isolation of the individual in his subjective world suggest a new view of man and a new poetic myth of the human condition; or rather, they convert an old view into a new fear. By their repudiation of superficial hope in human perfectibility, the early symbolists implicitly and explicitly denied the notion of transcendent meaningfulness in history, or of a redemptive historical goal to the individual's life.

The third step, after primitivism and decadence, towards the anti-historical disillusionment of the twentieth century, was the view of human nature as inherently aggressive. Such a view gained currency with the impact of Darwin. In Nietzsche, we will see the glorification of the virile man of prey who stalks the human jungle. In Freud, nature appears as eroticism and death. The "primitive" organic impulses in the human psyche loom as an unchangeably violent force, reducing all utopian dreams and historical ideals to childish delusions. In the "decadence" of twentieth-century arts nothing is left but skepticism of man's hope for some transcendent historical state. No substance remains here to any of man's illusions of the future.

But generally these pessimistic views belong to a later day. In the prewar years, the conception of man and nature presented in the arts—in music, and more directly in painting and literature— had not yet crystallized into a sweeping historical force. Despite occasional expressions of despair in the human condition, the intimation of historical futility had not yet become the dominant theme of prevailing aesthetic forms. Thereby the prewar arts showed the great gulf which separated them from postwar expressions of alienation. They were still far removed from the bitterness of an expressionist painter like Beckmann or of the Picasso of *Guernica*, and from the disarming moral doubts and existential frustrations of writers like Gide, Mann and Eliot. It may be said of prewar culture that despite the swelling current of pessimism and ahistorical outlook evident by the turn of the century, it still left room for a romanticization of the past, as in Rodin's heroic portrayal of the "Burghers of Calais," and for the counterpoint of hope in the future. The warning signs of a different age, however, were already in evidence.

Neither the arts nor the physical sciences of the prewar period directly precipitated the fall of transcendent historicity, though some of their characteristics undoubtedly contributed to its increasing momentum. For the mathematical sciences, perhaps their new theories had become too recondite, since the easier popularizations of eighteenth-century cosmology, to engage immediately the passionate involvement of large numbers of people, even among the intelligentsia. It remained for another field of science to exercise a direct impact on social philosophies at both the intellectual and popular levels. Philosophical doubt and historical pessimism were enhanced by the rise of indeterminacy and relativism, by the subjectivity of observations and the limitations of rational knowledge. But they did not depend on these currents, and they were certainly not new in the nineteenth century. It was historical experience itself that effected the greatest alteration in attitudes towards history. Insofar as science contributed indirectly —which it conspicuously did—its main impact was made by the branch that had the most relevance to historical consciousness because it provided a new evolutionary view of life.

3. Darwinism: The Untranscendability of the Human Condition

It was in 1859 that Charles Darwin published the *Origin of Species*, and biological evolutionism was launched on a new public career. Darwinism was to become by far the most widespread and popular scientific notion of the late nineteenth century. The subse-

quent application of evolution to social attitudes and political
values is so well known that it is one of the platitudes of intellectual history. The fact that despite sharp opposition, social Darwinism fitted readily into the discussions of its time is evidence that it
fell upon ground prepared by the very consciousness of historical
development that had been so much in fashion. Biological evolutionism is essentially an historicist view of nature, compatible with
the linear sense of time that had become well established in Western historical thought. Biology seemed to offer the most convincing and detailed scientific empirical confirmation of the historical-
ness of things.

The idea of biological evolution had long been in the air,
though hitherto only as one of several speculative theories devoid
of verification. Well before Charles Darwin, Goethe and Lamarck,
not to mention Buffon or Charles' own grandfather, Erasmus
Darwin, had held an evolutionary view of organic nature. What
was new with Darwin, besides the mountain of specific evidence
he amassed of the behavior of mammals and lower varieties of life,
was his provision of a central, unifying explanation for two of the
most remarkable characteristics of organic life. He sought a common answer for the presence of an enormous diversity of species
on one hand, and on the other for the similarity of many organic
functions and the essential unity of the life process in all organic
forms. To account for these two observations, Darwin proposed a
categorization of species, linked to a common source in a continuing evolutionary chain. The explanation of this linkage and the
key to the structure of Darwin's great study, was the notion that
species evolve because successive organisms tend to adjust themselves with increasing fitness to their environment through a process of selective biological adaptation. The history of organic
life arises as the result of natural selection, manifest in the
evolving capacities of various organisms to respond to all the
pressures around them, for example to find food, escape their
enemies and adjust to changing conditions of climate. Evolution
is also a consequence of sexual selection shown in the competitive ability to secure mates and to participate in the reproductive
process through which the advantages in the species are retained.

In different but mutually complementary ways, then, this natural selection spelled out one axial principle familiar to every reader: the survival of the fittest.

We need not repeat how this idea suited the existing social forces of late nineteenth-century Europe. Transferred from the field of biological organisms and applied to that of social institutions, the concept of evolution through the survival of the fittest could readily be used as a scientific justification of capitalist competition. Here it is the fittest individual competitor who comes out on top. But the principle seemed equally to justify socialist claims and predictions, such as the survival of the fittest class, the actual producer of wealth, and Marx could argue that Darwin seemed to support his view that it is the material needs of the human organism and its adaptation to the social circumstances of survival that determine actions and conscious behavior. Then, of course, social Darwinism could be enlisted to rationalize nationalism and aggressive expansion as the forms of survival of the fittest state.

On one hand, Darwinism lent itself to the doctrines of progress and the various confident expectations that had characterized earlier nineteenth-century thought, by proclaiming the continuing adaptability of each species. On the other hand, it destroyed the foundation for the faith in history as transcendence. While it corroborated the view of progress at the level of the evolution of biological efficiency and the greater refinement of more complex organs, it undermined the purpose of progress in man's search for release from the present human condition. But as long as Darwin's concept of cumulative adaptation to the environment left open the possibility of inheriting culturally acquired characteristics, it still left some purpose in our cultivating new forms of social behavior. As a social animal, man could improve the means of cooperation that are part of his evolutionary development. He could progress in his moral sense which, to Darwin, is also a consequence of the evolutionary process. Huxley argues that in civilization, the practice of what is "ethically best," or goodness and virtue, must replace ruthless self-assertion; human intelligence must contravene the cosmic struggle for existence. According to Spencer, who invented the phrase "survival of the fittest" and popularized the application of Darwinism to society, competitive struggle among individuals would ultimately give way to increasing cooperation, and war would give way to peace.

With the claim of the non-inheritability of acquired characteristics, even this idea of historical purpose seemed to be undermined. For what implicitly remains here is the impermeability of man's fundamental nature—which is seen as biologically determined—to historical and cultural currents. What we pass on in the basic structure of the psyche is the organism, which is presocial, and its drives, which are amoral. No social conditioning, according to later Darwinists, will result in our transmitting to our descendants less aggressive impulses. Nor can a culture uproot those impulses inherent in man's organic being. In fact, aggressiveness becomes necessary to the realization of material progress. Thus in the end, the biological concept of organic perfectibility constitutes a monument to man's moral disillusionment of achieving a redemptive state free of competitive hostilities.

Darwin himself was quite aware of the pessimistic implications of his work in the realm of human values and ethical considerations, to which it had not been directed but which could not long remain sealed to its conclusions. He fluctuated between the optimism implied in *The Descent of Man* and stated in the last chapter of the *Origin of Species,* and the pessimism of his private correspondence. It is not coincidental that Darwin's conclusion about nature paralleled Hobbes' view of the perpetual state of war, nor that Darwin conceded his debt to Malthus' pessimistic assertion about the tendency to a scarcity of food and the competitive struggle for life, which inevitably impose suffering on all but the select few. Darwinians saw nature as a state of war in which one species vies with another by preying upon it, and in which those who share the same needs or occupy the same biological station struggle to the death for the same limited resources and for the favor of mates. Meliorism, yes, but only in the machinery of life, not in any future overcoming of selfishness, conflict and war, nor in the establishment of a harmonious social order rooted in benevolence. To be sure, Darwin writes of the rise of moral consciousness and the formation of conscience as a consequence of man's social instincts and of the force of natural selection. But must one not conclude from his own work that since transcendence of the human condition is precluded by our animal nature, evolution can never repeal the law of struggle and suffering upon which it rests? Then history can only grind on, honing more finely the competitive tools of existence yet leaving unchanged the aggressiveness that is latent even in individual moral action.

Who is not acquainted with the bitter controversy that pitted Darwin and his defenders in the scientific community, Thomas Huxley and Herbert Spencer, against influential voices in the Christian churches, and especially against fundamentalists? The famed debate between Bishop Wilberforce and Huxley on whether man was descended from the monkeys—something Darwin, of course, had not claimed—was another round in the long conflict between churchmen and scientists. It is an apt cliché to say that where Copernicus had removed man's earth from the center of the universe, Darwin now removed man from his unique place in creation. But the uncompromisable difference lies neither here nor in the fundamentalists' insistence on the literal truth of Genesis. The real difficulty which liberal Christians could not brush aside, though perhaps few were aware of the problem, was in their differing views on the moral function of man.

Ironically, social Darwinism seemed compatible with the orthodox view of human nature inherently given over to lust and man's predaceousness. Both conservative Christianity and social Darwinism suggest a common unromantic view of history due to the fact that each sees man's life on earth bound by his lower instincts, his egotistic and aggressive impulses. But where Christianity calls upon the individual to attempt the moral restraint of his baser urges, most social Darwinists claimed that because these instincts are in accord with nature, they are to be welcomed and cultivated, whether at the individual or herd level. Spencer's hope of humanity achieving a morally improved and more peaceful world reveals itself as a liberal ideal incongruously grafted upon his Darwinian base. Most social Darwinists took the perpetuation of conflict for granted, certainly for the foreseeable future. Where

Christian conservatives at least had a transcendent refuge outside the historical arena, social Darwinists had none.

In sum, despite Darwin's recognition of the phenomenon of
conscience, the preeminent implication of popular Darwinism remained that man's biological impulses preclude a future state in
which he would overcome his animal behavior. Notwithstanding
Darwin's notion that human sympathy arises from man's social
needs and fulfills our gregarious nature, the view of most social
Darwinists was that our competitive instincts impede history from
ever progressing into a higher spiritual realm of moral consciousness. There is no use dreaming of man freed from the primitive
organic responses that tie us to the lower forms of life from which,
Darwin pointed out, we have emerged, and whose basic imprint
we shall always bear. While Darwinians and the believers in original sin understood the inherent hardness of human life in radically different ways, they converged unconsciously in their views
on its psychological and cultural consequences: the untranscendability through history of the competitive nature of society. Here
lay the basic conflict with liberal Christianity and its social application of charity, as it did, incidentally, with all other forms of
moral-historical faith—even those which, like Marxism, thought
they had found scientific support for their utopia in the principle
of natural selection.

Looking back over the natural sciences and arts of the
prewar era, we see a growing number of deutopianizing and dehistoricizing cultural forces. The period has been called appropriately, "the age of materialism." Idealism declined, and political
movements became more aggressive. Intellectual expressions were
but the reflections of powerful factors of alienation, resulting in
part from the mass currents of the second industrial revolution.
The unromantic hardness found in the undertow of intellectual
and artistic life had the effect of accumulating anxieties. But we
may wonder about the presumed interrelations between intellectual tendencies and mass movements, or between currents in the
arts and the sciences. Evolutionism, primitivism, indeterminacy—
these ideas have their autonomous roots in their respective areas
of human knowledge and experience. It would be rash to suppose

some "morphology of culture," and to seek, in the manner of Spengler, a cultural unity between the mathematical physics of Maxwell and the aesthetic impulses of Van Gogh. But then why do the disillusioning consequences of social Darwinism, for example, seem to reenforce the psychological effects of a principle in physics concerning an apparently unwinding universe? Why do they both converge in undermining the redemptive aspirations of man? The answer is, because they were fitted to a detranscendentalized view of Being and Becoming. Not only had our world perspective been secularized, but the substitute ideals of self-transcendence had largely failed.

When the sense of disillusionment arose among certain elites, it induced a search for corroborative ideas from other realms of thought. Scientific principles were then distorted to serve normative ends, as Darwinism was popularly used to justify individual competition. Forms of art that in an earlier day might well have been ignored or dismissed as personal aberrations, acquired disciples and thereby attained a new historical significance. In other words the common denominator of the new intellectual currents was simply the fact that they were all used to orchestrate a particular theme. It was the perspective itself that bestowed the appearance of coherence on disparate elements and unrelated theories. The tendency to anxiety arose not from the objective principles of science or from the aesthetic objectives of art, but from our ways of understanding and relating them in the changing outlook of historical experience and hopes. For the central issue, as always, was man's changing conception of himself and of the human condition. In Germany, upon the pessimism of Schopenhauer's dynamic blind will, Nietzsche imagined the realm of solitary supermen who laughingly peer down into the abyss.

4. *Nietzsche: Eternity and the Finality of Death*

Nietzsche's philosophy is a declamation to man's self-transcendence through his impulse to life. But we must pause to consider it in some detail because it presents or reflects many of the attitudes that characterized the growing despair of our conventionalized historical hopes and of their supposedly immortalizing function. In Nietzsche's violent iconoclasm and his denunciation of humanitarian ideals and utopian aspirations to equality and brotherhood, there is the expression of the growing countercurrents to the transcendent historical vision of a Condorcet, a Hegel or a Marx.

For Nietzsche, the exercise of creative power expresses man's need to dominate himself and the world. Cultivation of the nonintellectual energy of individual will becomes, for the one capable of it, the only saving moral quality. An aggressive self-assertiveness and the rejection of humanitarian concern for others reverse the Christian ethical ideals of self-sacrifice and meekness. It is the irrepressible urge to transcend the present into a new heroic age that sets apart, for Nietzsche, the individual hero, or superman, from the mass. In his godless world, this urge can only be founded on the religious pursuit of individual dominance, and hence on the consciously hard use of supposedly lesser men—those marked by their herd temperament—to serve one's own noble desires. Against what he regarded as the misplaced optimism of rationalist and romantic sentimentalists proclaiming the brotherhood of all men, Nietzsche glorified the natural impulses of the Dionysian personality who does not stultify his life energy through rational, social or moral restraints. While the hero must discipline himself to privation and to the iron control of his will, he must also respond freely to what Freud subsequently characterized as the impulses of the id, the healthy aggressive and voluptuous drives that constitute the vitality of life. For Nietzsche, the object of man's vital impulses remained the exhilarating sense of mastery over others and oneself. The mark of the superman is his supreme affirmation of life per se, not as existence but as power and creation. Like earlier romantics, Nietzsche proclaimed a return to nature. But where they had seen the natural order as ultimately benevolent, he saw it characterized by competitive violence and individual solitude that reveal the meaning of life only in the absoluteness of death.

The achievement of fulfillment and transcendence in the inspiration of creative passion was to be reserved to the select few, the heroic aristocracy of supermen who stand beyond good and evil to the degree that they are able to fashion their own world and their own meaning, since none exist elsewhere. The great enemy becomes Judeo-Christian morality with its emphasis on humility, charity and selfless love. Taking particular pride in the role of Antichrist, Nietzsche castigated the slave morality of Christianity, and its praise of the meek over the proud. Such an ethic, he argued, was a perversion of the natural order in which the competitive struggle prevailed and produced the dominance of the superior will.

Despite its initial appearance, this view was not Darwinian. Not the biological process of nature, but will and spartan asceticism would produce the superman of the future. For the hero appears first in the transcending imagination of those of born aristocratic temperament. Still, Nietzsche's faith in the emergence of a European race of neo-Renaissance men moved by aesthetic passions, fitted a competitive world, marked by the struggle of individuals to dominate. Thus he saw the morality of humility—which in Christian teaching accompanied the iron determination of a St. Paul and the unromantic theodicy of an Augustine—as a trick played by the mass of the weak to dupe the few men of strength out of their heroic vigor, which must constitute a moral law to itself.

Nietzsche's aversion to the doctrine of selfless charity and the ideal of moral egalitarianism extended from religion to the whole secular range of humanitarian ideals inspired by Judeo-Christian moral teaching. It applied to those secuarlized values inspired by the revolutionary and egalitarian implications of the brotherhood of man and the moral worth of each soul. He detested liberal politics and democratic aspirations, and for the same reason he despised the more radical egalitarianism of socialist thought, though his predisposition to violence did not appear alien to socialist revolutionism as exemplified by Sorel. But for the latter, elitism served a collective ideal. In Nietzsche on the contrary, it fitted a radical individualism. As for communism, Marx's ultimate moral objective—"from each according to his ability, to each according to his needs"—expressed the humani-

tarian faith and fellow-feeling which stood at the opposite pole to
Nietzsche's ideal of the isolation of the individual.

To achieve the race of supermen and the new aristocratic
morality, Nietzsche advanced an ethic of ruthless egotism and
power. The life-rejecting repression of the vital impulses of the
strong ego demanded by the priest, perhaps necessary to the control of the herd, would be exchanged for the life-affirming and
healthy will to power of the soldier-aristocrat. The weakness and
"uncleanness" of the sick was Nietzsche's pet aversion. But the
ethic of health and virility, we shall see, meant also the morality
of war and death.

Despite the indifference or hostility which first greeted Nietzsche's anti-Christian values, his pathomanic vision fitted the aggressive and militarist currents of his day better than genteel society cared to admit. Against the official Christian ideals affected by
the officer class and the occasional sentimentality still prevalent in
nationalism, the warrior ethic of Nietzsche bespoke the new hardness and militarization of prewar European life. Much as Nietzsche despised the ideal of the nation espoused by the military
class, his morality suggested the psychology of heroic attack that
characterized the mentality of young French and German officers.
Perhaps that is one reason why at the turn of the century he
achieved a *succès de scandale* and attracted disproportionate attention.

In any case, Nietzsche's proclamation of aggression and of
the vitality of a-rational life impulses was in tune with the cultural
undercurrents evidenced by the social philosophies of some of his
contemporaries. Sorel glorified the role of violence, and Bergson
looked to the primacy of prerational life forces, but with an important difference. While Bergson reflected in the early phase of
his vitalist philosophy a partly Nietzschean conception of the intuitive urge to life, which he translated into his famous idea of the
élan vital, his later thought moved towards an un-Nietzschean
humanitarianism and benevolence. Indeed, Bergson's conception
of some great men's transcendent fellow-feeling for mankind as a
whole, expressed in the idea of the unlimited "open society,"
stands in sharp contrast to Nietzsche's egocentrism. To Nietzsche,

the ideal of mankind is opposed to the ideal of the superman. For the author of *Thus Spake Zarathustra*, hardness is the first requirement of creative passion, and heroic self-fulfillment becomes possible only through a hard-hearted pursuit of individualistic objectives:

> And if your hardness will not glance and cut and chip to pieces, how can ye one day—create with me? . . . . This new table, O my brethren, I put over You: Become hard![1]

To attain this creative power, the higher man must discipline himself to develop toughness of will by welcoming pain, and ruthlessly using his inferiors to achieve his own heroic purpose. Only by scorning the herd notion of consideration for his weaker neighbor can man surpass himself. In an age when military life was becoming less glamorous due to the new technology of mass war, Nietzsche revived the idea of the valor of aristocratic antagonists. He yearned for the combat of heroes in which the individual is first of all a proud fighter, and peace is merely the prelude to battle.

This perspective is similar to Gabriele d'Annunzio's later glorification of war, epitomized in the chivalric code of the aviator-knight, and akin to that of the "hard romantics" of the political right, during the interwar years. Like Nietzsche, they sought in the comradeship of arms a moral ideal and an exhilaration which destroys, supposedly in order to recreate. For Nietzsche, the result was a steely self-control, single-mindedly turned to the deification of man, or rather of the heroic elect. For each superman must be above all the creator of his own personality.

Nietzsche's concept of a race of heroes carried individualism to its extreme limit in the glorification of the self-centered ego, seeking transcendence within itself. It was not a coincidence that Nietzsche was compulsively driven to break with virtually all his one-time companions, until he succeeded in isolating himself in his own thought and illusory reality. In his early years, he was close to Richard Wagner, whose "Ring" cycle seemed to embody the qualities of the Nietzschean superman. Sigmund and Siegfried are examples of the Germanic *Held*, which contrasts ironically with

Nietzsche's love of Mediterranean clarity and scorn of German
culture. Brünnhilde and Isolde, are supreme expressions of passionate death as the essence of transcendence, and Valhalla appears as the incarnation of a pagan "teutonic" creed of power and
will. But for all that, Wagner's perspective was too optimistic for
Nietzsche, too ready to gloss over the hollowness of things with
pompous symbols which appealed to the sentimentality of the
herd. Nietzsche's superman was a person of aesthetic refinement,
not of vulgar, bombastic tastes; it is a popular misconception to
think of his hero as a loutish caveman, or of the Dionysiac personality as one given to debauchery. As for Wagner, his run-of-the-
mill character proved itself, in Nietzsche's estimation, by the fact
that he eventually deserted the "hard" warrior ethic of the
Nibelungen cycle in favor of the "soft" Christianity of Parsifal.
So the composer and the philosopher parted in bitterness, and
Nietzsche moved closer to the solitude of his extreme individualism.

In a complementary vein, Nietzsche's hatred of all collective
entities that might limit the superior individual is nowhere better
demonstrated than in his detestation of modern nationalism. He
attacked the state, so popular in nineteenth-century Germany, in
language worthy of the anarchist Proudhon—though of course for
the French revolutionary socialist, the abolition of capitalist
power would lead to a free society of equals, not to the aggressive
individualism of a Hobbesian state of nature. For Nietzsche, the
superman stood above the nation and the law precisely because he
was beyond the ordinary conceptions of justice and ethics. The
crux of Nietzsche's philosophy of the Antichrist is that each man
stands alone, and must aesthetically fashion his own world, or else
accept the justified status of slave imposed by a stronger will.

Nietzsche's conception of the superman's transcendence involved an ambivalent attitude towards history, and an ambivalence in his expectations of the future. Despite Nietzsche's claim
that an historical sense is essential to good philosophy, his repeated anachronisms sometimes make him one of the most ahistorical of thinkers. He revolted against academic dicipline, and
dismissed the concern with historical knowledge in the formal

sense, along with all the other stifling conformities and routines of ordinary life. He bitterly criticized what he called the malady of history, or the misuse of the past. He attacked particularly the historical emphasis in the education of German youth and the danger of a people being overwhelmed by its memories until it perishes on the "rock" of "history."[2]

Nietzsche's conviction that little of worth had been said before him—or at least not since the time of Goethe—diminished his interest in the past, except in an ahistorical throwback to early Hellenic civilization. The atavistic reversion to a misinterpreted historical era is a typical repudiation of cumulative historical consciousness. Perhaps Nietzsche's anti-historicist bias against pedantic scholars had been reenforced by many nineteenth-century patriotic historians, whose moral object frequently was the glorification of the nation-state. On the whole, modern history seemed to Nietzsche a sordid record of the growth of slave morality into sickly egalitarianism and the democratic ideology of freedom for the mass. The French, who in many ways stood at the root of Western culture and still represented much that was best for a "good European" civilization, had degenerated lamentably since the seventeenth century. The Germans most of all had deteriorated into decadent placidity and disgusting self-satisfaction. That was why they had developed the worst political values and cultivated the most abject aesthetic tastes, as exemplified by the vulgarity of the Wagnerian rites at Bayreuth. In short, Nietzsche felt that the slavish study of history showed only the spread of false values and the loss of creative vigor and the joy of living. It threatened to impose the dead past upon the present.

But Nietzsche's contempt for traditional history disguised his own radically historicist perspective. He distinguished between the use and abuse of history, and stated that "man can only become man by first suppressing [the] unhistorical element in his thoughts. . . ." Criticizing "super-historical" men who "see no salvation in evolution [and] for whom the world is complete and fulfills its aim in every single moment," Nietzsche praises those "historical men" whose vision of the past turns them towards the future. His answer to the pedestrian misuse of history, and to the

abuse of historical memory as an escape from creative action, was
to "study history as a means to life."³ Every man and every
nation, he argued, needs a knowledge of the past, not for the sake
of knowing but for the sake of living subject to his will.⁴

In Nietzsche's view, the purpose of life must be realized in a
worldly, historical objective. Any supra-human goal or ahistorical
vision was forcefully repudiated in his affirmation of the death of
God and his deification of man. Nietzsche's sense of history was
based on the expectation that the new morality of the noble man
would be achieved within historical time:

> I love those who do not first seek a reason beyond the stars
> for going down and being sacrifices, but sacrifice themselves
> to the earth, that the earth of the Superman may hereafter
> arrive.⁵

The divine creative function of man was to remake himself
and thereby remake his secular historical world. This conception
had to be fitted into Nietzsche's doctrine of rebirth, or of eternal
recurrence, which required an ultimately cyclical sense of time at
the cosmic level. Yet within those cosmic cycles, there existed for
Nietzsche a meaningful linearity of time in the achievement of the
"positive," life-affirming ideal of man's vitality. Transcendent self-
realization must be located within the man-god.

In one sense, then, Nietzsche's view of the historical future
was optimistic and even utopian. It is the sense of holding the
future in himself that impels the superman to create. Yet withal,
there remained a deeply pessimistic note. It was not merely that
mankind disappointed or ignored Nietzsche, nor that the life of
the hero was hard and required grim determination. The hardness
of Nietzsche's philosophy was, above all, the self-enclosedness of
the free individual within his own ego. That is why the superman
had to become god in order to achieve transcendence: he had to
free the self of all limits. But such a liberation through aesthetic
power, which at best was reserved to the few, meant by its very
nature the destruction of the self. The ego cannot free itself
from all limits without thereby removing its defining attributes,
and annihilating its identity. Thus tranfiguration is equated with

mortality. "I have spoken my word, I am shattered upon my word: thus willeth mine eternal fate—as an herald I perish!"[6]

In Nietzsche, we see the most radical affirmation that the only purpose of life is self-transcendence—the individual's passionate going beyond himself. For Nietzsche, the heroic man makes his life meaningful, not for some ulterior purpose but for itself, in the consciousness of death and the absence of salvation. The "ring of the return" and the transcendent cycles of infinite recurrence express this fervent longing for eternity. Yet there is a critical dilemma in Nietzschean individualism: death is the key to self-transcendence, but the door it unlocks opens on the great void.

Nietzsche's universe is inherently meaningless; there is no ultimate value outside the self, either in the stars or in humanity. No absolute objective exists, neither in the secular state that he despised nor in the perfectibility of mankind, which he scorned. Neither heaven nor earth can provide the individual with a redemptive purpose, for that can arise only from his own creative will, and is limited to his own finite ego. Beyond this is nothingness. Thus Nietzsche's conception of self-transcendence is radically different from conceptions which had been traditionally cast in either religious or worldly frames of meaning, or in an historical perspective of human destiny.

The superman rises above himself by constantly reaching beyond his being at one moment, and exceeding himself in the future. Thereby he converts petty, ignoble selfishness into the noble egoism of creativity. Yet we must ask if in his passionate affirmation of transcendence as the ultimate principle of life, Nietzsche had not in effect denatured the eternity for which he longs or given it a radically different meaning that reduces immortality to ashes. How meaningful is an affirmation of life that has no ultimate, universal object, either secular or religious? The passionate yearning for eternal return does not overcome mortality; for the eternal here is but the ever-recurrent cycle of life and death, and thus never goes beyond them.

> I come again . . . —*not* to a new life, or to a
> better life, or to a similar life—

> I come again eternally to this self-same life,
> in greatest things and in least, that I may
> teach again the Eternal Recurrence of all
> things.[7]

Beneath the optimism of the historical triumph of the race of heroes lies the engulfing abyss of a life trapped in its own solitude and egocentricity. Nietzsche's overpowering longing for "deep, profound Eternity" is in effect but a death wish, expressed in the will to choose the right moment for dying. Only suicide remains as a consolation.

Nietzsche's raising of the mortal ego to the role of man-god means the isolation of both god and man in the finality of the self, unrelieved by the Faustian vision of universal historical purpose and right. Loosed from any frame of meaning *beyond* life and death, Nietzschean transcendence is characterized by its subjectivism and eternal finiteness. But does the eternal repetition of the finite constitute the achievement of the infinite? Does the eternal recurrence of death constitute immortality? Despite the defiant proclamation of a triumphant future, history becomes in effect an endless reenactment of the same human drama, without redeeming value or purpose.

Nietzsche had recalled attention to a long-neglected yet powerful element in human experience, namely that each free individual is alone, and ultimately remains an island. In doing so, he exposed the inadequacy of more optimistic historical solutions to the problem of transcendence. By forcing us to see the self-contradiction in our search for a transcendent meaning within a secular finite reality, such as the state, Nietzsche pointed to the great fallacy of our redemptive historicity. To live each moment as though it were eternity and each act a reenactment in an infinite cycle may involve a strange contradiction, but no more so than to eternalize a finite historical objective, whether it be democracy, an empire or mankind.

Others besides Nietzsche presented a nihilistic view of man, lost in the futility of the world and confronted with the emptiness in which he was ever falling. Before Nietzsche's time, Kierkegaard had emphasized even further the anguish of Being, and rejected with even greater vehemence than Nietzsche the easy cure of rational historical expectations. But at least he found an ultimate refuge in a hard, demanding faith. From the North were to come still other voices of anxiety: Ibsen, Strindberg, and later the films of Carl Dreyer and Ingmar Bergman. From Russia, came Dostoevsky's insight into the tormented psyche, struggling against the absurdity and purposelessness of life, or yielding to the suicidal impulse. Then in Germany, Heidegger was to come with his philosophy of *Sorge*, or "care," in consciously facing up, every moment, to the finality of death.

As certain historical goals had been approached during the nineteenth century—for example national unification of Italy and of Germany—the detranscendentalization of an ideal ostensibly serving a transcendent function could no longer be disguised. Gradually, the dim intimation of its self-contradiction, vaguely felt rather than realized, spread to the mass level. As other historical goals remained conspicuously distant, such as the achievement of social justice in industrial society, the failure to come significantly nearer to the transcendent objective produced disillusionment. It was history itself that defeated the historicist faith. Unrewarded hopes that might have had little social consequence in a non-secular or ahistorical frame, proved dismaying, just because the expectation of redemption had been largely historicized. The nineteenth century's historical ideals turned out to be largely self-defeating. Where they were substantially achieved, their success made them obsolete and psychologically useless: what purpose was there in sacrificing oneself for the establishment of the republican ideal once the republic had been instituted—and proven itself to be far from ideal? In Aulard's famous phrase, "*Que la République était belle sous l'Empire!*" The consequence of the achievement of the anticipated goals that had been functioning as transcendent historical values left a great moral vacuum. The ensuing letdown has been experienced by many nations. The grave problem for a society then becomes the question of whether it is in a position to create for itself some new version of its manifest destiny. But in late nineteenth-century Europe, many objectives that had served, perhaps for the better part of the century, as unifying ideal forces and an inspiration to both political conduct and personal values, ceased to have relevance. They could not be easily replaced. A society which had become geared psychologically to their service was left with a hollow and useless vision of self-transcendence by the very success of history.

In some cases, long-standing historical expectations had conspicuously failed of achievement. Thereby their status as a mystique supposedly incarnate in the historical process was jeopardized. The claims of rational or romantic progress towards a harmonious and just order appeared increasingly naïve as the age of *Realpolitik* wore on and as class hostilities, though changed in form, remained dramatically real in practice. The increasing concentration of industry and industrial power was met by large-scale workers' strikes in France and the United States, and the new mystique of the proletariat's revolutionary general strike.

Thus whatever "history" might have won on one front, it seemed to lose on another. The rise of new states which had fulfilled ardent national hopes in Central Europe brought with it new political problems and diplomatic tensions, and a readjustment of the power balance that engendered a profound sense of general insecurity in the pre-war situation. Imperialism no doubt provided relief from the maddening boredom of regimentation, intensified by the second wave of industrialization. But the sense of importance and excitement furnished by the sagas of colonial explorers, regimental colors and the reports of spectacular ceremonies was accompanied by growing anxieties. They were exemplified by the crisis of Fashoda, Mafeking, Tangiers, Agadir and others, not to mention the unresolved problems of Eastern Europe and the concern over the encirclement of Germany or, for others, over German power and ambitions. We have seen that if colonialism in the short run encouraged believers in progress by confirming the spread of "superior" Western civilization over the whole world, in the long run it left non-believers with new uncertainty. They were confronted with the patterns of culture and the values of other peoples, and sometimes came away with a sense of historical relativism and self-doubt.

It was war itself that dealt the *coup de grâce* to the transcendent historical vision and its redemptive hopes. After a century of comparative peace only sporadically interrupted, now by a short war in far-off Crimea, now by local wars in Bohemia, Eastern France or remote South Africa, the tragedy of 1914 shattered the historicist faith that man was making himself and his society increasingly rational, harmonious and moral. A century of faith in the progressive order of civilization ended in the most catastrophic loss of life since the Thirty Years' War, and the most devastating conflict modern European states had yet inflicted upon themselves. If it was true that human passions had, in a sense, failed history through man's inability to prevent the disaster, it was equally true that history had thereby failed man as a redeeming goal. To the extent that our expectations had become historicized, the collapse of historical consciousness as a moral force had undermined the possibility of redemption and the transcendence of mortality. With the sad resignation of a statesman of the old school closing the books on the old order, Sir Edward Grey remarked, "The lamps are going out all over Europe; we shall not see them lit again in our lifetime." And with the disillusionment of a prophet peering into the Pandora's box of the new age, Freud commented that it was just the sense of collapse over the outbreak of war which was unjustified because it consisted only "in the destruction of an illusion."[8]

X

THE COLLAPSE OF
REDEMPTIVE HISTORICITY

1. Relativism and Indeterminacy in Physics

It was in the context of the First World War and the German army's overrunning of Belgium that Thomas Mann had Adrian Leverkuhn say in *Doctor Faustus*:

> There is at bottom only one problem in the world, and this is its name. How does one break through? How does one get into the open? How does one burst the cocoon and become a butterfly? The whole situation is dominated by this question. Here too, . . . it treats of the breakthrough, in the capital essay on marionettes, and it is called straight out "the last chapter in the history of the world."[1]

Was transcendence not an ideal release at all, but only the final judgment and historical annihilation of the human puppet?

War underscored the violence and irrationality in man's nature, and reaffirmed the inherent arbitrariness of life and death. In the endless futility of trench warfare, history itself seemed to be offering psychological confirmation of its own randomness, and of the implacable barriers to any ideal order in the world. The one and a half million casualties of Verdun and the Somme suggested that even patriotic death had lost much of its meaningfulness in the grinding impersonality of modern mass war. Suffering and sacrifice, devoid for many of religious purpose, lost in addition any sense of redeeming historical consequences. A few conceived of themselves as modern knights in the manner of d'Annunzio or Richthofen. The rest were trapped in the mechanism and impersonalized industrial technology of death—the indiscriminate machine-gun and the even more indiscriminate gas. Total war precluded for most of them any individually meaningful gestures in the romanticized style of the old warrior-ethic, even had they conceived of some viable ideal that would be served thereby. Yet the very anonymity of modern combat was to appear in retrospect to many veterans in Germany, Italy and France as a more meaningful phase in their lives than the still more insidious boredom and frustration of their peacetime existence. They returned to an industrial world that, economically and politically, gave them nothing. Thus some looked back upon the comradeship of arms as the only time they had achieved a relative sense of importance and immediate purpose. Defective as the larger historical ideals of the war may have been, the front still contrasted favorably for many with the futility and disillusionment of the peacetime depression era.

For many of the intellectual and artistic elite, the fact of war served to crystallize the already incipient crisis of historical faith and the feeling of collapse of transcendence through historical time. From a sense of the incoherence of the civilized world, it was but a step to the intimation that history dissolves into a timeless abyss of cosmic unawareness or absurdity. Philosophical interpretations of the metaphysical presuppositions in the new conception of the physical sciences confirmed the mood of insecurity in the new cosmic probabilism and relativity. It was not that war-born attitudes and the indeterminacy in scientific thought were in any sense related. Science, it is true, depends in a general way on cultural conditioning. But scientific discoveries and principles emerge from the data and the autonomous needs of the discipline, not from intellectual fashions. The new concepts in the physical sciences derived, not from the climate of the age, but from physics. The argument that they both reflect the "ethos of the time" is as puerile as would be the claim that the War of the League of Augsburg reflected the "ethos" of Newton's *Principia*.

Nor can the First World War be held the cause for the mood of anxiety among certain elements of the intelligentsia and for the gradual communication of that anxiety to the upper strata of society, for we have seen that this mood had its roots in the nineteenth century, long before the assassination of the Archduke Francis Ferdinand. Yet the two independent levels of human consciousness represented by twentieth-century scientific thought and the legacy of war experience each produced consequences which had a common denominator, namely that the philosophical uncertainty attributed to one served to reinforce the pessimism emergent from the other.

The common element was not in the phenomena themselves, but in the psychological framework within which they were interpreted and linked. War accelerated the spread of anxiety which had already been found in the cosmological implications of new scientific formulations. The new scientific thought, in turn, seemed to many intellectuals to impart a cosmic meaning to the anxieties born of the war and of the other tangible frustrations of modern industrial society.

The revolution in physics, which began in the late nineteenth century, reached a climax in the work of Planck and Einstein during the first decade of our own. Its main consequences were new concepts of the atom and its nuclear structure, and of the nature of mass and energy. The results of quantum mechanics and relativity were translated into metaphysical concepts, summed up in the notion that relativism and scientific indeterminacy are the inherent and irremediable conditions of man's knowledge of the physical world. Indeterminacy, probability, relativity—concepts long familiar to philosophers—gained new status as the only scientifically "respectable" mode of thought. The consequence was that our scientific thinking came to rest upon a new conception of time.

It was 1905 that Einstein had presented the Special Theory of Relativity in a uniform field of motion, which he subsequently expanded into the General Theory. In the relativist framework, the measurement of time is dependent upon the field of movement of the observer. The mathematical formulation of this new theory rested upon the repudiation of the most basic assumptions about the absolute distinction of temporality and space. To be sure, the coherence and unity of physics was extended by the universality of relativity itself. But the point remains that Einstein's ideas had a shattering psychological impact. In precluding unconditional observation of duration, and thereby discarding the notion of absolute simultaneity of events, relativity denied the idea of a universally definitive sequence of objective time. Thus, to the degree that it is possible to transpose the measurement of duration from the coordinates of one field to those of another, it is equally impossible ever to break out of these relative relationships as such. There is no hope, then, of arriving at any ultimate temporal order.

Obviously, the physicist's conception of a time-space continuum and his new concept of the non-absolute simultaneity of events have no direct bearing on the historian's chronology. The Renaissance still comes before the Reformation! But is was largely upon the causal pattern and determinism of classical physics that many nineteenth century historians and social scientists had modeled their pretension to a positivist historical knowledge and to objective truth. Consequently the subjectivizing of scientific thought left history with no secure basis for its claim to certitude. Thus a radical relativism in history, which had its own rationale and independent roots, was encouraged and given added prestige.

In its own way, the historian's conception of time changed significantly, under the influence of the new social sciences and the comparative study of culture. The relativist approach to history had its roots in late nineteenth-century historical philosophies which rejected the notion of an absolute historical order wholly external to the observer and to the conditions of his observation. In our day many historians have even come to question periods once clearly delimited, such as the Middle Ages and its spurious "thousand years of darkness," or the Renaissance. The very terms have been taken as distortions, or at best as fictitious conveniences referring to categories of organization in our mind, rather than as distinct chapters in the actual development of our civilization. The reasons for these revisions, let it be noted, lie in the

historical evidence and not in ideas borrowed from other disciplines. But the predisposition to reexamine the evidence was itself
significantly influenced by the climate of revisionism, which owed
much to the general cultural impact of relativity. Where scientific
relativism denied any absolute time scale, relativist history challenged the definitive nature of our historical periodization. The
historian's counterpart to the scientist's statistical probability was
the partial indeterminateness of historical causality. Thus while
historical relativism did not derive directly from the relativism of
the physical sciences, it acquired from the latter a new compulsive
quality. In history as in all fields of knowledge, it seemed, the idea
of absolute truth is only the illusion preceeding man's fall from
innocence.

In post-Newtonian physics, the observer could no longer regard himself as a purely external element who has no impact on
an objective world he passively perceives. By his observation, he
intervenes in the situation, and thus subjectivizes it. Such a view
suggested a modified form of Kantianism. At least the classical
assumption of a clear distinction between subject and object in our
knowledge of an external world was challenged, this time not by
metaphysicians or philosophical idealists, but by science.

Applied to history, subjectivism meant asserting the insepa-
rability of the historian's own attitudes and concerns from the
historical explanation he offers. Just as in scientific relativity there
existed no objective time frame independent of the subjective
field of motion of the observer, so in relativist historiography there
could exist no ideally objective history that would be completely
divorced from the subjective characteristics of individual historians. The historian also affects the material he works with by the
very fact of his observation. He does not merely "expose" or
"discover" the data; he imposes a structure upon it. In the revi-
sionist perspective, he inevitably changes the object of his studies,
intruding his own organization upon the evidence. Thus while all
good historians contribute in some manner to our objective
knowledge of the past, they also further the subjectivizing of
history.

The question at issue is not whether man can ever attain

absolute historical truth, but whether such a notion even constitutes a meaningful ideal. For the problem is not the recognition of the obvious subjectivity of all historical accounts. It concerns rather the affirmation that subjectivism is inherent in the nature of historical thought. If so, it cannot be transcended, even as a hypothetical historical goal in our imagination. Even the ideal of a "perfect history" turns out to be a relative conception, valid only within a particular time and culture. The individual remains trapped in the limits of his own historical outlook, no matter how wide his range of vision. The consequence of radical relativism is the restriction of each form of meaning in history to the particular perspective of a period. It thereby prevents historicity from playing a transcendent role.

In 1927, Heisenberg announced his famed principle of indeterminacy in the measurement of individual atomic particles. He seemingly raised into a basic law of nature what had appeared, since Planck's quanta equations, as the disconcerting statistical probability of scientific knowledge. This much-abused conception became a catch-all for the most remarkable fantasies, including Eddington's analogy between "uncaused" movements of atoms and the free will of mind. For part of the European intelligentsia, the popularization of indeterminacy and of statistical approximation, added to the effect of relativity, was the last straw in confirming the nonfinality of scientific truth. It signified the impossibility of transcendent scientific certainty. Causality in the old sense melted away. What Hume had questioned philosophically in Newton's causal order, and Kant had labored mightily to restore by means of the categories of thought, was now ironically repudiated by science itself. Many a writer, philosopher and artist understandably concluded that the prewar undercurrent of insecurity and the doubt about all absolute values had proven itself justified. If even our most basic conceptions about the nature of the object world may be misleading, what hope remains of finding a Cartesian certitude in anything, least of all in the erratic process of human history? And in that case, how could relative historical values provide any objective redemption from man's sense of imprisonment in his own subjectivity and mortality?

2. Philosophies of Detachment and of Despair

The impact of scientific thought on Western civilization was manifest at two distinct levels of life. It was partly evidenced in the
technological changes the sciences engendered, and partly in the
philosophical notions they implied. In the long run, the technological applications and political effects of nuclear physics were to
have momentous consequences for all mankind. But in the immediate postwar context, it was primarily the philosophical ideas
suggested by science that had the most direct repercussions upon
segments of the European intelligentsia.

Since the seventeenth and eighteenth centuries, and the work
of Descartes, Leibnitz, Newton, Hume and Kant, the physical sciences have exercised a major influence on approaches to philosophical problems, especially in metaphysics and epistemology.
The nineteenth century saw the rise of other sciences that significantly influenced philosophy towards a new direction, notably towards historical thinking. Marx and Comte each proclaimed a
form of social science, or a discipline which they understood as
the rational scientific analysis of culture and society, approached
from an historical perspective. Then the great vogue of Darwinism
led some philosophers of the late nineteenth and early twentieth
centuries towards a biological frame of thought involving historical implications. Men like Spencer and Bergson understood science not as the formalization of a timeless system but as the
elaboration of an essentially evolutionary reality of organic forms.
They reflected different aspects of evolutionism and of its implicit
historicity. After the war, a powerful new current in philosophy,
largely prompted by modern physics and mathematics, made
many philosophers turn their backs on certain traditional problems. In the process, they disavowed the historicism that had
marked the nineteenth century—the century of Ranke, Burckhardt and Lamprecht, of Hegel, Dilthey and Marx.

To be sure, the temporal-historical outlook did not suddenly
disappear in twentieth-century philosophies. It had been too
deeply etched in the preceding trends of thought. The Marxian
view remained a powerful expression of a certain kind of historic-

ity and transcendence. The social sciences, especially in the sociological school of Weber and Mannheim, retained an essentially historical perspective. The lesson of Dilthey remained profoundly engraved in social and psychological ideas, in the work of men like Troeltsch and Jaspers. Dilthey and Rickert provided a psychological base for historical thinking clearly distinguished from the previous models of scientific analysis. In different ways, they both emphasized the role of value consciousness in our knowledge, and the unique quality of the life element in human history. These currents prevailed in some of the tendencies of postwar philosophical thought, primarily in Germany.

Furthermore, we may note that, continuing in the older tradition of metaphysics to offset the new philosophy of science, were a number of other thinkers whose ideas had significant historicist implications. Through them the impact of biology on organic and process philosophies was preserved deep into this century, serving as a counterpoint to the new ahistorical conceptions of science influenced primarily by modern physics. Alfred Whitehead, following an argument akin to that of Bergson, proposed that new levels of existence unfold spontaneously by a sort of biological development inherent in the very nature of Being. He formulated a metaphysical process of Becoming through an autonomously generative evolution that constantly achieves novelty, and thus transcends itself. The tradition of Hegelian historicism reappeared in the philosophy of Giovanni Gentile, who used it to defend the fascist state.

Finally let us mention the philosophies of history that occasionally provided a foil to positivistic thinkers and still gave direct expression to traditional historicist concerns. Spengler developed a radical historical relativism and irrationalism into the conception of cultural cycles. Collingwood and Croce preserved the imprint of Hegel's and Vico's ideas. Collingwood formulated the view that the consciousness of man's historical experience constitutes the true study of mind. Croce expounded a thoroughgoing historicism in which Being is conceived as the temporary phase of a continuous Becoming, and all knowledge becomes a form of historical knowledge. In a different vein, Cassirer's neo-Kantian philosophy and Jaspers' existentialism each involved a distinctive historical concern, and each in its own way presented the philosophical predicament of modern man in an historical perspective. Subsequently, Teilhard de Chardin fused in a uniquely personal theological perspective the concepts of historicist evolution and transcendence.

But by midcentury, the mainstreams of philosophical enquiry seemed to bypass most of these thinkers. The new schools developed philosophical techniques that dismissed the question of meaning in the universe, or postulated an existentialism presuming an inherent meaninglessness in man's historical experience. Few philosophers could take Spengler's wild speculations seriously. Even Cassirer's imposing historical approach to the study of man seemed relegated to the margins of philosophical interest. Whitehead, Croce and Bergson were generally shunted aside by newer philosophical currents amid which there was no room for any universal philosophy of historical Becoming.

Two milestones of modern philosophical thought, Russell's and Whitehead's *Principia Mathematica* and Ludwig Wittgenstein's *Tractatus,* led to philosophical schools concerned respectively with mathematical logic and with the analysis of language. Rudolf Carnap and the Vienna Circle developed logical positivism, and the Oxford group turned to linguistic analysis. The Cambridge, Vienna and Oxford movements led to novel currents in the philosophy of science. Some of the new-style philosophers were concerned primarily with the structure of an ideal language. Others considered the logic of ordinary linguistic usage, and some devoted their attention to the meaning of scientific statements. Basic to the positivists' approach was the effect of the new ideas in physics and their undermining of the ontological basis of the classical conceptions of space and time.

What is of primary concern to us in these new schools is the fact that they turned away from one of the classical motivations to philosophical enquiry, namely the search for an encompassing metaphysical order in the nature of things. While positivists sought unity in science and in the structure of language, they repudiated the idea of a supra-empirical Unity of Being, and hence of an ultimate transcendent meaning to their own lives. In effect, they converted the traditional philosopher's concern with the nature of Being into a concern with the nature of words. Small wonder that their more avid disciples frequently ignored the history of philosophy and its problems prior to their own time. Their penchant for particulars and their impatience with virtually all philosophical systems was expressive of their unwillingness to entertain the concept of a general speculative philosophical structure. With their technical objectives in view, they had little interest in the problem of transcendent meaning in history, or in the ethical role of historicist ideals.

It is true that there has been another major development in contemporary philosophy, one that does address itself to the problem of purpose in human existence. Its common denominator, amid a wide range of divergent concepts and principles, is the broad theme of existentialism, which proposes the individual's attainment of his "authentic Being" through the fearful encounters of conscious-making situations in life—above all the encounter with the irremediable consciousness of death. The essence of most existentialist thought is its emphasis on freedom. That is to say, it proclaims man free to determine his own self and Being out of the conscious choices he must make if he wishes to achieve the dignity of authentic human existence.

In the years after the Second World War, existentialism developed rapidly, both as a philosophical movement and as a popular literary fashion among youth. From the work of the German philosophers Heidegger and, to a lesser extent, Jaspers, it spread to France by means of the great influence of the writers Sartre and Camus, who gave it a distinctive stoic slant. Largely through their plays and novels, existentialism became a popular literary-philosophical movement, extending its artistic influence into Continental European and American thought.

Existentialist philosophy has significant repercussions on the consciousness of history. Though its emphasis is on the "presentness"—*Dasein*—of the individual, its conception of Being involves an awareness of past and future within individual experience which gives our Being in time its meaning. In other words, existentialist consciousness is not just consciousness *of* something, but consciousness *towards* something, and is characterized by a temporal-historical frame. We cannot here consider Heidegger's important formulation of historicity, namely that man's Being is, above all, a Being in time, and man's state an anxiety directed towards future objectives, ultimately towards death. We must take up elsewhere the theme of existentialism, and its significance to the categorization of historical consciousness in Heidegger's distinction between historicity (*Historie*) and history (*Geschichte*), between time and temporality. Let us simply note that the historistic awareness of Being in time here becomes necessary to the unfolding of our self-consciousness. The realization of authentic existence characterizes the distinctiveness of the individual ego. Thrown back in despair on its solitary resources, it must seek to create its own meaning out of the recognition of a meaningless universe.

Around these central themes there have developed three parallel lines of thought. One line, tracing back to Kierkegaard and running through Bultmann, Tillich and Berdyaev among others, involves man's search for a meaning-giving Christian eschatology within the fear and tragedy of human experience. In the second approach, represented by the philosophy of Jaspers, man seeks self-realization through transcendence within his existential condition. Applied to history, Jaspers' view anticipates a new historical epoch, a new creative axial phase in the historical process of the world. The third expression has left man to wrestle with the individual's confrontation of total void, and the dilemma of suicide, in the stark terms of a Camus. Here existentialism repudiates any external principle of organization, any cumulative meaning beyond one's own experience and self-consciousness. Thus the sense of despair and purposelessness, the fear of the randomness of the cosmos and of the inherent futility of an irrational history, wash out of our historical sense any ultimately meaningful values. At best, in the religious experience of a Kierkegaard, existential anxiety leaves room only for the disjunctive leap into the absurdity of belief—*credo quia impossibile.*

In the godless existentialist philosophy of Heidegger, the individual's resignation to his eventual disappearance into absolute nothingness constitutes a radical nihilism. It predicates the acceptance of despair as the price of freedom, including the despair of history. In Heidegger's conception, the essence of man's authentic Being is transcendence. By his existence, man transcends non-Being, which is itself a potentiality of Being. By his temporality, he transcends the present in his conscious Being towards the future. By freely determining his own individuality, man even transcends the world into which he has been cast. But there is here no higher reality or existence than man's conscious life. *Thus man can never transcend himself.*

Sartre argues that man by his free choice fashions his own essence. Out of the primary fact of his own existence and his Being in time, man forges "what" he is. He strives, by a process of negating his past, to transcend his mere existence, or his Being in itself, and to achieve the distinctive human quality of Being for himself. Both for Sartre and for Heidegger, it is the stark acceptance of the finality of death that releases man for the freedom of living self-consciously in his actions. If life here is a form of transcendence, *it is a transcendence limited by death; it is not a transcendence that seeks to reach beyond death towards immortality.* For the key to radical existentialism is the individual's conscious acceptance of one absolutely irremediable fact, namely his eventual non-Being and total individual extinction. The "existentiality" of death is man's reconciliation to nothingness. Only his consciousness of annihilation permits man to escape "falling" in the world, and to achieve authentic existence. Ultimately in existentialist thought, man is completely alone in the universe. He finds no outside support beyond his own life and death that will give him meaning, or that can hold out the hope of an eventual redemption.

In sum, man can find in radical existentialism no saving identification with any historicist ideal or with any value in the historical process. He must not look for a purpose in history that would give the false impression of liberating the individual from his finiteness and solitude. The ideal of formulating one's own values out of a remorseless acceptance of care and anxiety ends in Heidegger's support of National Socialism. With greater moral integrity, it leads to Camus' stoic affirmation of human dignity, expressed in the ever-present compulsion to make conscious choices. The necessity of freedom in the existentialist framework means that man must bravely and hopelessly confront the purposelessness of a random universe and the arbitrary quality of life. A sense of meaning created out of existential self-awareness must be limited to the individual's lifespan and death, rather than extend beyond them. Historicity is consequently further subjectivized and trapped within each person's mortality, from which it is incapable of offering any transcendent release. More than in the disengagement of positivism and of linguistic analysis, there appears in existentialism a final rejection of transcendent historical absolutes and of the redemptive power of the historical future.

3. Alienation in the Contemporary Arts

What some philosophers suggested at an abstract level became more familiar in the arts. Contemporary artists increasingly depicted the irrationality of man and the seeming absurdity of life. Under the powerful influence of Freud, they suggested the futility of eternalizing historical ideals and moral aspirations in a world of illusions and erotic dreams. Playing with a pseudo-Freudian imagery of the unconscious, they repeatedly proclaimed that the rational world was dead and sought to shock their audiences with the reiteration of this theme.

But not all the currents in the arts have manifested purposelessness or anguish. In fact, one response of the artist and the intellectual to historical frustration, or to the sense of a disintegrating world, has been to take refuge in the most messianic faith in the future, the last utopian conception of history—Marxism. Many idealists went to the libertarian tradition of the socialist movement. Others were drawn to the militant authoritarianism of quarreling Communist and Trotskyite sects. In any case, Marxism appealed to the strong impulse for social justice and to the artist's commitment in producing *art engagé*, such as the moving social criticism in Kaethe Kollwitz's etchings, the sarcasm of George Grosz, the bitter plays of Bertolt Brecht, and the cynical scores of Kurt Weill. The popularity of socialist idealism rested largely on the fact that amid the tide of postwar disillusionment, it still was attuned psychologically to the old progressive expectation of history.

But it was not the old appeal of socialism that constituted the novelty of the artist's and the intellectual's response to postwar conditions. In fact, even those artists who became Marxists in politics and ideology often revealed in their aesthetic style a profound anxiety and sense of man's doom contrasting ironically with the official optimism of their political faith. Sartre's ideological Marxism, it has been pointed out, contrasts curiously with his view of the solitude and freedom of man in a life devoid of all historical meaning and characterized by the inscription, "no exit." The charge of bourgeois decadence raised by Stalinists against *avant-garde* art is noteworthy because it manifests the uncase with which dogmatists of social progress viewed the alienation and implicit futility in current intellectual trends. The glorification of labor and the march of the revolution in history, portrayed in socialist realism, mark the psychological gap that separates a creed of historical hope, crude and trite as its expression may be, from the manifestations of historical pessimism.

The theme of alienation from history appears in two notable ways in the arts of the interwar years. One method involved the artist's isolation in a private aesthetic realm, an internal order in his discipline that insulated him from the chaos of the world around him. Cubism in painting and the architectonic style in atonal and neo-classical music, and in mathematically constructed "electronic" compositions, reveal this abstract structuring of form. The other method involved the artist's abandonment of himself to the irrationality of existence, as in dadaism and abstract expressionism or in the "random" sounds of John Cage. More frequently, the artist combined the techniques of the former with the sentiments of the latter, as in surrealism. Perhaps it is the allegories of Beckmann and the passionate rage of Picasso's *Guernica*—a painting which expresses outrage not merely at a particular act of wartime cruelty but at the inherent animal savagery of man—that best approximate in art the sense of human untranscendability and the anguish over history. But the most

direct expression of anxiety and historical despair is found in
literature.

Wherever one looks in contemporary writing, in poetry, in
drama or in the novel, one meets the same refrain of alienation
and purposelessness with respect to man's historical destiny and
fate. Eliot saw man floundering in a wasteland of meaninglessness
and of irretrievably lost innocence. Gide conveys the corrosive
doubt of the immoralist who achieves his freedom by the loss of
all impulse to life. In Pirandello and Kafka, we confront a night-
marish delusion of reality and the nihilism that engulf the individual. Brecht's dramas stressed man's brutality and inhumanity. In
The Iceman Cometh, O'Neill pointed out that only our preposter-
ous self-delusions permit us to endure existence in our goalless
world. And what contemporary work better suggests the pessimism of history than Günter Grass's symbolic and grotesque
picture of a stunted Germany in *The Tin Drum?* In another vein,
we find the devastating prophecies of a future totalitarian society
of dehumanized men presented by Huxley, Orwell and Wells.
Here detranscendentalization is completed in the robot man. Its
setting, we might note, is an historical forecast of the year 1984
or—does it really matter?—the day after tomorrow. In either
case, it marks man's "twenty-fifth hour."

XI

HISTORICITY AND
TOTALITARIAN PSYCHOLOGY

1. The Freudian School and the Illusion of the Future

Between 1893 and 1895, Sigmund Freud, a young Viennese
doctor, in collaboration with a senior physician, Dr. Joseph
Breuer, published some papers on the treatment of mental disorder, specifically on the psychological factors in hysteria. Over
the next half century, his work revolutionized many areas of art
and philosophy. Freudian psychology and the popularized distortions derived from it provided the common language of the new
literature and of the new explanations of human behavior, culture
and history. What concerns us here is how certain central elements
of Freud's thought had a direct bearing on contemporary attitudes
towards the historical process of civilization. More specifically, we
need to examine his view on the psychological impossibility of
approaching a redeeming utopia or any future transcended state of
man.

Freud, it is often noted, was inherently a rationalist, seeking
a scientific explanation of the unconscious workings of the mind.
In essence, much of his work was in the tradition of the eighteenth
century and the Enlightenment. His early therapeutic procedure
and clinical techniques indicate the decidedly rationalistic bent of
his psychology. But for all that, Freud was regarded as the modern prophet of the irrational and the unconscious. His thought

placed the unconscious in the center of our mental and psychological life. Indeed, while the basic instinctual drives of the id, notably the pleasure principle and the urge to aggressivity, can be restrained by the moral consciousness of the superego, and can be controlled by the mediating function of the conscious mind, they can never be removed. Thus their repression, which is necessary to civilization and therefore always present in history, only leads to psychological tensions or disturbances.

The Freudian image of the ego and its functional elements bears a significant resemblance to some of the dual and tripartite conceptions of the soul that were intuitively perceived in the Platonic and Christian conceptions of man. Of course, there remains the critical distinction, that in one case these drives are reproved as sin or lust, and in the other they are accepted as the natural characteristics of man's organic nature. More directly, Freud's analysis may be compared to Nietzsche's formulation of the aggressive impulses and the Dionysiac personality.

Turning to the general cultural and historical implications of Freud's categorical structure of the mind, we can see that they involve his predication of two fundamental conflicting drives of human nature, Eros and Thanatos—drives which manifest themselves in the dialectical impulse to sexuality and death, to creation and destruction. The death wish appears as an elemental psychic theme of the unconscious, expressed in the yearning to return to the safety of the maternal womb and the primal substance; this desire reveals itself in destructive passions, and sublimated suicidal or murderous impulses. That is why Freud denies the very possibility of a harmonious society. These conflicting unconscious drives underlie actions that may appear honorable to us, but are often the work of hidden motives for which our rationalized explanations are nothing but symbolic substitutes, acceptable to our moral sense and our culturally acquired guilt feelings. Through external restraints, the spontaneous emotional expressions of childhood become repressed to fit the needs of social harmony and conduct acceptable in civilized societies. It is civilization itself, therefore, that is the source of repression. Our historical future is inevitably trapped by the psychological contradiction between our natural desires and the necessary repressiveness of civilized life.

Underlying the process of inhibition is the gradual internalization of the moral sense of the superego which transforms acts regularly followed by punishments into forms of behavior deemed to be immoral. In this manner, civilization inevitably creates a crucial tension between the pleasure principle and the sense of right. When inadequately relieved by the release of psychological energies, these tensions engender the neuroses of our adult life. Particular neuroses may be clinically resolved by rational psychoanalytic therapy, *but the inherent conditions in civilization which constitute their source cannot.* Hence they will never permit a general rational solution to the psychic ills of man, or to the categorical problem of his self-alienation. In Freud's schema, therefore, the suffering of history remains untranscendable and all dreams of utopia, whether religious, rationalist or Marxist, appear as illusions. That is why, in his late essay concerning the impact of psychoanalysis on culture and society, *Civilization and Its Discontents,* Freud sees life as a continuing interplay of Eros and Thanatos that does not achieve any distinctive moral objective. In the end, Freud must reject the role of utopian prophet; he resigns himself to the irremediable condition of guilt-ridden, civilized man, and to the titanic struggle between man's conflicting motivations to life and to death.

Freud's insight into the relation of the unconscious to the rational process of thought prompted a great body of comments and exegeses, collectively exercising a dominant influence on many of our intellectual values, fashions and attitudes. It also bred a vast array of divergent commentaries and criticisms, some of them indirect reflections of the ideas they criticized. Freud's thought naturally underwent significant changes over the years, both in regard to the function of the libido, and the nature of the ego. Many of Freud's one-time students and disciples developed their own psychoanalytic theories, sometimes critically at variance with those of the master, to his bitter indignation. Adler branched off and repudiated much of Freud. He developed a form of individual psychology distinguished by his concept of inferiority feelings, aroused when man's basic drive for power and self-assertion is restricted. But the resulting psychological tensions, Adler claimed, can be resolved largely in terms of the individual's response to his social and cultural environment. The possibility of treating psychological disturbances by reducing the social stresses in life is an idea that also played a part in the work of neo-Freudians like Karen Horney and Harry Stack Sullivan. Here are implicitly hopeful psychological formulations which fit in with ideals of historical progress.

Erich Fromm began on orthodox Freudian lines, but later formulated a variant we may term psychoanalytic humanism. In his view, the sadistic and masochistic consequences of ego repression would be avoided through a cultural change that would remove the present frustrating social restraints upon the natural fulfillment of the ego. Fromm argues that this psychological aim could be achieved by means of the individual's refusal to continue repressing his individuality. A healthy affirmation of the self within a frame of rational and humanist values would provide a psychological salvation for our alienated individuality.

In another direction, Reich developed a curious variant on psychoanalytic theory. He exalted the release of sexual energy as the solution to the basic dilemmas in the psyche and identified creative force with the vitality of an erotic activity that becomes in itself the mystique of a new kind of life. Regenerative power occurs through eroticism, postulated as the organic counterpart to the inorganic principle of entropy and its natural dissipation of energy. For sexual activity, in Reich's view, counterbalances the death principle of the entropic "unwinding" of life.

Above all, it was Jung who developed out of the initial basis of Freudian presuppositions—against which he turned with increasing vehemence—a highly complex psychoanalytic theory. Jung departed from Freud's virtually monistic concentration on the libido. While continuing to use certain basic Freudian precepts on the role of the unconscious, he argued that there existed a range of autonomous and primal psychic experiences such that no one of them could be dissolved into another. Apart from the libidinal drive, he accepted the autonomous quality of other unconscious forces, for example the psychological reality of religious and mystic experiences, although there was no question that for Jung, too, these experiences frequently took the form of sexual phantasies and were inextricably interwoven with phallic symbolism. In dealing with these phantasy relationships, he elaborated his complex philosophical schema of psychic meanings and symbol interpretations, such as the representations of eternal circles, or *mandalas,* and of other supposedly primary and universal images in the unconscious. These images provide the heart of Jung's thought, namely his analysis of archetypal forms as the basic modes of human ideas and feelings.

In Jung's schema, archetypes represent the elemental models of all psychic experience. They run through the unconscious of all peoples and civilizations, reappearing in the veiled psychoanalytic imagery of their religions and myths. Pursuing the philosophical foundation of his psychological theory, Jung based much of his argument about the myth archetypes on the study of Eastern religion and the symbolism of folklore and epic poetry. For example, he found one archetypal form in the universal presence of culture heroes embodying man's gnostic urge to identify himself with God. Where Freud had been something of a cool rationalist, at least insofar as the clinical analysis of the unconscious was concerned, Jung was prepared to regard the irrational as something that had to be evaluated in its own psychoanalytic terms. His notion of a collective unconscious suggested yet a further departure from the distant Fruedian model of the ego.

Seen in historical perspective, Jung's collective unconscious was a radical new expression of an old notion, namely the existence of innate ideas. Jung's hypothesis constituted the irrational inversion of the familiar philosophical concept of *a priori* elements of thought. But his psychological approach presented the mental categories not as rational conditions of knowledge logically inherent in the nature of thinking, but as unconscious predispositions built into the processes of mind. Thus the notion of inborn ideas was drastically transformed. From a universal algebra of human consciousness it was made into the unconscious symbolism of man's psychic states and impulses.

While Jung insisted upon the quality of self-transcendence
within his mythopoeic schema, he regarded the prevailing modern
Western forms of transcendent objectives as psychologically
debilitating. Contrasting the West's tendency to seek transcendence outside the ego with the tendency in Hindu values to seek it
within the ego, or through the self's dissolution into the cosmic
One, Jung repudiated psychologically the standard Western model
of redemptive purpose. That is to say, he rejected the notion of
ego-transference to an historical ideal external to the self, or to a
specific objective in time. In his philosophical speculations, history
often served Jung as a source of knowledge or of profound insight.
But historicity and the idolization of historical values were alien
to his outlook. Against the continuing force of archetypal symbols, rational historical intentions and sentimental hopes remain
insignificant. Against the weight of the collective unconscious,
man's conscious aspirations have little effect. The objective meaning of historical goals disappears under the great myth structure
imbedded in the human psyche.

Psychoanalytic thinking came to pervade the Western intellectual atmosphere. It affected the frame of modern values, and
exercised a growing impact on our attitudes towards history. The
ideas of Freud, or popularized notions supposedly derived from
his work, became the new intellectual fashion of much of the
intelligentsia. Some of the optimistic versions of psychological
theory, postulating the hope of social readjustment, personal release and sexual freedom, encouraged a naïve utopianism with
evident historicist implications. *Avant-garde* youth often saw in
psychological postulates a new liberation from artificial restraints
and cultural inhibitions. They tended to translate their iconoclasm
into a radical revolution of cultural values affecting not only sensual behavior but other moral and social customs. Some socialists
combined vaguely Freudian principles with the economic analysis
and historical ideals of Marxism. Thus they joined the hopes of a
classless society with those of a revolutionary liberation of the
personality seen in psychoanalytic terms.

But Freud's own views clearly did not constitute a utopian
sense of imminent human liberation. They involved rather a stoic

acceptance of the permanent struggle of life and a fatalistic resignation to the limited prospects of mankind. It was this disillusioned aspect of psychological thought that seemed most in keeping with the currents of twentieth-century history and with the tragic events of the interwar years. The so-called advance of civilization, Freud concluded, left no way out of the dilemma of frustration and self-estrangement. The necessary price of the increasing complexity of civilization, he argued, was the ever more disturbing sense of guilt mirrored in the intensification of aggressive political movements. In this sense, Freud's view fitted the rise of new totalitarian regimes. Conversely, they seemed to confirm his analysis of the basically irrational nature of the psyche in the unconscious determinants of thought and in the violent passions of the id. The outcome of thousands of years of civilization, scientific advance, humane moral teaching and rational ethic was Dachau.

2. *Psychological Forces and Totalitarian Movements: The Elites*

Erich Kahler sees in totalitarianism the internal breakdown of the ego structure. The theme of a depersonalizing individual response to the forces of modern industrial civilization and war has become a cliché of modern social criticism. In the psychological perspective of Fromm, a critical object- or group-transference of feelings and identity generates a disintegrative effect on the ego. In Germany, for example, it is obvious that endemic economic dislocation, national political frustrations and class insecurity constituted the material-historical conditions for the rise of Hitler. But the full impact of National Socialism appeared only in the collapse of the inner balance of the individual personality, which revealed itself in the attempt of many Germans to escape personal responsibility for failure through commitment to a totalitarian movement. By participating in the mass cult, the individual sought to overcome the sentiments of futility and purposelessness largely engendered by the postwar despair of a meaningless history.

At the turn of the century, the flight of the intellectual seemed to shift to new forms of political exoticism. Autocratic ideals and authoritarian movements attracted certain student groups and militant youth. After the war, new conditions of life washed away much of what remained of democratic and socialist ideologies. The old radical appeal of humanitarian objectives gave way to a new revolutionary force of totalitarian movements. It is an axiom of historical thinking that during times of crisis, political currents generally tend towards the extremes. Applied to the interwar years, the principle of polarization may be mislead-ing. The movements of National Socialism and Communism, for example, are more alike than they are opposite to one another in respect to the totalitarian aspects of party organization and the ruthless methods of control. On the other hand, they are wholly divergent in their ultimate goals, their concept of man, and their view of history. But in any case, the fact remains that the rising political currents of the twenties and thirties were preeminently anti-democratic.

Viewing society from a conservative and aristocratic perspec-tive, José Ortega y Gasset criticized the political forces of indus-trial mass society which, he argued, have become obsessed with the magic of numbers. He finds the dehumanizing condition of modern life in the increasing effect of the lowest common denomi-nator of mass values, reflected in the new glorification of a totali-tarian herd instinct. Along comparable lines, Julien Benda advanced his critique of the intellectual leadership's betrayal of its traditional responsibility to stand for what amounted to universal spiritual values. Meanwhile the totalitarian movements both men feared were arising in various parts of Europe.

In Paris, the bitterly anti-Semitic and anti-republican na-tionalism of Charles Maurras' *Action Française* achieved a certain popular notoriety in the Latin Quarter. In Italy, Pareto's theory of the elite served to justify the idealized opportunism behind the mystique of Fascism, while a few ardent Fascist youths were briefly inspired by the flamboyant chauvinism they appropriated from d'Annunzio. Alfredo Rocco provided a rationalization of the to-talitarian state and of Fascist laws. But perhaps it was Weimar Germany that best reflected the ideological crosscurrents of the postwar years.

German cultural history of the twenties presented a strange

juxtaposition of conflicting political values. On one hand, Berlin became the center of a sophisticated cosmopolitan intelligentsia responsive, at least in the abstract, to the social-democratic values of the Weimar Republic. But on the other hand, Germany's intellectual life also offered the reverse picture, suggested by the striking public response to Oswald Spengler's *The Decline of the West.* Despite Spengler's belated disavowal of Hitler, his ideas foreshadowed National Socialist values, and appeared to serve the Nazi cause. In his combination of historicism and the repudiation of liberal progress, he reflected the psychological conditions which had led others to the refuge of a totalitarian movement and to the deceptive image of self-transcendence it presented.

Spengler's place in our study of historical values rests primarily on his affirmation of a philosophy of cycles marked by the necessary decline of each civilization, including our own. He pictured Western civilization as having irretrievably passed its peak of cultural creativity, condemned henceforth to an autumn or early winter of inevitable decline. This view seemed to others to express deep-rooted historical pessimism, though Spengler himself denied it. He claimed rather to find in Western man's worldwide economic organization and technical efficiency the new "extensive" opportunities for meaningful activity, now that our world had been forced to abdicate from the "intensive" development of its culture. But spiritual dynamism and Faustian originality lay beyond the powers of a waning civilization that had crossed the dividing line from creative vitality to stagnant intellectualism, reflected in the arid life of the modern cosmopolis.

In Spengler's schema, the eighteenth and nineteenth centuries saw the last sparks of our cultural élan. They marked the barrier separating sterile twentieth-century society from its cultural roots, as Hellenistic civilization was separated from the age of Pericles. Small wonder that those who read *The Decline of the West,* or the far greater number who merely heard about Spengler's work, should take from him a radical relativism of all values, art and philosophy that could but end in a corroding intimation of historical pessimism.

Many German intellectuals sought a refuge in the security of an emotional commitment to totalitarian destiny and to the convincing claim that history was inevitably on their side. What is surprising in the growth of National Socialism is not that it attracted large numbers of lower-middle-class followers, but that its brutal anti-rationalism and pathological hates appealed to many intellectual Germans, often educated in the ethics of Kant. In this regard, Hannah Arendt has suggested interestingly that it was a moral rationalization based on a ludicrous transposition of Kantian imperatives which justified even the semi-educated and unintellectual Adolf Eichmann in his deliberate participation in the efficient organization of genocide. From our point of view it is significant that a movement whose propaganda was, in Hitler's words, aimed at the lowest level of emotional responses and was intentionally couched in vulgarisms directed to enflame mobs, should nonetheless attract educated followers. It drew support from class-conscious and Kultur-oriented German university professors such as Sombart and Heidegger. Why was it that this latter-day Satanism should come to represent in Heidegger's view a new departure, a chance of authentic Being? Why did many musicians like Gieseking and Richard Strauss accommodate themselves to the regime—some, no doubt, out of indifference or naïveté, but others out of conviction—if not for that sense of destiny they ironically sought in it, transcending themselves through their secularized goal?

But among totalitarian movements, it was not those based on a doctrine of militant nationalism or upon an ideology of racism that attracted the predominant support of the alienated intelligentsia, but the Communist Party. It combined the traditional Marxist appeal and humanitarian socialist ideals with the discipline of a centralized party structure and a promise of ultimate revolutionary success against bourgeois regimes, or later against fascist aggressions. When compared with the largely bourgeois Social Democrats, they had the psychological advantage with many young intellectuals of an apparently uncompromising ideology of revolution, at least until 1935. After the Stalin-Laval agreement, they enjoyed, until the Molotov-Ribbentrop pact, the new advantage of being the most militant group in resisting the expanding power of Mussolini and Hitler. Thus partly despite, and partly because of, the totalitarian practices of Stalin, Communism drew many European intellectuals into a cosmopolitan ideological community, and provided them with a common denominator of social values and of historical aspirations.

In a chaotic world, totalitarian certainty becomes an asset, appealing even to many intellectuals. Totalitarianism combined with the ideal of freedom provides an almost unbeatable combination. It is a commonplace to remark that as the sense of purpose atrophied in non-totalitarian systems of values, it was only totalitarian parties that provided the ideological assurance of participation in the "movement of history," and offered to many an alienated intellectual the psychological satisfaction of his urge to dominate, by permitting him to conceive of himself as a part of the elite of the new society. One observer comments that totalitarian leaders "achieve a vicarious immortality through membership in the Inner Party, since the mind of the Party is collective and immortal."[2] While Communism and National Socialism stood at opposite points in their ideological goals and political objectives, they tended to join like the two ends of a near-circular arc in their totalitarian characteristics. Thus it is not surprising that they shared, in appealing to intellectuals, the use of an explicit or implicit historical futurism.

To be sure, totalitarian historicity represents a fundamentally flawed historical consciousness, in that it actually seeks to exclude much of the past from the "living record of events." It tries deliberately to dissolve certain events into nothingness, historically speaking; it reduces some individuals into non-existence in the historical legacy, as if they had never lived. Thus the Nazis, for example, skipped over centuries of historical development in their return to pseudo-primitivism. They erased certain personalities such as Heine and Mendelssohn from their historical memory and undertook the symbolically revealing act of book burning. The Communists glibly rewrote their history to achieve the "non-existence" of disfavored personalities.

The historical annihilation of persons and events is a quite different phenomenon from the exercise of historical prejudices that attack or even distort the elements and figures of the past they oppose without, however, obliterating them. In other words, totalitarian historicity is distinguished not merely by its bias—an attribute it shares with much non-totalitarian thought—but by its attempt to preclude any open-ended re-examination of its historical myths. Only a totalitarian regime has the discipline to seek control, not only over men's attitudes towards something, but over its very mention in public or private life. For the intellectual, the promise of historical oblivion is generally a far more radical punishment than mere condemnation; it threatens to destroy him by wiping out his relationship to the ideal object that gives meaning to his life.

Totalitarian historical consciousness appears in Stalin's deleting the very identity of his victims from Communist hagiology. It appears in Hitler's consignment of past and present Jewish intellectuals to eradication from Nazi consciousness and to exclusion from German culture. To the true believer, this vitiated historical sense offered an historical and moral goal, absorbing his identity in that of the group, whether the nation or the class. To the intellectual, it signified identification with the power of the mass movement and with the collective salvation of the party. Ironically, the psychological attitude of the totalitarian mystique rested upon an historical perspective that was perhaps more attractive to the intelligentsia, inclined to seek a meaning to life in its ideal vision, than it was to men whose satisfactions are often more immediate, namely their comforts and their families. For many an intellectual, only totalitarianism still provided an option of hope and purpose, at the price of individuality. And only communism still seemed to provide the surviving form of the old rationalist faith in human progress, as it later appeared to non-Western intellectuals to be the last form of historistic ideals they had once learned from Western liberalism. In his nightmare version of Stalinist totalitarianism, 1984, George Orwell suggests that the key principle of the regime is that the control of the past makes possible the infallible determination of the future, and that the total control of the present determines our memory of the past. Expressing the ultimate communist trust in historicity, cast in the negative mold imposed by his defeat and exile, Trotsky wrote in the concluding chapter of his biography of Stalin: "The vengeance of history is more terrible than the vengeance of the most powerful General Secretary."[3]

Little point would be served in providing here the long catalogue of artists and intellectuals who during the interwar years found an answer to the anxiety of historical purposelessness in joining the enthusiastic sect-life of the Stalinist left before, in numerous cases, eventually leaving it again in greater despair or disgust. Koestler, Spender, Silone, Crossman and others have given us the classic view of the psychological yearning and historicist ideals that took them into the movement, and their disillusionment in the god that failed which took them out again. Huxley, Wells and Orwell produced brilliant and terrifying satires of totalitarian life. Koestler, above all, described with chilling realism the party's mechanisms of belief and power, even to the self-hypnosis of its disciples. Not incidentally, the last offer of Gletkin to Rubashov in *Darkness at Noon* is to bow to the dictate of the party in return for a guaranteed place in the eventual history books. His implicit alternative is eternal oblivion through the elimination of his name from the historical record. Such was the bond that tied totalitarian ideology to the historical transcendence of man's mortal condition.

3. Totalitarian Mystique and the Frustrations of History: The Masses

It was not, however, the process of ideas alone that brought on totalitarianism, nor was it the intellectuals' responses that provided the dynamism of totalitarian movements. In the last analysis, the decisive evidence of historical disillusionment must be found among the masses rather than the elites. Its roots must be sought, not in the ideological commitments of intellectuals or artists, but in concrete historical circumstances, notably the aftermath of war, the economic conditions of the postwar years and the political frustrations that accompanied them.

The major factors in the masses' experience of postwar history were the disintegration of democracy and the growing failure of the quest for collective security and peace. Underlying these developments was the debilitating impact of economic depression. These impersonal forces combined to make the individual feel increasingly powerless to affect his destiny. Beyond the dehumanization of slums, which could be cured, the worker on an assembly line came to sense the intrinsic spiritual estrangement of the industrial environment long protested by poets and philosophers. Even the glamor of technological successes could no longer veil the anomie in the metropolis, nor prevent the sentiment of depersonalization from entering mass consciousness. The feeling of historical futility which had previously been the mark of intellectual and artistic elites now filtered down to the popular levels of mass society. From the anxiety engendered by the increasing routinization of life and the anonymity of a bureaucratic society it was but a step to the sense of history as an abyss.

The popular arts, particularly films, testify to the diffusion of anxiety. The films of totalitarian countries were for the most part characterized by glorification of the historical destiny that expressed the dogmatic or ideological appeal of the regime. The use of pseudo-history, tying in a contrived national tradition with the shrill claim of a transcendent historical future was strikingly conveyed by the Nazi propaganda film, *Triumph of the Will*. Motion pictures made in the Soviet Union, such as Eisenstein's *Potemkin*, generally displayed the same propagandistic quality and proselytizing use of history. On the other hand, films made in non-totalitarian countries did not conform to a monolithic motif and purpose. Such pictures were of all types, including fictionalized pseudo-historical dramas, but they were generally devoid of conscious ideology. Their most prevalent themes were escapism at the mass level and disillusionment in the art film, where the idea of alienation constantly recurs, as in *The Cabinet of Dr. Caligari*. The most revealing note is struck in the classic films of Chaplin, which achieved universal popularity. Behind the slapstick, the social satire and the optimism of the occasional happy ending, there is a constant undertone of sadness. The distinctive mood of Chaplin's great tragi-comedies, such as *City Lights* and *Modern*

Times, is that of the pathetic individual, lost in the modern social and industrial world.

Yet the idea that attitudes simply filtered down from the elites to the mass must give us pause. The sense of disorientation at the top certainly had repercussions at other levels of society. But the relationship of moods involves as much a parallelism of experiences as a link of cause and effect. There were several autonomous factors in the currents of popular movements that account for the occasional compatibility of responses among intellectuals and masses, despite their mutual suspicions.

It would be misleading to suppose that the lower middle class took directly from the elite its notions of disillusionment and meaninglessness suggested in the new art, science and psychology. It tended rather to dismiss such *avant-garde* manifestations as further support for its distrust of the intellectual who stands apart from the common sense of ordinary men. Popular disillusionment was not simply a filtering down of skeptical sentiments or moral doubts from philosophical relativism or from psychoanalysis. It had its independent sources in historical experience, in economic problems and in the insidious disintegration of personality under long unemployment or job insecurity.

But after these considerations have been duly noted, the fact still remains that a significant relationship between popular attitudes and intellectual movements appears evident. When the dominant classes, which had traditionally formulated and maintained a sense of the universal and some scheme of transcendent values, came to proclaim their own uncertainty and to announce the relativity of all things, a mood of general disorientation was likely to take hold. When the elites abdicated a sense of reason and purpose, the lack of direction dimly felt to prevail at the top sifted down, not necessarily in the same specific terms. It came to pervade the general atmosphere of society. To be sure, there was a culture lag of generations; this time lapse was spelled out in the distance not only of decades but of different historical experiences. Nonetheless, the war, the subsequent dislocation and the great depression provided a common psychological stimulus and cultural context. These dramatic developments made up an overpowering historical force under which responses of uprootedness and fear cut across intellectual and class lines. It is in the events of the postwar decade that we find the material-historical causes of the distinctive temper of the age, namely its insecurity in diplomacy and in social and economic matters, as well as in the currents of thought.

After a brief flash of hope in the new world of democracy, the problems of peace intensified the wartime legacy of popular lassitude and discouragement. President Wilson managed for a moment to infuse the Allies with a stirring vision of the war to end wars. But the realities of the Versailles Treaty soon disillusioned the great powers and left the smaller states with chronic fears. The Germans felt they had been victimized; the French found security as elusive as ever. The English discovered they had eaten up their capital assets with little to show for it except chronic unemployment. The Italians woke up to see their irridentist ambitions unfulfilled. The years of trench warfare followed by postwar economic collapse and inflation eroded what was left of the patriotic enthusiasms with which many workers had answered the call to arms in 1914. The chain of subsequent events seemed to justify the warning of revolutionaries who had proclaimed that only the upper bourgeoisie and the munitions makers had any stake in the defense of capitalist nations.

Except in Czechoslovakia, the hopes for democracy and economic prosperity did not last long in Central and Eastern Europe. Autocracy marked by occasional chaos characterized most of the new independent states carved out of the old empires and living under the leaky roof of the League of Nations. In Western Europe, France found herself confronted with the endemic consequences of her population decline and lagging industrialization. Class rigidity, which had already marked the social reality behind the veneer of *la belle époque*, hardened the arteries of French economic life. After the war, these stresses were aggravated by chronic inflation and a freezing of status patterns. The limping quality of French government and its parliamentary instability were the inverted reflections of a stultifying paralysis in the economic and social order. The war had caused a devastating hemorrhage in the ailing republic, maiming and killing young men upon

whose productive and reproductive capacities the country depended—hence the great psychological weight of the so-called
"hollow years."

As for England, she found herself an exhausted nation. Ruled
without imagination by an upper class of serious-minded medi-
ocrities and well-meaning old men, she staggered through the interwar decades with a faltering economy and a fading imperial
grandeur. The new dominant Conservative Party had lost the
"spring" of Disraeli's day, not to mention his social vision, and
Labour produced no popular counterpart to Gladstone. Condemned to the oldest factory equipment in the world, Britain had
to face the newer technology of industrial rivals who had by-
passed her in productivity. These "disadvantages of forwardness"
showed in her lagging coal industry and debilitating unemployment rate.

Even the pre-war escape from personal insignificance into the
vicarious thrill of imperialism was closed off as power visibly
shifted from the old European nations, westward to the United
States and eastward to Japan. In contrast to the explosive colonial
expansion of the pre-war era, the postwar situation was marked by
a hiatus of power and a moment of self-doubt. It was soon followed
by a painful retreat, with many a violent backlash, from advanced
imperial positions. Past the point of colonial ascendancy began a
slow decline that was to culminate in the growing momentum of
decolonization in midcentury. The dominant relation of the West
to the non-Western world was to be revolutionized.

Closed in upon themselves, Europeans increasingly had to
face up to the drabness of the industrial civilization they had
created. Perhaps few things were more suggestive of historical
pessimism and the decline of the West than this collective devolution of European power, and the disabusing of the old attitude
that the historical destinies of people were settled in the chancel-
leries of Paris, London and Berlin. The self-assurance that Western Europe was the political and intellectual center of the world
suffered a further hard blow with the revolutionary role suddenly
assumed by Moscow, and the hold of the Third International over
many of the best minds of the time.

It was the Soviet Union that provided, in the course of

postwar events, the model of the revolutionary movement converted into a totalitarian party regime. We shall not discuss here
the familiar history of the 1917 revolutions, the seizure of power
by Lenin, or his conception and development of the monolithic
party. Nor shall we describe the emergence of Stalin and the insti-
tutionalization of revolutionary terror during the heightened
despotism of the first two Five-Year Plans and the great purges.
Suffice it to say that what made the new regime totalitarian, as
distinct from merely autocratic, was the use of violence and intimidation to secure monolithic party control over every aspect of
national life. To achieve its historical objective, the totalitarian
party claims in theory to absorb all individual and group energies.
It seeks to consolidate the whole range of activities of its members, and later of all citizens, under its effective domination. Consequently totalitarianism dissolves the distinctions between the
private and public realms. It makes all personal concerns a matter
for the actual or potential exercise of central authority. It establishes intentionally arbitrary and fluctuating dividing lines between
legal and criminal behavior so as to reduce the trust in rational
decisions and to intensify the dependence on party leaders. In essence, the party seeks to monopolize power for its own sake.

We have already seen, in the context of revolutionary
France, that violence is first used in the development of a totalitarian regime as an exceptional means to secure control, but then
is transformed into terror. It becomes the use of force for intimidation, and the resort to arbitrary punishment for the purpose of a
cathartic act of sacrifice in the name of a messianic ideal. This
change marks the process of demonification of secular redemptive
historicity. Violence then becomes self-justifying. In the Nazi
regime, for example, the purge was supposed to serve political
conformity, racial purity and the elimination of potential rivals. In
the Soviet Union, it was intended to serve ideological orthodoxy,
industrial development and centralized despotism. In both cases,
the routinization of violence exhibits the classical contradiction
between freedom and historical utopianism. It leads to the absorption of the idea of liberty into a presumed higher ideal. During
the nineteen twenties, the emergence of Stalin's totalitarian power

set the pattern of single-party regimes based on mass propaganda and the normalization of terror. It set a precedent for the extreme centralization of authority and the arbitrary use of force in the name of historically redeeming objectives such as "The Fatherland of the Proletariat" or "The Thousand-Year Reich."

Meanwhile, in Italy, a single-party regime had also emerged from the frustrations of war and the crises of peace. Rising to power largely through the economic disintegration, political chaos and class hatreds he skillfully exploited, Mussolini proclaimed opportunistic goals for the Fascists. He also promised to cure the stagnation of Italian national life that went back to the period after unification, and he held out an historical vision of the future. Fascist dictatorship was despotic, arbitrary and often brutal. But it was not conclusively totalitarian. The purge and murder were little used after Matteotti's assassination, and pluralist tendencies were not wholly dissolved in the centralism of political power. Still, according to Mussolini's definition of totalitarianism, the role of the party made Fascism an incomplete model for the later dictatorship of National Socialism.

Italian corporatist theory provided the mystique of transcending the class struggle through the idolization of the state. Fascist practices established precedents in the use of youth movements, in the military training and regimentation of young students, and in the indoctrination of labor. Illegal force and intimidation were used by the party militia. Above all, Mussolini developed the use of hypnotic mass propaganda to proclaim an historical destiny—the glorious revival of imperial Rome. All these notions were to achieve their completed forms in the more highly organized totalitarianism of Germany, with its more developed industrial techniques and mob psychology.

The history of the Weimar Republic and its collapse under the depression of 1929 need not retain our detailed concern. The effects of the Versailles Treaty, of the Spartakist rebellion and the early *putsches*, and the impact of reparations constitute a familiar story. The Ruhr occupation, the effect of inflation on the insecure lower middle class and the critical unemployment of the early thirties are key elements of a well-known drama. They were

HEAVEN, HELL, & HISTORY

set against the background of an inherited Prussian military tradition and authoritarianism that manifested itself in the legacy of a rigid social hierarchy and a reverence for the state. These forces were given new impetus by the rage of anti-Semitism and by the personal spell of Hitler.

Such in brief is the conventional explanation of the rise of National Socialism. Through the function of the party, Hitler transformed these various elements into a totalitarian movement endowed with an apparently transcendent historical force. For in the end, as an aberration characteristic of our time, totalitarianism reduces itself to one essential feature: *the manipulation of the masses through the monolithic control of industry, propaganda and police power by a party elite, proclaiming a manifest destiny that enflames mass aspirations to some messianic historical goal.* Totalitarianism can establish itself only as a mass movement dominated by a minority. The elitism of party leadership is an essential ingredient of totalitarian regimes; the mass character of the movement is the essential factor of totalitarian psychology. Both find their common focus in an aborted historicity.

It is the rise of totalitarianism as a major mass phenomenon that distinctively stamps the history of Europe in the interwar years. Though the intelligentsia were often drawn to totalitarian movements, it was primarily the masses that found in them an escape from their present condition of existence and from the futility of history. The course of events during the twenties and thirties accelerated the flight to extreme political parties. Thus there occurred a polarization of political forces, contradictory in their ideologies and in their conceptions of freedom and justice as well as in their view of human destiny, but essentially alike in the key functions of their historical mystiques.

4. Totalitarianism and Historicity

With the historical mystiques of totalitarian mass movements we reach the end of our survey of the rise and decline of transcendent historicity. We have come to its last phase, namely the disintegration of historical consciousness and the desperate response thereto in the form of totalitarian values. Two characteristics of the new mass movements express this final quality of desperation: the cult of irrationality, and the cult of leadership as a substitute for the individual's lost identity.

Mass ceremonies, like the *Parteitag* or May Day pageants, showed the role in totalitarianism of an irrational appeal to emotion. With its official Marxist ideology, the Soviet Union's Communist regime claimed to pursue purely rational and scientific policies. But its practices belied its theory. No less than other totalitarian parties, it relied on the psychological mass effect of revolutionary symbolism, with all its rites, iconography of leaders, and uncritical glorification of Stalin. National Socialism, on the other hand, frankly reveled in its appeal to the unconscious, or to the so-called dynamism of organic vitality below the level of reason. Yet it, too, needed to develop a rationale of sorts, an efficient ordering of its use of irrationality. In each case, the rationale constituted the technique of organization and the irrationale constituted the source of power, or the bond of unity that made a mystique out of an ideology.

The redemptive role of totalitarian irrationality has nothing to do with the notion of progress. Some totalitarian movements, such as Stalinist communism, suggested a theoretical hope of ultimate human perfectibility and a vision of eventual human happiness. Others did not. But in neither case did this issue have any bearing on the transcendent psychological function of the mystique. It was the fact of identification itself and the sense of historical purpose, not the question of meliorism or of man's general well-being, that constituted the transcendent quality. Indeed, Mussolini specifically rejected the eighteenth-century idea of progress, and emphatically repudiated its corollary, the hope of permanent peace. Affirming that the domination of the strong is the destiny of man and that war is an ennobling experience, both fascism and National Socialism developed an outlook that precluded the progress of humanity and yet sought to affirm a transcendent value to history.

Mussolini, Stalin, Hitler—the crux of the totalitarian elite dominating the mass and incarnating its will, is the principle of

charismatic leadership. It is the leader who gives symbolic historical presence to the movement's ultimate goals and personifies its
manifest destiny. Once again Stalin's career proves the most ar-
resting, because in his case the cult of personality of the later
years was so obviously in contradiction with doctrine. Fascism
and National Socialism never pretended to a policy other than the
idolization of the *Duce* or the *Führer*. Consequently it was natural
for Nazism to exhibit the most thoroughgoing example of government by charisma. The will of Hitler and the objective of Germany were defined as one. The dictator who identifies himself
absolutely with the destiny of a people makes himself the alter ego
of his disciples. In a society where transcendence is bound up with
a secular redemptive purpose, he inevitably becomes to his followers the vicarious instrument of their historical immortalization.

The totalitarian despot, incarnating the very "salvation" of
his followers, presents the final measure of how far the Judeo-
Christian idea of a savior in history had deteriorated in its devolution from the divine to the secular. He shows how much the idea
of historical transcendence had been vitiated by the actual detranscendentalization of historical objectives. In non-totalitarian
charisma, a Churchill or a de Gaulle may embody an extraordinary historical dimension to his followers. He may epitomize their
national aspirations. Yet there remains inherent in the non-totalitarian value structure a place for a man's private realm of life, and
an approach to self-transcendence independent of the public ideal.
Therefore the leader does not fully absorb the individual's prospects for vicarious immortality, as the totalitarian dictator purports to do. This distinction is crucial. For it is the misuse of
historical redemption that distinguishes the totalitarian outlook,
which identifies transcendent values with the will of the providential despot, from the charisma of democratic leaders, such as
Jaurès or Gladstone. It is its relentless psychology that characterizes totalitarian charisma, and it is its unlimited nature that defines
its messianic-historical function. Totalitarianism constitutes the
price for idolizing man's historical future and for deifying man
as creator of all transcending historical value, whether that price is

paid in the dehumanization of the labor-camp or in the self-motivating sadism of the death-camp.

Totalitarianism arose primarily because the apparent solidarity of the movement or party offered some reply to historical pessimism. It stood against the current of historical purposelessness for the affirmation of meaning in human affairs on which the older historicist values had defaulted. Totalitarianism was but the political and psychological converse to the democratic or progressive historicity that it had replaced and whose redemptive function it took over—in demonic form.

We may conclude that totalitarian historicity was the culmination of the attempt to impose a secular value on mass society and to give historical ideals a redemptive force. In Germany, the disillusionment of the elites and the masses led to what Hermann Rauschning called "the revolution of nihilism."[4] With its exaltation of power, the movement temporarily disguises the self-contradiction of secular immortalization through historical consciousness. One source of this development was the "desertion of the intellectuals" whose flight to irrationality left Western values in a state of disarray. Another source was the effect of industry on mass society that left many people lost amid the things man had made. That is why totalitarian parties could achieve power only in industrialized countries, or more characteristically in countries undergoing forced industrialization. Only under these conditions could effective centralized controls be organized and the appeal of mass values be applied, for the sense of personal insignificance and therefore the dread of historical oblivion were heightened.

The increasing depersonalization of life converted a simple historical pessimism into a desperate search for new purpose. It precipitated the self-estrangement of the solitary individual who sought refuge in a totalitarian movement intended to disguise the absurdity of his historical illusions. Mass society imposed a new violence even on hopes of progress, which could have a redeeming certainty only if all individual actions were theoretically predetermined and all individuality eliminated. Then even humanitarian ideals became essentially dehumanizing, as under the rule of

Stalin. The utopian impulse to liberate mankind here served a relentless craving for power and a ruthless exploitation of men. Thus by different means the impact of totalitarianism crystallized the terror of history, which is symbolized today in the potentiality of man's nuclear self-destruction.

In the end, totalitarianism reveals itself to be the belated price of the burdening of historicity with the weight of salvation. The totalitarian pathology of modern civilization is a result of the historicizing of our values, and the development of a redemptive secular historicity, that had grown during the last centuries. Demonic historicism took root because there existed a contradiction inherent within our historical ideals, which had sought to achieve secular transcendence and immortality within historical time. When this historical faith came to face the contradiction between its secular utopian goal and the redemptory task of literally immortalizing the alter ego, it underwent a tragic collapse. The consequence of this failure was the demonic intensity of modern totalitarian movements. Perhaps the feeling of terror inherent in the intimation that man may not be able to transcend his present condition and momentary existence is best captured in a chilling page from Kafka's *The Trial*:

> These are difficulties which the man from the country had not expected to meet; the Law, he thinks, should be accessible to every man and at all times, . . .

He watches the doorkeeper and decides it is best to wait; the doorkeeper gives him a stool. He sits down and waits, for days and for years. Often he tries to be allowed in; the doorkeeper grows weary with his entreaties.

During the first years, he curses his fate; later he grumbles under his breath. His sight grows dim: is the world darkening, or is it his eyes that are failing him? Yet from beneath the door of the Law he now sees a permanent radiance of light.

> Now his life is drawing to a close. Before he dies . . . the whole time of his sojourn condenses in his mind into one question, which he has never yet put to the doorkeeper. He beckons the door-keeper, since he can no longer

raise his stiffening body . . . "What do you want to know now?" asks the door-keeper, "you are insatiable." "Everyone strives to attain the Law," answers the man, "how does it come about, then, that in all these years no one has come seeking admittance but me?" The door-keeper perceives that the man is at the end of his strength and that his hearing is failing, so he bellows in his ear: "No one but you could gain admittance through this door, since this door was intended only for you. I am now going to shut it."[5]

EPILOGUE

Our study has followed the rise and decline of historical consciousness as a basic expression of redemptive hope and as a major form of immortalization and self-transcendence. It has considered the career of historicity over the last three centuries of Western civilization, beginning with its rise from an attitude of the elites to its development into the motivating force of new mass movements. We have seen its manifestations in doctrines that postulate human progress as well as in aggressive nationalisms that deny the idea of perfectibility or the hope of peace. We have found its expression in various forms of idealism and also in certain materialist objectives that are used to serve a transcendent function. Over the last century, we observed its accelerating decline as the course of historical events brought out the inherent self-contradictions of modern historical thought, which manifested themselves in totalitarianism. Thus, we suggested, the moral crisis of our times was in large measure a consequence of the collapse of redemptive historicity.

Meanwhile the sense of transcendent meaning in history has not been entirely lost in modern consciousness. A secularized form of it survives in Marxism and still exercises a major impact, particularly in non-Western societies. Quite different manifestations of transcendent historicity appear in modern Christian thought, in the work of theologians like Niebuhr, Tillich, Berdyaev, Maritain and d'Arcy to name a few, and of religious-minded historians like Christopher Dawson and Arnold Toynbee. In different ways, these thinkers have sought a reflection of the ultimate through the unfolding of man's historical experience, and especially through the development of his historical consciousness.

Of all modern historians, it is probably Arnold Toynbee who is most closely identified, in the public view, with the notion of a transcendent and universal meaning in history. For superimposed upon the rhythms of growth and decline of civilizations which he presents, Toynbee intimates the possibility of humanity's continuing upward trend. Using the simile of mankind scaling a mountain while countless numbers slide off its precipices, or referring at other times to a point on the edge of a wheel which, through its constant revolutions, keeps moving forward, Toynbee cautiously envisages man's eventual achievement of a universal civilization. While he sometimes regards man's future with foreboding, and suggests that present civilization may well follow its predecessors into history's graveyard, he foresees at other moments the possibility of a higher synthesis of world culture and religion. In his vision, religion and history become essentially fused. Here there is still a "heaven-journey" of the human soul, expressed in man's historical striving and in the tragedy of his failures. It is no doubt because of Toynbee's intimation of a potentially transcendent historical purpose that, despite the sharp criticisms of many professional historians, he enjoys a comparatively high reputation and wide lay following among part of the reading public. Amid the growing number of implicitly relativist and nominalist historians who shun the idea of any unity of meaning in man's historical record, Toynbee stands out with his bold, if disputed, reaffirmation of the value of history, to find a universal order and goal in human experience.

We must leave to our next volume the systematic discussion of historical philosophies of the nineteenth and twentieth centuries. We have deliberately left them out of the present study because we have chosen to concern ourselves rather with the popular and philosophical uses of historical consciousness, and with the cultural role of historicity as a general form of awareness in modern Western civilization. In the psychology of historical-mindedness which we must now study, we will consider the essential elements of historicity and their cultural impact on the forms of thought and action. Here we will need to take up the work of historical thinkers from Ranke, Burckardt and Dilthey to Collingwood, Huizinga and Pirenne. We shall have to study the consequences for historicity in the ideas of Weber and Mannheim,

272 HEAVEN, HELL, & HISTORY

among others. We will consider the general formulations of civilization by historians and social philosophers like Dawson, McNeill, Sorokin, Toynbee and Voegelin. For the moment, suffice it to say that despite the imagination of a Toynbee, the preeminent tendency of modern thought has been towards a continuing detranscendentalization of historical consciousness. This trend has done little to dispel, and much to encourage, the fear of a goalless future. It has induced the sense of history as man's purgatory beyond which no heaven exists.

In the next volume, our first task will be to show how the faith in history of previous generations was eventually exported to other civilizations, specifically those of China and India. We shall see the utopian sense of historical expectation provide a common denominator of historicity through much of the world. In China, it was to influence a civilization that had traditionally been historical in outlook but that had not conceived of history as a linear teleology nor as a transcendence of the human condition. In India, it was to transform a civilization that had tended to avoid historical consciousness. By the twentieth century, many of these traditional attitudes had changed. Sun Yat-sen, astringent in his criticism of Western cultural influence, nonetheless came to couch his "principles of the people" in a redeeming perspective of future progress and national destiny. Gandhi, committed to the reaffirmation of Indian village economy and values, nonetheless availed himself of Western political ideals, such as nationalism, in his spiritual mission and his rejection of Western domination. Thus we shall see that the West, in exporting its ideologies of democracy and egalitarianism as well as its technology and mode of production, also transmitted something more subtle. Buried in its visible exports and political doctrines was the sense of historicity which Victorian missionaries unconsciously took with them wherever they settled.

We shall see that at the time when the sense of redemptive historical purpose was declining in Western countries, it was taking root in non-Western cultures. As a consequence of imperialism, it was implanted into civilizations to which it was philosophically and psychologically alien. Here was an ironic situation: faith in the redeeming quality of the future became a characteristic of many underdeveloped nations at the very time it was collapsing in the culture which had given it birth. This fact provides one reason why the historicism of Marxist teaching proved appealing to intellectuals of the non-Western world. Educated in the history-oriented values of Western schools and European political doctrines of the nineteenth century, they found that only socialist ideals still proclaimed the image of the future they expected. Only non-Western societies today preserve the full intensity of the redemptive sense of history.

Our second task will be to analyze the ontological nature and the essential structure of historicity, whose career we have traced in the present volume. We must shift our attention from the questions of the background and the evolution of an idea to the consideration of its distinguishing traits and characteristic functions. Why does man seek to liberate himself from his condition of existence or from his present state? What is the nature of his impulse to transcend himself and to break out of the mortal limits of the ego? We will see that, at the basic psychological level, the impulse to transcendence is a manifestation of the drive to survival, projected upon man's awareness of an open-ended future. The yearning for transcendence is a form of the will to life, recast in the perspective of eternity. Its aim is the realization of a vicarious form of existence, achieved through a sense of eternal meaning attached to human experience. We will therefore have to examine the consequences of man's recognition of himself as a temporal being, living within the infinities of past and future. For man ceases to be satisfied with immediate gratification of his desires when he realizes that each moment of contentment or pleasure must pose anew the question of tomorrow, and foreshadow the absence of ultimate fulfillment. In short, transcendence is to be seen as the impulse to life itself, transformed into an urge to continue living by our awareness of individual mortality, of oblivion and of endless time.

We will see that the concern with self-transcendence and redemptive immortalization does not seek to deny the obvious fact that most men are preeminently motivated by immediate concerns rather than by moral considerations, and preoccupied by pressing material needs and personal matters concerning themselves and their families rather than by ideologies. Few people are moved primarily by long-range impersonal values; even when they think they are, their apparent motivation is often but a disguise for more selfish interests. Only rarely does a man's taking stock of his life lead to a significant redirection of his energies, truly motivated by a new moral commitment to humanity. Thus we will see that our emphasis on transcendence is *not a form of ideological explanation*. Self-transcendence is an expression of man's basic urge to being, transmuted by his consciousness of time and death into a desire for continuing happiness, and hence into a yearning for immortality. Ideal values are but the psychological consequences of this drive; they are not identical with it. Consequently it is not the specific ideal objectives that attract a following as much as the sentiment of human solidarity they provide. The crucial redeeming quality is the sense of participating in "the movement" —whatever its objective—for its own sake, as an expression of the individual's ongoing life.

The rationale of transcendence begins with the psychology of immortalization, understood as the natural consequence of man's realization of time and futuricity. It is the recognition of our eventual mortality that leads us to seek extension of our own ego and to look for some form of its survival, both directly as a soul, and indirectly through some legacy to posterity. It prompts us to find a vicarious embodiment of the self in a timeless reality, or to seek an identification of our ego with an indefinitely continuing ideal in the future. Our task will be to show the relationship between this basic impulse of the psyche and the conception of transcendent historicity. We will see, for example, that individualism and activism emerge as the distinctive attributes of the historical mode of transcendence. For it is only in historical consciousness that man reaches for immortality, not by passively losing his individuality or by merging his identity in that of the tribe or the family, but rather by exercising a personal impact on the course of events. He identifies himself with an historical ideal, yet strives to retain his individuality. Moved by a sense of historical destiny to be realized by individual will and action, he seeks to leave his unique imprint, however small, on the shape of things to come.

Our last question will concern the central problem of this study, namely whether a new sense of self-transcendence can be formulated out of the collapse of historical expectations and values that would prove relevant to our present experience. Can one meaningfully refashion a conception of historical purpose in human affairs without falling back on a formulation of some "ultimate" teleological goal? Can one conceive of a redemptive historical consciousness that presupposes no absolute ideals, yet that escapes the inherent frustration of relativism? In answer to these questions, we will see whether a transcendent value can be found, not necessarily in particular ideals, but in the universal distinction all cultures make between right and wrong, or that is to say in the very impulse of human consciousness to idealness itself.

In his incisive book on *Cosmos and Myth*, Mircea Eliade has pointed out that our linear view of history had lost the security of the cyclical pattern of emulation and of ritual re-creation that used to relate primitive man to the cosmic myths of his culture. Consequently when in the Western view of time and of historical destiny the individual lost his sense of a final goal, or even of a direction of movement, he was left in a moral void. Western man found himself facing a relentless process of historical change heading into an endless emptiness. The grinding force of historical tragedy intensified the individual's feeling of impotence, converting it into the terror of oblivion within the infinite abyss of time. Detranscendentalization left man without any escape from annihilation, either beyond worldly reality or within it.

From history as the road to heaven for Condorcet we had come down to history as purgatory. Many disillusioned individuals, however, experienced an existence devoid of all redemptive purpose as an eternal imprisonment in futility. Faced with the nihilistic alternatives of suicide or a life of despair, they concluded that an unendingly meaningless history was Hell.

NOTES

Chapter II

1. Cited in Paul Hazard, *European Thought in the Eighteenth Century* (trans. J. Lewis May; London: Hollis & Carter, 1954), p. 142.
2. Thomas Hobbes, *Leviathan* (ed. Michael Oakeshott; Oxford: Clarendon Press, 1960), p. 82.
3. John Locke, *The Second Treatise of Government*, Ch. II, para. 6.
4. John Locke, *Essay on Human Understanding*, Bk. II, Ch. I, para. 1; Bk. I, Ch. II, para. 15.
5. *Considérations sur les Causes de la Grandeur des Romains et de leur Décadence* (ed. Gonzague Truc; Paris: Garnier, n.d.), p. 101.

Chapter III

1. "Introduction," *Ancient and Modern History*, in *The Works of Voltaire* (trans. by Tobias Smollett, revised by William T. Fleming; New York: St. Hubert's Guild, 1901), XIII, 9-10.
2. "Introduction" to *The Age of Louis XIV*, cited in Fritz Stern, *The Varieties of History* (New York: Meridian Books, 1956), pp. 41-42.
3. Jean-Jacques Rousseau, *Emile* (trans. Barbara Foxley, London: Everyman's Library, 1955) p. 253.
4. *Ibid.*, p. 252.
5. *Ibid.*, "The Creed of a Savoyard Vicar," p. 239.
6. Letter to Voltaire, August 18, 1756, cited in Charles William Hendel, *Jean-Jacques Rousseau, Moralist* (2 vols., London: Oxford Univ. Press, 1934), I, 227.
7. J. J., Rousseau, Second Part of "Discours sur L'Inégalité," in *The Political Writings of Jean-Jacques Rousseau* (2 vols., ed. C. E. Vaughan; Oxford: Blackwell, 1962), I, 169.
8. J. J. Rousseau, *Émile*, p. 244.
9. *Ibid.*
10. *Ibid.*, p. 217.
11. J. J. Rousseau, *The Social Contract*, Bk. IV, Ch. II (in *Social Contract: Essays by Locke, Hume and Rousseau* [New York: Oxford Univ. Press, 1948]), p. 273.
12. Vaughan's "Introduction" to the Project for Corsica, in J. J. Rousseau, *The Political Writings*, II, 297 and 350.
13. J. J. Rousseau, *The Social Contract*, Bk. IV, Ch. VIII, p. 306.
14. Antoine-Nicolas de Condorcet, *Sketch for a Historical Picture of the*

Progress of the Human Mind (trans. June Barraclough; New York: Noonday Press, 1955), p. 175.

15. *Ibid.*, p. 199.
16. *Ibid.*, pp. 176, 178-79.
17. *Ibid.*, pp. 200-1.
18. *Ibid.*, p. 193.
19. *Ibid.*, p. 196.
20. *Lectures on History*, cited in Franklin Le Van Baumer, ed., *Main Currents of Western Thought* (New York: A. Knopf, 1956), p. 439.
21. "An Essay on the First Principles of Government," *loc. cit.*, p. 439.
22. Cited in Bruce Mazlish, "History and Morality," *The Journal of Philosophy*, LV (March, 1958), 233-234.
23. Crane Brinton, *Ideas and Men* (Englewood, N.J.: Prentice-Hall, 1963 ed.), p. 289.
24. A. N. de Condorcet, *op. cit.*, pp. 201-2.

Chapter IV

1. *Arthur Young's Travels in France* (ed. Miss Betham-Edwards; London: G. Bell, 1892), p. 27
2. *Ibid.*, p. 61.
3. L. G. Wickham Legg, *Select Documents Illustrative of the French Revolution* (2 vols., Oxford: Clarendon Press, 1905), II, 216-17.
4. L. G. W. Legg, *op. cit.*, II, 217, 218.

Chapter V

1. Victor Hugo, "Hernani" (trans. Camilla Crosland), in *Three Plays by Victor Hugo* (ed Helen A. Gaubert; New York: Washington Square Press, 1964), pp. 3-4.
2. Literally: "Endure awhile, you are so beautiful!" *Faust*, Pt. II, Act V, ll, 582.
3. "Wer immer strebend sich bemuht, den können wir erlösen," *ibid.*, Pt. II, Act V, ll, 936-37.

Chapter VI

1. "First Thesis" in "Idea for a Universal History," in I. Kant, *On History* (trans. Lewis W. Beck, *et al*; Indianapolis: Bobbs-Merrill, 1963), p. 12.
2. Georg W. F. Hegel, *The Encyclopedia of Philosophy* (trans. Gustav E. Mueller; New York: Philosophical Library, 1959), pp. 122, 124.
3. *Ibid.*, pp. 195 and 69–70.
4. *Ibid.*, p. 103.
5. G. W. F. Hegel, *The Philosophy of History* (trans. J. Sibree; New York: Willey Book Co., 1944), pp. 16, 18.
6. *Ibid.*, p. 457.
7. *Ibid.*, p. 172.
8. G. W. F. Hegel, *The Logic of Hegel* (trans. William Wallace; Oxford: Clarendon Press, 1892), p. 167.
9. *Ibid.*, p. 168.

10. G. W. F. Hegel, *Hegel's Philosophy of Right* (trans. by T. M. Knox; Oxford: Clarendon Press, 1942), p. 10; also commentary, p. 302.
11. G. W. F. Hegel, *The Philosophy of History*, p. 9; see also *The Logic of Hegel*, p. 10.
12. G. W. F. Hegel, *Hegel's Philosophy of Right* (trans. T. M. Knox; Oxford: Clarendon Press, 1942), p. 216.
13. *Ibid.*, p. 217.
14. *Ibid.*, p. 183.
15. *Ibid.*, p. 218.
16. *Ibid.*, p. 218.
17. *Ibid.*, p. 155; see also *The Philosophy of History*, pp. 39, 47.
18. G. W. F. Hegel, *The Philosophy of History*, pp. 341–42.
19. In his study of Hegel, Walter Arnold Kaufmann repudiates the traditional interpretation of an Hegelian pseudo-eschatology (*Hegel; Reinterpretation, Texts and Commentary*; New York: Doubleday, 1965).
20. *Ibid.*, p. 19.
21. *Ibid.*, p. 16.
22. *Ibid.*, p. 41.
23. G. W. F. Hegel, *The Logic of Hegel*, p. 269.
24. G. W. F. Hegel, *The Philosophy of History*, p. 41.
25. G. W. F. Hegel, *Hegel's Philosophy of Right*, pp. 182–83.
26. *Ibid.*, p. 160.

Chapter VII
1. William Wordsworth, "The World is Too Much With Us," ll. 1-3.
2. Quoted in John Morley, *The Life of William Ewart Gladstone* (3 vols. in one [New York: Macmillan, 1952], III Bk. X), 529–30.

Chapter VIII
1. Auguste Comte, *A General View of Positivism* (trans. J. H. Bridges; Stanford, California: Academica Reprints, n.d.), pp. 379, 381.
2. Extract from "A Memoir of Mazzini," cited in Franklin Le Van Baumer, *Main Currents of Western Thought*, p. 501.

Chapter IX
1. Friedrich Nietzsche, *Thus Spake Zarathustra* in *The Philosophy of Nietzsche* (trans. Thomas Common; New York: Modern Library, 1954), p. 240.
2. Nietzsche, *The Use and Abuse of History* in *The Complete Works of Friedrich Nietzsche*, ed. by Dr. Oscar Levy, Vol. II, Pt. II (*Thoughts Out of Season* [trans. Adrian Collins]), pp. 91, 95, 99.
3. *Ibid.*, pp. 11, 14, 15.
4. *Ibid.*, p. 30.
5. F. Nietzsche, *Thus Spake Zarathustra*, p. 9.
6. *Thus Spake Zarathustra* (trans. A. Tille, rev. M. M. Bozman; London: J. M. Dent [Everyman's Library], 1933), p. 197.
7. *Ibid.*, p. 196.

8. Sigmund Freud, "Thoughts for the Times on War and Death," in *Civilization, War and Death* (ed. John Rickman [Psychoanalytic Epitomes, No. 4], London: Hogarth, 1939), p. 6.

Chapter X

1. Thomas Mann, *Doctor Faustus* (trans. H. T. Lowe-Porter; New York: A. Knopf, 1948), pp. 307–8.
2. Cited in Stephen Jay Greenblatt, *Three Modern Satirists*, Waugh, Orwell and Huxley (New Haven: Yale University Press, 1965), p. 71.
3. Leon Trotsky, *Stalin* (London: Hollis & Carter, 1947), p. 383.
4. *The Revolution of Nihilism, Warning to the West* (trans. by E. W. Dickes, New York: Longmans, Green, 1939).
5. Franz Kafka, *The Trial* (trans. Willa and Edwin Muir; New York: A. Knopf, 1955), pp. 269–71.

SELECTED READINGS

THE literature on transcendence and its relation to history is vast. Much of the work in this area has been done by nineteenth- and twentieth-century German philosophers and historians, particularly from Wilhelm Dilthey to Ernst Troeltsch and Friedrich Meinecke, into modern existentialism, notably of Martin Heidegger. Besides philosophical discussions in the work of Heinrich Rickert, Alois Dempf, Heinrich Barth, Walter Ehrlich and Jakob Mühlethaler, to cite a few, there are psychological treatments by Ernst Bloch, not to mention relevant discussions in Freud and Jung. These ideas appear from another point of view in sociology and the sociology of knowledge, from Georg Simmel and Max Weber to Alfred Weber and Karl Mannheim. The literature on utopianism is extensive, including significant treatments in German by Paul Tillich and in French by Roger Mucchielli. The issue of meaning in history and self-transcendence appears in much of the theological literature, such as in the work of Jakob Taubes and Erich Frank among others. Evolutionary philosophies such as those of Henri Bergson and especially Alfred N. Whitehead and Pierre Teilhard de Chardin involve closely related issues. Humanist approaches appear in the work of Max Scheler, Erich Kahler and Erich Fromm. There are innumerable relevant discussions in the philosophy of history, among which we may note the recent work of Paul Weiss for its appropriate chapters. Among contemporary philosophies of history relevant to our concerns (leaving aside the work of Arnold Toynbee and Pitirim Sorokin), that of Eric Voegelin stands out for the early period. What follows here is in no sense a bibliography; it is merely a brief list of readings dealing with several of the questions involved.

Arendt, Hannah. *Between Past and Future*. New York: Viking Press, 1961.

———. "History and Immortality, *The Partisan Review*. New York. XXIV, Winter, 1957.

Berdyaev, Nicholas A. *The Meaning of History*, London: G. Bles, 1936.

Berlin, Isaiah. *Historical Inevitability*. New York: Oxford University Press, 1955.

Borkenau, Franz. "The Concept of Death," *The Twentieth Century*. London. CLVII, April, 1955.

Bultmann, Rudolf. *The Presence of Eternity; History and Eschatology*. New York: Harper, 1957.

Bury, John B. *The Idea of Progress*. New York: Dover Publications, 1955.

Cairns, Grace E. *Philosophies of History*. New York: Philosophical Library, 1962.

Cassirer, Ernst. *The Myth of the State*. New Haven: Yale University Press, 1946.

Cohn, Norman. *The Pursuit of Millennium*. Fairlawn, New Jersey: Essential Books, 1957.

Collingwood, Robin G. *The Idea of History*. New York: Oxford University Press, 1956.

D'Arcy, Rev. Martin. *The Sense of History, Secular and Sacred*. London: Faber, 1954.

Eliade, Mircea. *The Myth of the Eternal Return*. Trans. Williard R. Trask. New York: Pantheon Books, 1954. Also published under title *Cosmos and Myth*.

Hazard, Paul. *European Thought in the Eighteenth Century, From Montesquieu to Lessing*. Trans. J. Lewis May. London: Hollis and Carter, 1954.

———. *The European Mind, 1680-1715*. London: Hollis and Carter, 1953.

Higham, John. "Beyond Consensus: The Historian as Moral Critic," *The American Historical Review*. New York. LXVII, April, 1962.

Hoffer, Eric. *The True Believer: Thoughts on the Nature of Mass Movements*. New York: Harper, 1951.

Jaspers, Karl. *The Origin and Goal of History*. Trans. Michael Bullock. New Haven: Yale University Press, 1953.

Löwith, Karl. *Meaning in History*. Chicago: University of Chicago Press, 1949.

Mazlish, Bruce. "History and Morality," *The Journal of Philosophy.* New York. LV, March, 1958.

Morgan, Arthur E. *Nowhere Was Somewhere: How History Makes Utopias, and Utopias Make History.* Chapel Hill, North Carolina: University of North Carolina Press, 1946.

Niebuhr, Reinhold. *Faith and History: A Comparison of Christian and Modern Views of History.* New York: Scribners, 1949.

Polak, Frederik L. *The Image of the Future.* 2 vols. New York: Oceana Publications, 1961.

Popper, Karl. *The Poverty of Historicism.* London: Routledge and Kegan Paul, 1957.

Seidenberg, Roderick. *Anatomy of the Future.* Chapel Hill, North Carolina: University of North Carolina Press, 1961.

———. *Posthistoric Man: An Inquiry.* Chapel Hill, North Carolina: University of North Carolina Press, 1950.

Stern, Alfred. *Philosophy of History and the Problem of Values.* 's-Grevenhage, Netherlands; Mouton and Co., 1962.

Susman, Warren I. "History and the American Intellectual; Uses of a Usable Past," *American Quarterly.* Philadelphia. XVI, Summer, 1964, No. 2 Part 2.

Talmon, Jacob Leib. *The Origins of Totalitarian Democracy.* New York: F. A. Praeger, 1960.

———. *Political Messianism: The Romantic Phase.* New York: F. A. Praeger, 1960.

Tillich, Paul. *The Interpretation of History.* Trans. A. N. Rasetzki and Elsa L. Talmey. New York: Scribners, 1936.

Troeltsch, Ernst. *Protestantism and Progress.* Trans. W. Montgomery. Boston: Beacon, 1958.

Tuveson, Ernest Lee. *Millennium and Utopia.* Berkeley: University of California Press, 1944.

Weber, Alfred. *Farewell to European History.* Trans. R. F. C. Hull. New Haven: Yale University Press, 1948.

INDEX

Verlaine, Paul, 210
Versailles, Treaty of, 260, 263
Vico, Giovanni Battista, 17
Voegelin, Eric, 272
Voltaire, 25, 26-27, 38, 41, 49-54,
69, 77-78, 88, 145

Wagner, Richard, 114, 129, 221-222
"Walk, The" (Schiller), 130
Wallace, Alfred Russel, 188-189
War of the League of Augsburg, 231
Weber, Max, 237, 272
Weber, Carl Maria von, 114
Weill, Kurt, 242
Weimar Republic, 252, 254, 263

Wells, H. G., 244, 257
Whig Party (Great Britain), 32
Whitehead, Alfred North, 238
Wilberforce, Bishop, 215
Wilhelm Tell (Schiller), 130
William II, Kaiser, 164, 195, 197
Wilson, Woodrow, 260
Wittgenstein, Ludwig, 238
Wordsworth, William, 129
World War I, 201, 229
World War II, 239

Young, Arthur, 84, 85
Young Italy (organization), 123